JULIA GENTRY

BOLD

101 Daily Devotionals to DREAM BOLD and LIVE BIGGER

Uninhibited Publishing

BEND, OREGON

BOLD: 101 Daily Devotions to Dream Bold and Live Bigger
Published by Uninhibited Publishing
Bend, Oregon

Copyright ©2025 by Julia Gentry All rights reserved.

No part of this book may be reproduced in any form or by any mechanical means, including information storage and retrieval systems without permission in writing from the publisher/author, except by a reviewer who may quote passages in a review.

All images, logos, quotes, and trademarks included in this book are subject to use according to trademark and copyright laws of the United States of America.

Amplified Bible (AMP). Copyright © 2015 by The Lockman Foundation. All rights reserved.

Amplified Bible, Classic Edition (AMPC). Copyright © 1954, 1958, 1962, 1964, 1965, 1987 by The Lockman Foundation. All rights reserved.

Contemporary English Version (CEV). Copyright © 1995 by American Bible Society. All rights reserved.

English Standard Version (ESV). *The Holy Bible*, English Standard Version. Text Edition: 2016. Copyright © 2001 by Crossway Bibles, a publishing ministry of Good News Publishers. All rights reserved.

GOD'S WORD Translation (GW). Copyright © 1995, 2003, 2013, 2014, 2019, 2020 by God's Word to the Nations Mission Society. All rights reserved.

King James Version (KJV). In public domain.

The Message (MSG). Copyright © 1993, 2002, 2018 by Eugene H. Peterson. (NavPress) All rights reserved.

New International Version (NIV). *The Holy Bible*, New International Version. Copyright © 1973, 1978, 1984, 2011 by Biblica, Inc. All rights reserved worldwide. *All Bible verses in this book are taken from this translation unless otherwise noted.*

New King James Version (NKJV). Copyright © 1982 by Thomas Nelson. (Thomas Nelson Publishers) All rights reserved.

New Living Translation (NLT). *Holy Bible*, New Living Translation. Copyright © 1996, 2004, 2015 by Tyndale House Foundation. (Tyndale House Publishers, Inc.) All rights reserved.

The Passion Translation (TPT). Copyright © 2017, 2018, 2020 by Passion & Fire Ministries, Inc. All rights reserved. ThePassionTranslation.com.

ISBN: 978-1-7357859-5-0 paperback
ISBN: 978-1-7357859-6-7 hardcover
SELF-HELP/Spiritual

Interior design by Victoria Wolf, wolfdesignandmarketing.com
Cover Design by Donna Cunningham, BeauxArts.Design

QUANTITY PURCHASES: Schools, companies, professional groups, clubs, and other organizations may qualify for special terms when ordering quantities of this title. For information, email dream@thejuliagentry.com.

This book is dedicated to my mom. Your life is an example of living at the feet of Jesus. Your impact is eternal. Thank you.

MY GIFT TO YOU—
Let's Go Even Bolder, Together

Because you said yes to dreaming boldly with God, I want to say thank you with a special gift just for you.

As a reader of this book, you now receive **FREE access to my companion course, BOLD**—an immersive video experience designed to walk with you, step-by-step, through each day of this devotional.

This course was created to do more than inspire you. It's here to activate you. You'll get:

- Daily video teachings that align with each devotional entry
- Encouragement and insight to help you go deeper in your journey
- Support to help you move from inspiration to transformation
- A chance to cultivate daily rhythms of bold faith, courageous leadership, and Kingdom impact

Whether you're an auditory learner, craving accountability, or just wanting more from your devotional time—**this course is for you.**

Simply scan the QR code and enter the code **IAMBOLD** at checkout to access the full experience—for **FREE**.

Introduction

SCRIPTURE GIVES US A POWERFUL and enlightening promise in Acts 2:17 (The Passion Translation): *This is what I will do in the last days—I will pour out my Spirit on everybody and cause your sons and daughters to prophesy, and your young men will see visions, and your old men will experience dreams from God.*

The question isn't if we're living in the last days—we are. The real question is: Are we aware of the prophetic words, visions, and dreams God is pouring out ... and are we actively responding to what He's saying?

I propose something bold: The issue isn't with God—it's with us.

Although dreaming bold and living big for the Lord do make an impact in the world around us, your greatest impact will always come from consistent, intentional time spent with the Lord. Because when you spend daily, intimate time with Him—your heart starts to beat like His. Your mind is transformed by His truth. And your dreams become His dreams ... the kind that actually change the world.

In John 15:7 (English Standard Version), Jesus says, *If you abide in me, and my words abide in you, ask whatever you wish, and it will be done for you.* Often we fixate on the promise—"ask whatever you wish, and it will be done"—but miss the deeper invitation to "abide in me." This is the foundation of His divine framework and ultimately how we bring heaven to earth. Abiding.

The word *abiding* means to remain, stay, or dwell in a particular place over time. It's a fixed state. It's actually calling us to make our home in God—to live, breathe, and be sustained by His presence. The gift of abiding is not about getting results; it's about deep, ongoing communion with the Lord. Abiding in God means staying connected to Him even when life is tough, our dreams seem impossible, when our prayers seem to go unanswered, and/or when circumstances don't align with our expectations. It's about having His Word not just in our minds but also deep in our hearts, shaping how we think, feel, and act. The abiding life *is* God's dream for each of us, and when we encounter His presence, we can't *not* experience the abundant life He promises.

Jesus himself said, *'I came that they may have* and *enjoy life, and have it in abundance [to the full, till it overflows]'* (John 10:10 Amplified Bible). The word *"abundantly"* is not about quantity but about the extraordinary *quality* of life Jesus promises us. It's a life so rich in meaning and depth that it transforms the way we live our lives. This high-quality life with the Lord becomes the foundation from which we are called to dwell, to dream, and to create—every single day. From this place of abundance, we can access the promises of God; receive prophetic words, visions, and dreams; and ultimately tap into His divine plan for our lives. This is where the best ideas, innovations, and even business plans are birthed—from the abundance of life in Christ. Then we must live to tell about it.

Scripture says, *Faith by itself isn't enough. Unless it produces good deeds, it is dead and useless* (James 2:17 New Living Translation). A dream without action is no dream at all. In order to walk in full alignment with God's will and fulfill the dreams He has placed on your heart, you'll need to develop the spiritual discipline to sustain your journey through the highs and the lows, the good days and the hard. Spiritual discipline is the ability to control one's behavior and actions to achieve a goal or maintain a standard of conduct, despite the craziness of life, the obstacles that try to keep us down, and our own disbelief and doubt that try to detour us. Developing this kind of discipline isn't always convenient or easy, but it's always worth it.

When we live from this place of abiding, walking in faith on the daily, we become agents of heaven on earth. We make our reality look more like His. We shine the light of the Father into a very dark world. As Matthew 5:13–15 (New International Version) reminds us: *You are the salt of the earth. … You are the light of the world. … Let your light shine before others, that they may see your good deeds and glorify your Father in heaven.*

This is the power of dreaming with God.

This is the power of partnership.

This is how we bring heaven to earth.

BOLD is a daily devotional designed to support you in creating a life that both abides in the Lord and is full of abundant possibilities while also instilling the habit and practice of pursuing your God-given dreams on the daily. That means you will learn how to develop the *mindset, heartset,* and *dreamset* required to dream bold, lead big, and make an impact with and for the Lord.

My prayer is that this devotional will ignite a fresh fire for the Lord and the revelation He so freely gives. I pray you are awakened to divine dreams and a vision for your life and that you become hungry for heaven's realities. I pray your life begins to display the full promise of the very prayer Jesus taught us to pray: *Manifest your kingdom realm, and cause your every purpose to be fulfilled on earth, just as it is in heaven* (Matthew 6:9–11 TPT). And may you learn to not just pray this prayer, but may you also become this prayer, co-creating with Him to bring heaven to earth.

Dream stacking is a phrase I've coined and can be defined as *the discipline and practice of setting and achieving small, manageable dreams on the daily.* So most of all, I pray you commit to the daily discipline it takes to make every single one of your dreams a reality, bringing heaven to earth as you learn how to "dream stack" as if your life depends on it. Because, come to find out, it does.

Introduction

May your life be marked by boldness—bold dreams, bold prayers, and bold actions. May you walk confidently in the plans God has for you, stepping out in faith and courage to bring His Kingdom to earth. May every decision you make be rooted in the confidence of His promises as you live fearlessly, knowing that with God, all things are possible. May your life be a radiant reflection of His glory.

Dream bold. Live bigger. Make an impact for the Kingdom.

Dream on the daily.

Why 101

"101? WHY 101, GOD?"

He didn't give me a direct answer—but I admit, my curiosity got the best of me, so I decided to dig a little deeper. God always has this incredible way of knowing just how to draw me in.

When God speaks to me, He doesn't reveal the whole picture all at once. He gives me pieces, like clues to a puzzle. Proverbs 25:2 says, *It is the glory of God to conceal a matter; to search out a matter is the glory of kings.* This means God doesn't keep things *from* us as punishment but does so *for* us. As we seek Him with all our hearts, we don't find just our answer, we find His glory. The journey He invites us on is one of continually deepening our understanding of His heart, refining our character to reflect His, and ultimately leading us to places beyond our wildest dreams. This process is more than discovery; it's a divine partnership.

"101."

I wrote it at the top of my page. Then I leaned in.

Since that moment, I've learned so much about the power behind this number and the significance it has in our lives. You hold those findings now in the palm of your hand, and I pray they blow your mind and open your heart as they did for me.

The pattern of this number is first seen throughout Scripture in profound, pivotal moments:

Genesis 1:01 *In the beginning God created the heavens and the earth.*

Numbers 1:01 *The Lord spoke to Moses.*

Joshua 1:01 *After the death of Moses the servant of the Lord, the Lord said to Joshua.*

Judges 1:01 *After the death of Joshua, the Israelites asked the Lord, "Who of us is to go up first to fight against the Canaanites?" The Lord answered, "Judah shall go up; I have given the land into their hands."*

Psalm 1:01 *Blessed is the one who does not walk in step with the wicked ... but whose delight is in the law of the Lord, and who meditates on his law day and night.*

John 1:01 *In the beginning was the Word, and the Word was with God, and the Word was God.*

Revelation 1:01 *The revelation from Jesus Christ, which God gave him to show his servants what must soon take place.*

Come to find out, the number 101 symbolizes the spirit of bold, courageous action—a call to act now! It signifies abundance, progress, and forward momentum. These verses share the connection of the number, and they also reveal something deeper—something powerful for you to discover as you begin your own 101-day journey with the Lord.

God speaks. He speaks in so many ways—through His Word, through His creation, through people around us. He's always speaking. The real question isn't if He's speaking—it's are we really listening?

Sometimes we say we're listening, but if we're honest, it's more like when my kids nod their heads without hearing a word I say. We can do the same thing with God—nodding along but missing the heart of what He's trying to reveal. God wants to speak truth into our lives. He wants to reveal Himself. But it's on us to tune our spiritual ears to hear and sharpen our spiritual eyes to see what He's saying.

God creates. And everything He creates is in alignment with His Word. Two words to take note of here: *create* and *alignment*. Here's the truth: You were made in the image of God. Just as God created the heavens and the whole Earth with intentionality and power, you were designed to create too. Creativity is not just something you do, it's who you are. It's woven into your origin and destiny. When you are grounded in this identity, feasting on His revelations, you will express it in how you live your life. You will create with Him. Dream with Him. I truly believe when we as believers fundamentally understand this, together we will play a role in bringing heaven to earth.

Beyond that, everything He creates is in perfect *alignment* with His Word. He doesn't act randomly or without purpose—everything He does follows divine order. When we realign ourselves to His will, His way, and His timing, we open the door to *exceedingly, abundantly -above* (Ephesians 3:20 New King James Version) what we could ever hope for or imagine. Life, of course, has its way of throwing curve balls, leaving us feeling off-balance and affecting how we view ourselves, the world, and even our relationship with the Lord. That's when a realignment becomes necessary. Like a chiropractor's adjustment, sometimes all we need is a slight shift to breathe deeply again and see things from God's perspective.

God guides. When God gives us a bold dream, He doesn't promise to show us every step along the way. Instead, He calls us to trust Him and follow Him, step by step, as He leads us in paths of righteousness. It's easy, though, to feel overwhelmed by life and put those dreams on hold—ignoring them, downplaying their importance, feeling stuck, or taking no steps at all. When you feel the dream is too big or life is too challenging, you're in luck, because you will not do it alone. He will lead you in paths of righteousness, but the journey will require both boldness and consistent discipline to keep in step with the Lord.

Spiritual discipline is about growing in holiness as God matches your character with His revelation. His discipline is rooted in love and affection as He aligns your heart and mind to His will, training your habits and behavior to match the glory He's revealed to you. For me, this is the ultimate form of "dream stacking." Being that God is a big God and His plans for you are huge, He's going to give you bold dreams that seem bigger than you, maybe seem "improbable" or even "impossible."" Dream stacking is where you build a life of consistent, disciplined growth in the Lord through daily steps that lead to larger breakthroughs while growing within you the character to support the weight of the blessing.

What to Expect in This Devotional

TOO OFTEN, I SEE PEOPLE READ the Word of God without ever applying it. Others carry a dream without realizing it's actually a divine invitation to partner with God in bringing heaven to earth. And then there are those who long for change but lack the spiritual discipline to truly walk it out. But what if—what if—reading God's Word, aligning with His truth, and dreaming with Him could be the very path that turns revelation into reality?

In the pages ahead, you'll find 101 devotions that will provide you with a daily opportunity to bridge the gap between revelation and transformation, God's dreams and your reality, learning and growing. I will show you the right formula to dream bold, live big, and make an impact for God's Kingdom as you revel in His revelation, align your life with His truth, and dream stack those God-given, bold dreams as if your life depends on it! It's called mindset, heartset, and dreamset.

Here's what I mean: Your mindset is how you think—your beliefs, thought patterns, and mental agreements that either align with truth or limit what's possible. Your heartset is how you feel and process the world—your emotional posture, capacity, and willingness to respond to God with vulnerability and boldness. And your dreamset is how you move—it's the actions, the decisions, and the courageous steps you take in pursuit of the bold dreams God has entrusted to you.

Revel: Each day begins with a fresh passage of Scripture and a thought-provoking devotional designed to blow your mind by connecting the timeless truths of Scripture to the real-life situations you're walking through. I encourage you to truly revel in it—take time to be deeply delighted and overjoyed by its truth. Don't just read it. Don't just learn it. Become it. This isn't about just understanding the Word—it's about learning how to apply it to every area of your life. God's Word is alive and powerful, and when you approach it with expectancy, it brings fresh revelation and real transformation. So revel in the revelation—let it light up your heart, your thoughts, and every part of your day as you carry the light of His Word into everything you do.

Align: Each day, as you reflect on God's Word, let Him go to work on your heart—aligning you more and more with His truth. Alignment happens when you position your heart to agree with and come into partnership with the Lord. It's a proactive process, bringing your mind, heart, and actions into agreement with His Word. Every day, you'll have the opportunity to look back on the previous day and take accountability (account for your ability) for the steps you did—or didn't—take.

From my own experience, after a few days, this part may start to feel repetitive—but that's the point. It's also why it's the most important. We become what we practice and we can't expect what we don't inspect. Daily heart alignment is essential to becoming all God created you to be because it takes spiritual discipline to consistently bring your actions into agreement with His truth. Don't skip this part. It's the small, consistent practices—especially the ones no one sees—that create the biggest, most eternal impact. I will try to keep it interesting, but be OK when it feels boring—because guess what? You can do hard things. And you can do boring things too.

Dream Stack: Each day, you'll be prompted with a question designed to help you clarify and take your next BOLD step. Like "stacking your wins" means intentionally celebrating small victories to build momentum, stacking your dreams is the same—only the focus is on what God has placed in your heart, not your fears, your to-do list, or anything else competing for your attention outside His will and call on your life. Though this too will feel a bit redundant in nature, that's the point. These daily questions are designed to build the tactical discipline you will need to see your dreams come to life. Everyone wants the glory, but few want the grind. We all want the destination, but not everyone is willing to walk the daily path to get there. Dream stacking will help you move your dreams forward one intentional step at a time—every day for 101 days. (And yes, that's 101 BOLD steps!)

I encourage you to dedicate at least thirty minutes each day to this process. There will be days you want to skip. Don't. There will be days it will feel hard. Do it anyway. Like brushing your teeth, this isn't something you do once and forget about. It's about building a habit of connecting with God until that becomes a lifestyle. Remember, everything you're wanting is on the other side of the work you're avoiding.

Revel in His revelation, align with His truth, and build upon every bold dream He's ever given you as you stack your dreams every day for the ultimate win—bringing heaven to earth.

DAY 1

Fully Devoted

I counsel you to buy from me gold refined by fire, so that you may be rich, and white garments so that you may clothe yourself and the shame of your nakedness may not be seen, and salve to anoint your eyes, so that you may see. Those whom I love, I reprove and discipline, so be zealous and repent. Behold, I stand at the door and knock. If anyone hears my voice and opens the door, I will come in to him and eat with him, and he with me.

—Revelation 3:18–20 ESV

THIS ISN'T YOUR TYPICAL DEVOTIONAL. This is a move of God, and it starts within you. He's chosen you. Will you choose Him back, all-in, fully *devoted*?

The word *devotion* is not only an act of prayer or personal worship, but a wholehearted love, loyalty, and enthusiasm for a person or cause. It's a deep allegiance, a zeal for something or, better yet, *someone* that shapes our lives and choices. In fact, devotion speaks to a self-dedication—an all-in commitment.

Learning this got me asking a lot of questions I now pass on to you:

- What are you devoted to? What excites you?
- What are you enthusiastically loyal to? Even all-in for?
- What receives your zeal and your dedication? Or perhaps the better question to ask is *Who* receives your zeal and dedication?

To live in devotion to God is to step beyond half-hearted living, past fear and worry, into a place of wholehearted love and enthusiasm for Him. When you're devoted solely to Him, you're willing, energized, and motivated—walking in the passion and fire of God.

What if your daily dreaming with the Lord wasn't just about the "right" steps or even "bold dreams" but was also about developing the *right heart* committed to *His* dreams? That would be a heart fully alive committed to Him?

Today's passage paints a picture of Jesus standing outside the church while the congregation gathers without Him. How often do we find ourselves going through the motions—attending church, participating in activities, learning about God's Word—without truly inviting Jesus into the center of our hearts? How often do we approach our faith without zeal, full devotion, or complete surrender?

And still, there's Jesus—standing at the door of our hearts knocking—because He desires more than a surface-level relationship—He wants in! He doesn't want us merely attending church or going through the duties of Christianity; He wants to take up residence in our hearts. He wants to be present in *every* area of our lives. This is a "come to Jesus" moment when you realize that while you've given Him some access, you may not have given Him *all* access.

The good news is, in Christ, there is no condemnation. This passage offers hope as Jesus stands outside the door patiently waiting for us to invite Him in. So how do we let Him in? It begins with repentance—turning away from what holds you back from going all-in and offering yourself fully to Him. Not just parts of you, but every part—your pain, shame, pride, anxiety, fear, and limited understanding. It also means surrendering your hopes, dreams, goals, and ambitions to Him.

We often look to the world for answers, validation, and fulfillment, but Jesus alone is the source of lasting satisfaction and true, eternal treasure. Material things and worldly status will fade, but when we fully surrender to Christ, we receive His "gold"—riches that are found in a deep, abiding relationship with Him. This wealth is eternal, transformative, and life-giving as our hearts become fully aligned with His. True riches are found in a life wholly devoted to Him.

Today, I encourage you to open the door of your heart in a new way. Repent and seek Him with full devotion, zealously pursuing a deeper relationship with Jesus. He is knocking—will you answer? Will you let Him in? Will you be *fully devoted*?

Take a moment today to recommit your heart to God. Let this renewed devotion ignite something fresh in your soul, giving you the freedom to dream with Him again. Those dreams you carry aren't random; they're placed there for a purpose—His purpose. And as you walk in full devotion to the Lord, your life will be transformed. More than that, you'll begin to reflect Jesus more and more, becoming a living expression of heaven on earth.

※ ※ ※ ※ ※ ※

Revel: Today is Day 1. Take a moment to reflect and take inventory of your heart. What or, better yet, who are you truly devoted to? Examine your priorities, desires, and affections. What would it look like to live being excited and enthusiastic for the Lord? How would that shape your decisions, relationships, and daily actions? Consider the way your life might look if you were fully devoted to Him.

....

....

....

....

Day 1 Fully Devoted

Align: Over these 101 days, purposefully set aside time to be with Jesus and align your life with His Word. Align your mindset, heartset, and dreamset with His truth so you can boldly live out the fullness of His revelation. Start today by taking a moment to close your eyes and pray—not just any prayer but one that's genuine, full of heart, and fully devoted. Ask God to bring every area of your life back into alignment with Him. Take inventory of where you are right now in that alignment and where you truly want to be. Let the journey ahead help you close that gap, step by step, as you move closer to Him

....

....

....

....

Dream Stack: Start today by writing down one or two dreams you will focus on for these 101 days. Write them here as a personal commitment to yourself and the Lord. Then ask yourself: What is one thing I can do today to make this bold dream happen?
Let this be the beginning of an intentional pursuit of His plans for your life.

....

....

....

....

DAY 2

Dream Bold

The members of the council were amazed when they saw the boldness of Peter and John, for they could see that they were ordinary men with no special training in the Scriptures. They also recognized them as men who had been with Jesus.

—Acts 4:12–14 NLT

BOLD.

We all have preconceived notions about this word, don't we? I know I did. For the longest time, I would not have described myself as bold. Sure, I caught glimpses of it when I did something brave or spoke out in moments that required courage, but boldness always seemed fleeting—here one moment, gone the next.

I admired people whose lives were marked by boldness—the ones on the front lines who defied the odds and faced battles head-on. But me? I didn't think I fit that mold. Maybe you feel the same way.

Yet here we are, embarking on a journey to dream bold dreams, pray bold prayers, and take bold action. So we better start rethinking what boldness truly means. And here's the good news: Biblical boldness isn't what you think.

The world may define boldness as being outspoken and courageous, running toward the thing you fear without feeling fear. But when we unpack the Scriptures—when we look at the lives of those who were bold for the Lord—we see a different picture. One that may surprise you and, I hope, encourages you.

In my opinion, no one embodies boldness in the New Testament quite like the apostles we see in the book of Acts. These are men who spoke life in the face of death, declared truth among the lies, and extended love behind prison bars. Their lives are a profound example of boldness because they were rooted in something much deeper than most are. In today's passage we see why. It says that Peter and John were ordinary people doing extraordinary things simply because *they were with Jesus*.

It wasn't Peter and John's education or status that made them bold. It wasn't natural talent or fearlessness. It was their time with Jesus that empowered them to be bold. I believe that Biblical boldness isn't about how large your dreams are or how brave you feel—it's about the depth of your relationship with the Lord and your obedience to what God is calling you to do. Simply put, boldness is the willingness to say yes to Jesus. And come to find out, the more you spend time with Him, the easier it is to say yes to Him!

I am here to tell you today, if you want to be bolder, spend more time with Jesus. When you spend time with Him, you fall in love with Him and develop a selfless desire to obey him. Real obedience is birthed out of love, not fear. Therefore, boldness flows from an intimate connection to Jesus. It's not something we muster up on our own; it's something the Spirit empowers us to do. Boldness is Spirit-led, not self-led.

Would Paul have chosen prison, rejection, and hardship if they were up to him? Probably not. But Paul was *willing*—willing to say yes to God, no matter the cost. Paul's boldness was not based on his own strength but on his dependency on God. That's the heart of boldness.

Boldness doesn't mean you never face fear or doubt; it means you simply choose to trust and obey God even when the path is uncertain. Boldness means saying yes, even when you want to say no. Though obedience isn't always convenient, it's always worth it.

As you dream with God, He's going to challenge you. He's going to ask you to step into things you've never imagined, to think in ways that stretch you, and to act with the kind of faith that will take you beyond your comfort zone. He'll blow your mind with what's possible, and He'll shift your perspective on what's true. But here's the beauty of it: As you depend on Him, you'll discover that with God, nothing is impossible. All He needs is your Yes!

Boldness is a life of intentional connection with the Lord and ongoing obedience to His will. It's trusting God in the face of adversity and moving forward even when plans don't unfold the way we expect. It's staying committed to God's presence and purposes, even when the dreams seem impossible. Boldness isn't about never feeling fear; it's about choosing to trust God in spite of fear.

May your life be marked by your Yes! to Jesus—empowered by the Spirit and fully connected to the One who can do immeasurably more than all you ask or imagine.

※ ※ ※ ※ ※ ※

Revel: How does this fresh revelation of boldness shift your approach to your walking with the Lord? Dreaming with Him? Where is God calling you to step out in boldness in your life? Today, lean into His strength and give Him your wholehearted Yes!

....

....

....

....

Day 2 Dream Bold

Align: Reflect on yesterday—what was the one action you committed to in your Dream Stack that would move you closer to your dream? Did you follow through on it? If not, what held you back?

....

....

....

....

Dream Stack: What's one step you can take today to manifest your dream? Manifest means to show or display, so what action will demonstrate you're serious about the dream God has given you? Write it down and make it happen.

....

....

....

....

DAY 3

Shine Bright

[Jesus said,] 'You are the light of the world. A town built on a hill cannot be hidden. Neither do people light a lamp and put it under a bowl. Instead they put it on its stand, and it gives light to everyone in the house. In the same way, let your light shine before others, that they may see your good deeds and glorify your Father in heaven.'

—Matthew 5:14–16

YESTERDAY WE LEARNED THAT *bold* isn't something you feel; it's someone you become as you spend intentional time with Jesus. The closer you get *to* Him, the easier it is to step out *for* Him.

Outside of Spirit empowerment, *bold* also means having a strong or vivid appearance—being striking and bright. I'd like to propose that those with the *boldest* dreams shine the *brightest* for the Lord.

Too often we think of dreaming as a waste of time—unrealistic, impractical, or even selfish. We come up with reasons why we don't have enough time, resources, or abilities. Then we hear people say, "Dream big!" and we chase that artificial sense of significance as though it's the answer we've been looking for. But not only is "big" not the answer, it's also never something you heard Jesus say.

Jesus never encouraged us to chase after big dreams or greatness for our own sake. Though the world may equate dreaming big with personal success or fame, Jesus calls us into closeness with Him. It's from that intimacy that bold dreams are born—dreams that are aligned with His Kingdom and shaped by His heart for the world. So really, it's not about how big the dream is, but how near we are to Him and how willing we are to obey what He's asking of us.

As believers, it's our responsibility to make this side of heaven look more like heaven and to boldly show up for Him, to dream with Him, to *shine bright* because of Him. In today's passage, we see that clearly.

I've heard it said countless times that the world is growing darker, but perhaps the light is getting dimmer. When we shrink back into comfort zones and avoid stepping out in faith, we dim the very light we're called to carry Let me remind you that darkness is just an absence of light, so the darkness has no real power. When the light reveals itself, darkness dissipates. Therefore, blaming the dark for being dark doesn't solve the problem, and when we spend too much time criticizing the darkness—whether in our culture, communities, or even our own hearts—we can lose sight of our own true responsibility, which is to turn up the brightness of the light within us.

Dreaming with the Lord is about *boldly* showing up—for Him and with Him—in a world that desperately needs more than just a vision board. It needs an *encounter* with Jesus. It needs the bright light of a Savior, and like the moon reflects the sun, we are designed to reflect the light of Jesus. I'm here to remind you today that playing small doesn't reveal the testimony of Jesus. He didn't call you to play it safe; He called you to be the light of the world—to step boldly into your calling and reveal His transformative power through your life.

We cannot lower the standard of Jesus—the *Light*—to accommodate the darkness we see around us. Not only do we need to speak *light* into the darkest places, but we also need to *be* the light by reflecting Jesus into the world. We need to be a people who are boldly dreaming with the Lord, believing in miracles, stepping out in faith, and partnering with the dreams, visions, and prophetic words that He has placed in our hearts. When we do this, we radiate the truth of Christ and become beacons of hope and transformation, a testimony to God's power in the world. No matter how dark the world becomes, even a small amount of light can go a long way.

It's time! It's time to stop focusing on the darkness and instead shine brighter. It's time to partner with what God is doing, to dream the dreams He is dreaming, and embrace the call: *Be the light.*

May your bold dreams shine bright!

※ ※ ※ ※ ※ ※

Revel: Do you see how your bold dreams reflect the light of the Father? Are you allowing your light to shine bright or have you covered your light to accommodate those around you?

Today, be encouraged. Jesus is the light of the world, and all you need to do is spend time with Him, learn from Him, and recommit to dreaming with Him. Then, like the moon reflects the sun, dream bold and shine bright! The world *is* waiting.

....

....

....

....

Day 3 Shine Bright

Align: Pause and reflect. What was the bold step you committed to yesterday—the one that was supposed to move you one step closer to the dream God's placed in your heart? Did you do it? If yes, celebrate it! If not, be honest with yourself—what got in the way? Was it fear, distraction, doubt, busyness? This isn't about shame or guilt; it's about awareness. Growth requires honesty, and honesty opens the door to transformation. Don't just move on—learn from it. What needs to shift today so you do follow through?

....

....

....

....

Dream Stack: Today, what is one step you will take to move closer to the dream God's given you? Write it down. Make it happen. Remember, a dream with no action is no dream at all.

....

....

....

....

DAY 4

Heartset: How's Your Heart?

God rewrote the text of my life when I opened
the book of my heart to his eyes.

—Psalm 18:24 The Message

HOW'S YOUR HEART?

Well, that's a loaded question, isn't it? It's also the reason why women often avoid me at the park—they know I'm not there for small talk about the weather or the news. I want to know how their heart is. Though it's not a complex question, I have found it's very hard for one to answer.

Usually when I ask, "How's your heart?" I get one of two responses. One, there's an outpouring of "all the things," with emotions spilling all over the place. We call these people oversharers. Or two, there's a dumbfounded, blank stare. These are our analytical friends who cringe at the thought of a conversation about the heart.

But *heartset* is universal—it influences all of us, whether we're aware of it or not.

If your *skill set* is the framework of your abilities and talents, and your *mindset* is the framework of your thoughts, your *heartset* is the framework of your emotions—it's the posture and alignment of your heart. It's the emotional framework through which you experience life, guiding how you feel, perceive, and make decisions. Heartset influences how you approach life—your dreams, relationships, and even your faith.

We live in a world that celebrates skill set and is obsessed with mindset but often disregards or forgets the importance of *heartset*. Truth be told, you can have all the skill set and mindset in the world, but without a whole heart—an open, aligned heart—you will struggle and fall short of the full life Jesus promises. But a heart that is healed, open, and connected to God has the capacity to live out the bold dreams He has placed within you.

So, *how is your heart?*

The heart is no small matter in Scripture. It's mentioned over 500 times in the New International Version and more than 800 times in the King James Version. The world might say, "Follow your heart," but God never tells us to follow our hearts—He tells us to follow Him. At the same time, we often hear from the pulpit, "The heart is deceitful," which can be true if our hearts are not focused on God. But the deeper truth is that God created your heart, and He does want all of it.

Though the idea of giving the Lord our whole heart makes sense, why can it feel so hard to do? Honestly, life. Life happens—failures, setbacks, hurts, mistakes. It's easy to allow these experiences to cause us to shut down, numbing ourselves to avoid future pain and guarding our hearts. Or we may allow our emotions to get the best of us, completely dominating our lives, causing us to follow every feeling we feel rather than standing on God's truth. The issue isn't that emotions are invalid; it's that unprocessed emotions lead to confusion, and confusion always leads to a guarded heart and a lifetime of small talk.

I'd like to propose that small talk is a result of a guarded heart. Watch the next time you're at a park or out with friends; be aware of how much conversation is happening without much of anything actually being said. Why? Because we are guarding our hearts.

Ultimately, a guarded heart is a broken heart, and every broken heart needs healing. Healing isn't a moment in time, nor does it happen automatically; it's a process. People say, "Healing takes time." But the truth is, time alone doesn't heal all wounds—healing is an intentional journey that requires your ongoing participation and care. And it's a path we must learn to walk with grace and consistency. But where does one begin?

The Scripture reading for today reminds us God can and will do remarkable, inconceivable, and most improbable things with your life, but first, you must open the book of your heart before His eyes. Essentially, you start by giving your whole heart to the Lord, because only in Him do you find wholeness and completion.

Though I hesitate to minimize your healing journey into a three-step guide, here is the process I have found effective for healing and wholeness.

1. **Take your heart to Jesus.** This doesn't magically solve all your problems, but it does shift your focus. Too often we let the problem or pain become our focus—our "god." But the Bible tells us to bring our troubles to Him: *In this world you will have trouble. But take heart! I have overcome the world.* (John 16:33) When we take our hearts to Him, we shift our focus from our pain and proactively give it to the One who has already overcome.

2. **Set your heart on things above.** The next step is learning to keep your heart anchored in Him. Take Him your heart, yes, and let Him keep it! Scripture tells us to *Set your hearts on things above, where Christ is.* (Colossians 3:1) *Set* is a fixed state. It's not temporary; it's permanent. When your heart is set on Him, on heavenly realities—rather than the things of this world—everything changes. You begin to live from heaven's perspective, and this transforms how you navigate daily life. This is what it means to experience heaven on earth, letting God's truths shape your every step.

3. **Put your heart into it.** This means engaging with a healed, whole heart in all you do—not just going through the motions but doing everything wholeheartedly as an offering to God. Scripture says, *Put your heart and soul into every activity you do, as though you are doing it for the Lord himself and not merely for others* (Colossians 3:23 TPT). You'll be amazed at how transformative and healing it is when you approach each task with your whole heart.

Day 4 Heartset: How's Your Heart?

When you learn to continually bring your heart to the Lord on the daily, He will heal and restore you over and over again. This restoration happens through an ongoing process of opening your heart before the Lord (take your heart to Jesus), resting in Him (set your heart on things above), and pursuing what pleases Him (put your heart into it).

Watch as those small talk conversations turn into meaningful connections, opening deep wells of understanding for someone on their journey toward revelation. Watch how everyday moments transform into opportunities to share Jesus, support someone in their struggles, or encourage someone in their faith journey, whether they know God or not. A healed heart expands your capacity to truly care.

Today, begin to reestablish a divine heart healing by opening the book of your heart before the Lord. Let Him refine, realign, and renew your heart. He is faithful, and He will write a beautiful story with your life!

Revel: How's your heart? Acknowledge whatever your answer may be, then offer it up to Him. Now close your eyes and sit back in the Lord. Imagine yourself opening the book of your heart before his eyes. Let Him write His truth upon your heart.

Align: As you look back on yesterday, what bold move did you commit to for your dream? Did you follow through? If not, what resistance showed up—was it a story, an excuse, or a mindset that tried to hold you back? Now ask yourself: What truth do you need to lean on today to realign your actions with God's Word and stay on track with what He's calling you to build?

....

....

....

....

Dream Stack: What is one bold step you can take to make your dream a reality? Remember, steps of faith are rarely easy—they stretch you, challenge you, and often feel uncomfortable in the moment. But staying stuck? That's even harder. So if it's all going to be hard, choose the hard that moves you forward. Choose the hard that leads to growth, freedom, and the future God has for you. Choose the right kind of hard. Write it down and make it happen.

....

....

....

....

DAY 5

What's the Point?

Consider it pure joy, my brothers and sisters, whenever you face trials of many kinds, because you know that the testing of your faith produces perseverance. Let perseverance finish its work so that you may be mature and complete, not lacking anything.

—James 1:2–4

HOW CAN "JOY" AND "TRIALS" exist in the same sentence?

It seems contradictory at first, but maybe it's because God sees something we don't. Too often, our focus is on the win—the result, the dream, the happiness that comes from the destination. And while there's nothing inherently wrong with that, if our goal is purely the outcome, we miss the deeper purpose. We miss the point. We worship a God who is victorious—He's already won the battle.

This means we aren't striving *for* victory; we are living *from* victory. With this assurance, our striving can cease, our fears can be silenced, and we can recognize that the journey—whether painful or pleasant—isn't about the end result. It's about what's happening *within*.

You are the point.

When you understand this, you unlock a joy that transcends outcomes. This joy doesn't come from reaching the goal but from becoming who God created you to be *through* the process regardless of the obstacles. The point is your character being refined so you can be everything God created you to be.

Today's passage from the book of James powerfully captures this truth: *Consider it pure joy, my brothers and sisters, whenever you face trials of many kinds, because ….* The word *because* is key here, reminding us that God doesn't allow trials without purpose. The passage continues: *because you know that the testing of your faith produces perseverance.* This proves that it's not merely about reaching the end goal but about what the process cultivates within you—perseverance, maturity, and wholeness.

Though God is not the author of pain, He works all things together for good if we allow Him to. That means trials are tools in God's hands, shaping us into who He created us to be. He uses the trials not to break us but to make us into the mature, complete children He always intended us to be—lacking nothing. Our trials aren't just hurdles to overcome but also opportunities for growth.

If you're facing a trial today, the Bible calls you to embrace it with joy because God is doing deep work—within you. He's refining you, preparing you, and creating within you a character that reflects His glory. He's working out of you what can't go with you to heaven. What you're going through isn't just about the destination or the dream; it's about you—about who you're becoming in the process.

You're the point.

Instead of resisting the process, be grateful. In fact, be full of joy! Say, "I see what you're doing here, God. Though I don't like it, I know that you love me and you're refining me. Thank You for refining me. Thank You for using every trial to bring out the best in me. Though this tests me, it won't break me. You're shaping me into everything You've promised I would be." Joy isn't found in escaping the hard times; it's found in knowing that God is using everything for our good.

■ ■ ■ ■ ■ ■

Revel: Take a moment to consider the challenges you're facing right now. What if God's primary focus isn't the dream you're pursuing, but the person you're becoming? What if His goal is to shape you into someone mature, fully equipped, and reflective of His Son Jesus?

Spend time in His presence asking not just about the dreams He has for you but also about the person He's forming you to be. Ask Him to reveal more about the character He's developing within you and how He's using this challenge to shape you even more into His likeness.

....

....

....

....

Align: Look back on yesterday—what bold step did you commit to? Did you follow through or did something get in the way? Why or why not? Be honest. (Yes, this might feel repetitive. Yes, you'll face this check-in every day for the next ninety-six days. That's the point. Don't resist it—lean in and let discipline do its deep work.)

....

....

....

....

Day 5 What's the Point?

Dream Stack: What's one bold step you can take today to keep your dream in motion? Go all in. Your future self will thank you! Note it here and take accountability for it tomorrow.

....

....

....

....

DAY 6

Let It Burn

The earth was rocked at the sound of his voice from the mountain, but now he has promised, "Once and for all I will not only shake the systems of the world, but also the unseen powers in the heavenly realm!" Now this phrase, "once and for all" clearly indicates the final removal of things that are shaking, that is, the old world order, so only what is shakable will remain. Since we are receiving our rights to an unshakable kingdom we should be extremely thankful and offer God the purest worship that delights his heart as we lay down our lives in absolute surrender, filled with awe. For our God is a holy, devouring fire!

—Hebrews 12:26–29 TPT

MANY YEARS AGO, I was asked, "What's your burn?"

I had no idea at the time how much that question would shift my understanding of my spiritual walk. Now I pass that same question onto you: What's your burn?

As we explored in yesterday's devotional, the troubles and trials of life, though not caused by God, are always used by Him to shape us into maturity and completeness—reflecting Jesus. That means nothing goes unseen by God, and nothing is wasted. God's ultimate goal for us on this side of heaven is to look more like Christ. That is the *why*.

But how does God accomplish this? How does He refine us into His image?

Through His refining fire.

As humans, we are often shaped by our upbringing, experiences, personal interpretations, external influences, and even unprocessed pain. Even in the best environments, we are still born into sin. That means that as we grow in our walk with the Lord, we must be reshaped by Him, refined in Him. This is not a one-time event—it's an ongoing process of alignment between us and a holy, righteous God who wants us to become more like Him.

Sooooooooo, I must ask: Have you felt this pressure recently? Maybe you've sensed a shaking—within you or around you, in your circumstances, in your family or business. Maybe you've felt it within friendships or within the church you attend. Perhaps you are being refined.

For some, refining feels like relentless pressure. For others, it may seem like one obstacle after another or like a series of emotional, financial, or relational struggles. But no matter how it manifests, the refining process is always spiritual. *Always.*

Today's Scripture invites us to take a holy pause and consider the refining fire in our own lives—where God shapes, purifies, and prepares us for more. The term *refining fire* refers to the process of purifying precious metals like silver or gold. Through intense heat, impurities rise to the surface and are removed, leaving the metal in its purest form. Likewise, God uses the trials and difficulties of life to refine our faith and mold us into Christ's image. Though it's easy to believe that things are happening *to* you, we must remember that in the Kingdom, things always happen *for* you. What feels like a shaking or even breaking is God transforming us into the truest, purest form of our God-given identity. It's uncomfortable at times, but it's always purposeful.

I encourage you to let the shaking you feel break off the old mindsets, habits, and beliefs that no longer serve you. Let the pressure shape you so you reflect more of Jesus. Let the refining fire purify you and sanctify you for the Lord. Let the tension you feel draw you closer to God, not push you further away. Allow it to strengthen your resolve, to separate your dreams from your fears, to tear down anything that stands against the truth of Christ.

Hardship is inevitable, but the choice to allow it to refine you into Christlikeness is up to you. Don't resist the fire; surrender to it. Though you may feel pressed and shaken, be unmovable.

This is the hour to be refined, purified, and set apart. It is an hour to embrace the new and let go of the old as you are shaped and refined to be His ready Bride—His set apart people.

May you feel the burn and may you become the refining fire.

Revel: Pause and reflect on the purpose of the refining fire. What area of your life feels the most pressure or where do you feel the most *burn*? Consider how God might be using this season of your life to refine, purify, and strengthen you.

As you reflect, ask Him to reveal anything within you that stands in opposition to His will. Invite Him to burn away the impurities, refine your heart, and prepare you for the greater purposes He has in store.

Day 6 Let It Burn

Align: Pause and reflect on yesterday. What bold step did you commit to that would move you closer to your God-given dream? Now get honest—did your actions actually align with that intention? What worked? What didn't? Where did you move in faith? Where did you hesitate? This is what alignment looks like: noticing where your mindset, heartset, and actions line up with God's truth—and where they need a little course-correction.

Give yourself extra time today to practice both grace and intention. Alignment can feel awkward at first—not because you're doing it wrong, but because you're building something new. As I always say, "Awkward until awesome, messy until miracle." Keep showing up. Alignment becomes strength when you practice it.

....

....

....

....

Dream Stack: Today, what is one action step you will take to move closer to your dream? No one said it would be easy, but they did say it would be worth it. Write it down. Take the step. Watch God move.

....

....

....

....

DAY 7

Fully Present: The Power of Caring More About Less

> Whatever you do, work at it with all your heart, as working for the Lord, not for human masters, since you know that you will receive an inheritance from the Lord as a reward. It is the Lord Christ you are serving.
>
> —Colossians 3:23–24

"HOW TO LIVE MORE PRESENT."

This is one of the most common Google searches today, yet it's one of the hardest things for most people to master. Think about your own life—where do you wish you were more present? What's holding you back from that?

The number one reason we struggle with being present is that we're constantly busy. Somewhere along the way, the American dream morphed into the pursuit of busyness. Our society constantly shouts the message "He who does the most, the quickest, wins." Everything pushes us to be faster and better and to do more. We stack our to-do lists to the max, cram our schedules to overflowing, and spend countless hours and loads of money trying to learn how to multitask, close deals faster, and hustle harder than everyone else.

This culture of doing feeds our need for approval, affirmation, and belonging—until it doesn't. We eventually reach a point where we sit down, reflect, and realize we aren't happy—we're tired, drained, or exhausted, and certainly not present. Once we can admit we're "feeding the need," trying to fill a bottomless pit, we can pause and realign with God's original design.

Today's verse from Colossians allows us to see that living present isn't a starting point; it's a result of something. We see clearly that living present isn't about adding more to your plate. Living present is a *by-product* of something so much deeper—it's the result of learning to care more about fewer things and caring for them with your whole heart, as unto the Lord.

I call it "caring more about less."

Consider running water: It may seem gentle and unassuming at first, but when its strength is concentrated into a single point, it becomes a powerful force of nature. When water is channeled or focused into a narrow stream or jet, its pressure and intensity increase dramatically, allowing it to cut through solid materials like rock or metal with precision. This focused force can carve deep canyons over time or, with modern technology, be used in high-pressure water jets to slice through steel. The power lies in the concentration—what is soft and flowing in its natural state can have immense strength and impact when directed with focus.

As believers, our lives should be marked by strength and impact. Our lives should be marked by whole hearts working for the Lord. That means *caring more about less* is a life focused on living for an audience of One. It means keeping your eyes solely on Jesus; He is your target, your source, your everything—your reason why. Heck, He's your new boss. When His voice becomes the most distinctive voice in your life, He has this beautiful way of refining you (as we learned yesterday) and showing you what truly matters.

God is a God of divine order, so as He becomes your top priority, He gives you the ability to focus on fewer priorities that align more with His purpose for your life. Then it's about proactively eliminating anything that distracts you from what He has called you to do, focusing on what He has called you to do, and doing it with your whole heart. Not half-heartedly, not for approval from others, and not in a rush, but with full devotion as if you're doing it for the Lord—because you are.

The real key to living more present isn't just about being in the here and now—it's also about being with the Lord and discerning what He is saying and doing what He's called you to do, unapologetically. When you live in that awareness, caring more about less, the natural result is a more present life.

Today, I encourage you to care more about what God thinks and less about the opinions of others. Care more about what He's called you to do and less about what others say you should do. Care more about doing fewer things with your whole heart and less about doing everything with only half your heart.

PS This will be hard.

PPS You can do hard things.

■ ■ ■ ■ ■ ■

Revel: Take a moment to reflect on the distractions and less important things that are pulling your attention away from what matters most—keeping your focus on Jesus. Write down anything that comes to mind: tasks, habits, a job, people-pleasing tendencies, or anything else that keeps you from a real connection with Him.

Now, based on the dream God has placed in your heart, identify the fewer, more significant things that align with your purpose, calling, and dreams—the things you want to devote yourself to with your whole heart. How can you intentionally remove distractions and care more about less? (Yes, you can do hard things!)

....

....

....

....

Day 7 Fully Present: The Power of Caring More About Less

Align: It's time for a truth check-in. Did you follow through on what you said you'd do yesterday? Be real with yourself—because real growth starts with honesty.

If you did, awesome—keep showing up and staying consistent. If you didn't, take a moment to pause and ask yourself what got in the way and why?

Remember: You are who God says you are, but you're also shaped by what you practice daily.

....

....

....

....

Dream Stack: Today, what is one small action step you will take to move toward your dream? Even the smallest steps make the greatest impact—and aren't you curious as to what will happen if you keep taking steps?! Write it down, commit to it, and celebrate when you make it happen.

....

....

....

....

DAY 8

Habit Loops: Breaking the Cycle

You say, 'I am allowed to do anything'—but not everything is good for you. You say, 'I am allowed to do anything'—but not everything is beneficial.

—1 Corinthians 10:23 NLT

DO YOU EVER FIND YOURSELF REPEATING the same mistakes? Maybe you vow to break a bad habit, only to find yourself back in the same place two weeks later. Or you take ten steps forward, only to fall twenty steps behind, despite having the best intentions.

It's tempting to shrug it off and say, "Well, that's just who I am," or to pretend the pattern isn't there. But deep down, you know it's a cycle that needs to be broken. The good news is you're not alone—and the even better news is there's a way out.

As believers, one of the most important things we can do is recognize our patterns. Those things you keep doing that you don't want to do? The habits you want to quit but feel stuck in? Jesus died not only for our sins but for the destructive patterns in our life as well. Scripture tells us that *if the Son sets you free, you will be free indeed* (John 8:36). That freedom isn't just for someone else—it's for *you*.

But let's be real: Breaking free from habit loops can feel overwhelming, and it's easy to spiral into blame, shame, and guilt. Questions like "Why do I keep doing this?" or "What's wrong with me?" often arise, but they rarely offer real answers.

It's been said the quality of your questions determines the quality of your answers. So instead of asking "Why do I keep doing this?" consider shifting your focus to a new question:

"What do I want most versus what do I want now?"

What we want *now* often leads us to avoid pain, choose the path of least resistance, or indulge in temporary fixes that make us feel good in the moment. But what we want *most* speaks to the deeper desires that can transform our future—if we start making decisions based on where we're going, not just where we are.

- What you want *now* might lead you to avoid difficult conversations, but what you want *most* is true connection, which requires courage and vulnerability.
- What you want *now* could mean hitting the snooze button because you're tired, but what you want *most* is to be healthy and strong, which requires getting up and showing up for yourself at the gym.
- What you want *now* might be relief from the pain, but what you want *most* is complete healing, which means walking through the pain to find freedom.

Both paths are hard. So here's a truth: *Pick Your Hard*.

Paul, in 1 Corinthians, sheds light on the same struggle we face in balancing our freedom with discernment. Today's verse reveals the tension of living as believers. We know we have freedom in Christ—He fulfilled the law and set us free from the limitations of this world. But true freedom in the Lord requires a deeper awareness that our choices should reflect His nature. While we *can* do many things, not everything aligns with God's best for us.

This means making decisions based not just on immediate desires but also on what we want most—a heart and mind in tune with God's will. When you're truly aligned with Him, anything outside of His will becomes a clear no, or as my seven-year old says, "That's a nope on a rope." It's about making choices that reflect His character and bring lasting growth.

Just because you have the freedom to do something doesn't mean it's the best choice for your well-being or your relationship with God. Shifting your focus from short-term satisfaction to long-term transformation opens the door to breaking free from limiting beliefs, bad habits, and unhealthy patterns you find yourself in so you can step into the abundant life God has for you.

The real question is: Will you choose the path of temporary relief, which may seem easier now but brings greater difficulty later, or the path of discipline, which is tougher at first but leads to lasting transformation? Both will be hard. Pick your hard. The choice is yours.

Revel: What do you want *now*? What do you want *most*? How can you shift your focus to what matters most, allowing God to guide your decisions past the here and now?

Spend some time during your dream stacking time to create a few daily habits to support you in what you want most. Then schedule those habits and don't quit.

Day 8 Habit Loops: Breaking the Cycle

Align: Take a moment to reflect on yesterday. By now, you should be noticing patterns—patterns in how and with what you spend the most amount of time. What are these patterns telling you? How can you be even more intentional with your time and energy moving forward? Are your day-to-day actions in alignment with the dream God's given you? If not, where can you close the gap today?

....

....

....

....

Dream Stack: Today, what is one specific step you will take to manifest your dream? Remember, there is no such thing as try. You either do or you don't; you never try. Write it down. Get 'er done.

....

....

....

....

DAY 9

Think Higher: The Thing Above the Thing

'For my thoughts are not your thoughts, neither are your ways my ways,' declares the Lord. 'As the heavens are higher than the earth, so are my ways higher than your ways and my thoughts than your thoughts.'

—Isaiah 55:8–9

IT'S SO EASY TO GET CONSUMED by the here and now. Every season of life feels permanent, every struggle overwhelming, and every triumph all-consuming. But as believers, we know this isn't the full story. The truth is that God's perspective is vastly different than ours. While we often focus on a single moment, He sees the whole picture—the beginning and the end.

God created the world with eternity in mind. That means His thoughts are higher, greater, and better than ours. Today's Scripture is the ultimate invitation into thinking differently or, shall we say, *thinking higher*.

To think higher means to lift your gaze beyond the immediate and intentionally align your thoughts with His. This isn't about invalidating your thoughts; it's about acknowledging His as the ultimate truth. His perspective allows you to see things in their true context—where what seemed overwhelming suddenly appears manageable when viewed from a divine vantage point. It's exchanging your "thing" for His "thing above the thing."

Consider for a moment driving to the airport in a busy city like Los Angeles or Denver. The traffic can feel like it's bumper to bumper, and all around you is the hustle and bustle of the people hurrying about their day. Thousands of people passing by, most you'll never know by name. Towering overhead are more skyscrapers and other buildings than you can count. If you were to stop long enough to take it all in, you could become completely bogged down, even overwhelmed, or maybe lost in translation.

Then you board one of those planes flying overhead and within a few minutes, you're soaring high above it all. Everything that once felt so big and daunting now appears to be as small as an ant hill. Is it as small as an ant hill? Of course not, but with a new vantage point, your perspective on everything changes.

Thinking higher is like boarding that plane with God—not diminishing the reality of what we face but gaining the perspective to handle it as He sees it. When you align your thoughts with God's, you gain fresh insight into your circumstances, whether they're joyful or difficult, and you can better act in alignment with His will, and when you're in His will, you think like He thinks. That means, even on your best days, His plans are *still better*, and on your worst days, He offers hope beyond the pain.

Today, what's "your thing? Maybe it's the fear, worry, or financial distress you've been experiencing or the day-to-day grind. Maybe your thing is a relationship seemingly falling apart or an unexpected doctor's report. Or maybe your thing is your dreams and your goals, your hopes and desires. No matter what your thing is, lean in with God and begin to ask Him for his thing above the thing.

When you are deeply rooted in the knowledge of God's higher purposes, it transforms the way you approach everything. You're no longer bogged down by the fleeting pressures of the world. Instead, you're empowered to do earthly good, to bring the light of heaven into the darkness around you. Allow Him to elevate your vision today.

Ask God to help you see beyond the trees. Seek His perspective and let your heart be awakened to His higher calling. As you do so, you'll find that even in the midst of the most ordinary moments, you are equipped to do extraordinary things for His Kingdom. May you become so heavenly conscious, so eternity-minded, that you have the capacity to do even more earthly good.

※ ※ ※ ※ ※ ※

Revel: What's "the thing" that's keeping you from seeing God's "thing above the thing"?

Take a moment to recognize the worldly distractions, comforts, or pressures that leave you feeling superficially satisfied, overwhelmed, or hopeless. These things often cloud God's higher purpose for your life. Begin to realign your focus by shifting from a temporary, earthly mindset to an eternal, heavenly perspective. When you do this, you'll be empowered to make an even greater impact here on earth.

Day 9 Think Higher: The Thing Above the Thing

Align: So ... about yesterday—did you actually take that step toward your dream, or did you get distracted by snacks, scrolling, or sheer avoidance? No judgment here, just keeping it real. What tripped you up, and how can you course-correct today as the bold dreamer you are?

....

....

....

....

Dream Stack: What's one bold move you can make today toward that God-size dream of yours? Please note that taking action is not about waiting for the perfect mood or a sign from the heavens (unless it's coffee falling from the sky). You might not always feel ready each day—but the truth is, you have feelings; you're not your feelings. Write your bold move down. Do it despite how you feel.

....

....

....

....

DAY 10

From "Why, God?" to "What, God?": A Shift in Perspective

What no eye has seen, nor ear heard, nor the heart of man imagined, what God has prepared for those who love him.

—1 Corinthians 2:9 ESV

IT'S HUMAN NATURE TO ASK QUESTIONS like, "Why, God? Why is this happening to me? Why do bad things happen to good people? Why does this have to be so hard?"

Asking why is a natural response to pain and confusion. If you've found yourself asking that question, it would make you human, not crazy. But I've learned that this question can create a significant roadblock in our walk with God. It can prevent us from experiencing the full work He wants to do in and through us.

When we ask, "Why, God?" we often begin to question His goodness and open the door to doubt. Think about it for a moment. The last time you asked that question, where did it lead you? Chances are it focused your attention on what God wasn't doing, the pain He wasn't healing, and the answers you didn't have. And how did you feel after asking? Exhausted. Disappointed. Lacking faith. Why? Because you had partnered with doubt.

This happens because our human nature has a negativity bias. Our minds are wired to look for evidence to support our fears. So when we ask, "Why is this happening, God?" We find answers that reinforce our doubts. We start believing that God isn't good, that we can't depend on Him, and that He's distant from our struggles. This doubt spirals into a false reality.

Don't get me wrong—the desire to find the answer behind the question "Why, God?" is real and valid. Yet if we're not careful, we may seek the miracles of God without embracing the mystery—both of which reveal His sovereignty and the depth of our true need for Him. We all long for more of His revelation, His power, and His majesty. But the truth is, we often struggle with the mysteries. We must recognize that some questions will never get answered on this side of eternity, and that's not because God is not good. Remember, as our passage from today tells us, *No eye has seen, nor ear heard, nor ... heart ... imagined, what God has prepared for those who love Him.* Did you catch that? He is *that* good.

The minute we try to diminish the power of God to fit the things we can understand, we forfeit the ability to see His mighty hand and majestic miracles. Truth be told, it's both His mysteries and His revelations that sustain us. It's both His mysteries and His revelations that guide us through the hard times. Believe it or not, it is the same mystery and revelation of God that led Him to create the heavens and the earth that also sent Jesus to the cross. It's the same mystery and revelation that holds the universe (and your life) together right now in ways beyond our comprehension.

So today, I want to invite you to ask a better question, one that will align you with God's work in your life: "What, God?"

By asking "What, God?" you will shift your focus away from doubt and onto His majesty. It invites you to look beyond your immediate circumstances and into a greater reality—His. When you ask, "What, God? What are You doing?" you force your physical eyes to see through a spiritual lens and observe that He is working, even in the midst of your hardest of moments. The question allows you to lift your eyes from your limited viewpoint and behold His goodness and majesty. It takes the focus off *your* timing, *your* plans, and *your* will—and places it on His.

Best of all, this question is an invitation to partner with what He is doing instead of doubting Him for what it appears He's not doing. As we seek Him—asking for His divine plan, calling upon Him in the midst of our circumstances—Scripture promises that God faithfully reveals himself to those who seek Him. When He does, we can truly partner with Him. The question then shifts from simply, "What are you doing, God?" to "What are you doing, and what do you want me to do about it?"

Though we may not always fully grasp what He's doing, we can rest in His goodness and trust that His plans far exceed anything we could imagine. Trusting the Lord is what unlocks the peace that surpasses all understanding. It also gives us the faith to walk closely with Him, partnering with His majesty, whether we're in the valley or on the mountaintop … even if it's just one step at a time. It keeps our focus on Him, not the outcome.

When we shift our focus to who God is and what He *is* doing, we gain a clearer perspective. We realize that even when life feels like it's falling apart, God is not finished. Our story isn't over. Eternity is already set in motion, and we are invited to step into the flow of His divine purpose as we marvel at His majesty. Trust Him, then partner with Him in what He is doing.

Revel: What "why" questions are you bringing to God right now? How can you shift from asking, "Why, God?" to "What, God?"—as in, what is He doing in your current situation?

Take time to consider what He is doing, then figure out how you can partner with His majesty and His mystery in this moment.

Day 10 From "Why, God?" to "What, God?": A Shift in Perspective

....

....

....

....

Align: Let's be honest—reflecting on what you did or didn't do yesterday can stir up all kinds of emotions. It might feel awkward or irrelevant, or even trigger some guilt or shame. But I encourage you to lean in because this part matters. Reflection isn't about perfection; it's about progress. We are what we practice, and what we practice becomes permanent.

This isn't just a box to check; it's a chance to learn, grow, and become more of who God created you to be. Alignment is about integrity between your intention and your action, your belief and your behavior, your dream and your discipline. When you stop and assess, you give yourself the gift of clarity and the opportunity to course-correct.

So pause and reflect: What bold step did you say you were going to take yesterday? Did you follow through? If not, what held you back—and be honest with yourself here. Was it fear? Distraction? Doubt? Laziness in disguise? Now dig a little deeper: Why did that stop you, and what truth do you need to stand on today to get back in alignment?

Growth doesn't happen by accident—it happens on purpose. And today is another chance to choose purpose, on purpose.

....

....

....

....

BOLD

Dream Stack: Based upon the revelation God gave you in your reveling time, what is one action you can take to manifest your dream that's in alignment with His majesty and greater plans? Put it at the top of your to-do list and make it happen!

....

....

....

....

DAY 11

SHIFT from Fear to Faith

Even though I walk through the darkest valley, I will fear no evil, for you are with me.

—Psalm 23:4

HAVE YOU EVER FOUND YOURSELF struggling with fear?

Wait, let me rephrase that: Do you remember the last time you struggled with fear?

Whether it's the fear of failure, rejection, or uncertainty about the future, fear is something we all face. We may try to ignore it, push through it, or pretend it doesn't exist, but fear feels real—and it's powerful.

The Bible never downplays fear, yet God doesn't coddle us when we're afraid. When David faced Goliath, God didn't tell him, "Don't worry; it's no big deal." When Mary became pregnant with the Son of God, He didn't say, "Oh, Mary. Don't stress; people will understand." Instead of shaming us or dismissing our fear, God gives us a powerful way to deal with it—"Fear not!"

This simple command is powerful and the pattern-interrupt we need, especially because it's followed by a guarantee He is with us always. Just telling you to "fear not" is one thing, but giving you the ultimate reason why you don't have to fear is another. Scripture tells us to "fear not" and acknowledge His presence. So how do we handle fear? The answer is simple: Shift our focus.

Overcoming fear starts with redirecting your attention, shifting your focus from problem to presence. In today's passage, we see David make that exact shift. He acknowledges the reality of where he is—the darkest valley—and yet, he boldly declares he will not fear. Why? Because God is with him. Let's pause here. I'd argue that the most powerful words in this verse are the first two: *even though*. That phrase is packed with purpose. It means "despite the fact that" and reminds us that courage isn't the absence of darkness—it's the presence of God in the middle of it. David didn't deny the valley, but he refused to let it define his response.

The Bible consistently tells us to be strong and courageous, not because fear doesn't exist, but because *God is with us*.

- *Be strong and courageous. Do not be afraid; do not be discouraged, for the Lord your God will be with you wherever you go.* —Joshua 1:9
- *When I am afraid, I put my trust in you.* —Psalm 56:3
- *Do not be anxious about anything, but in every situation, by prayer and petition, with thanksgiving, present your requests to God.* —Philippians 4:6

In each of these verses, God shifts the focus away from fear and onto His presence. Though fear is real, it doesn't have the final say. If you're feeling overwhelmed by fear today, don't simply try to muster up the strength to ignore it. Instead, pay attention to what you're focusing on. Fear is a by-product of misplaced focus. It comes when we focus on our problems.

The enemy wants you to believe that fear is practical and responsible, but it's not. It's a lie designed to get you off course. Fear disrupts your focus, and today, it's time to shift your gaze back to the face of Jesus. When Peter walked on water, it wasn't because the storm had calmed, but because his eyes were fixed on Jesus. When Daniel was in the lion's den, his attention wasn't on the lions but on the Lord. And when Esther approached the king, her focus wasn't on him but on her true King. Faith arises when we focus on Jesus.

Faith was always God's original design; fear is merely its counterfeit. It is by faith that we believe God created the heavens and the earth (Genesis 1:1). It is by faith that we are saved (Ephesians 2:8). It is by faith that we trust not in what we can see but in what we cannot see (2 Corinthians 5:7). Fear, in essence, is misguided faith—faith in the wrong things. Instead of accommodating your fear, displace it by shifting your focus. Fix your eyes on Jesus and let Him be the reason you "fear not!"

Today, make the shift. Don't force yourself to have more faith—simply allow your faith to flow as a natural by-product of looking to Jesus. Look beyond the waves and beyond the fear, and keep your gaze firmly fixed on Him.

Revel: What fear is weighing most heavily on your heart right now? Take a moment to reflect—have you been focusing more on your problem or on God's presence?

Pause and rest in the Lord's presence—don't rush and don't overthink it. Quietly plead the blood of Jesus over each fear, and as you do, let your faith rise as you shift your focus from the problem to the power of God's presence.

Day 11 SHIFT from Fear to Faith

Align: All right, real talk—let's rewind the tape. Look back on yesterday: Did you actually take that step toward your dream, or did Netflix win again? No judgment, just honesty. If you didn't make the move you said you would, ask yourself what tripped you up. Was it fear, distraction, overwhelm—or maybe just forgetting? (Hey, it happens.)

Now the good news: You're not stuck. Today's a fresh start. Identify what stood in your way, give it a name, and plot your comeback. Because you, my friend, are way too bold to let yesterday's setback steal today's step. Let's realign and keep moving forward!

....

....

....

....

Dream Stack: Regardless of what you did or didn't do yesterday, what's one action you can take today that will move your dream one step closer to reality? Make sure to write it down—you'll want to reflect on it tomorrow.

Remember, you were born to dream—and each step you take brings you closer to making it happen.

....

....

....

....

DAY 12

The Truth About Doubt

But when you ask, you must believe and not doubt, because the one who doubts is like a wave of the sea, blown and tossed by the wind.

—James 1:6

YESTERDAY, WE TALKED ABOUT FEAR. Today, let's focus on doubt—a struggle that is distinctly different from fear. If you've ever wrestled with doubt, you know what I mean.

Fear declares, "I *am* afraid." Doubt, on the other hand, asks, "*Am* I afraid?" Fear is decided. Doubt is undecided. Doubt doesn't mean unbelief—it means you're stuck in indecision, wavering between belief and disbelief. That's why doubt feels so exhausting. You go back and forth, wondering, *Can it happen? Yes, it can! No, it won't. Maybe it will. What will?* And it drains you because you're caught in limbo, or as James says, *blown and tossed by the wind,* aimlessly drifting with no firm direction on what you actually believe.

But what if doubt isn't as bad as you might think? In fact, what if doubt is an opportunity in disguise? Rather than seeing doubt as a threat, consider it an invitation to confront critical conversations. As we mature as believers, there is so much we don't know and so much we continue to learn about who God is and the plans He has for us. On top of that, life, with all its ups and downs, forces us to confront important questions that need answers: What do I really believe? Is God trustworthy? Is His power enough for my situation? These aren't negative questions—they're moments of indecision presenting you with a chance to seek God's wisdom and truth.

Consider how a child grows. Their first ten years are pure absorption of life—discovering what's possible and what everything means. They're in constant learning mode, asking questions, seeking to discover, and ultimately shaping their beliefs about themselves, other people, God, the world as a whole. As a parent training your child in the Lord, every question they ask becomes prime real estate for shaping both their minds and hearts with God's truth.

Now imagine if they asked you those fundamental questions—What do I really believe about God? Is He trustworthy? Is His power enough for my situation?

What would you say to your child?

I hope you would confidently declare the goodness of the Lord, speak of the power of salvation, and point to the unshakable foundation of living a life of faith in God, all by using the Word. I pray you would lead them to Scriptures that reveal His faithfulness and countless miracles, building a sense of awe and reverence for who God is. I'd hope your child would be so captivated by the revelation of Jesus they would carry that truth within them for the rest of their life.

What if your own questions and doubts provided you with the same opportunity? What if the very moments you find yourself questioning God's power or His faithfulness are ripe opportunities to dig deeper as you would for your child? What if your doubt is giving you the chance to make a conscious choice about what you actually believe, using the Word of God as your anchor?

Here's the key: As you bring your big, bold questions to God—about life, His Word, provision, healing, whatever it may be—be confident in who He is. He is the great I AM. Just because you don't have all the answers yet doesn't mean He isn't still the answer. That's the power behind today's Scripture.

As you approach Him with your questions, don't let the weight of your circumstances—or the ache of the unknown—cause you to doubt Him. Doubt will always try to toss you around like waves. But when you come to Him, trusting who He is, you anchor yourself in unshakable truth.

It's not wrong to have questions, but where you seek your answers is crucial. Come to Him with the assurance that you will find the answers. Come to Him knowing that He is the answer. Come to Him knowing He is your source of truth and stability. Just because clarity hasn't come yet doesn't mean it won't.

I want to encourage you in this today: Let every moment be an opportunity for the Word of God to shape (or reshape) your heart. Even doubt, if brought to God, can become the soil in which faith grows stronger. Let your questions lead you back to His promises, which are found not in the fleeting opinions or facts of the world but in the unchanging truth of His Word.

From now on, when you encounter doubt, don't let it toss you around. Let it ground you deeper in your faith. Consciously choose to trust God's truth, which is reliable, timeless, and unfailing. Use doubt as a signal to anchor yourself into His promises. Don't let the waves of uncertainty pull you away from Him—let them draw you closer to the unshakable foundation of His love and strength. Then take Him at His Word.

Today, the choice is yours: What will you believe?

Day 12 The Truth About Doubt

Revel: Is there an area in your life where doubt has begun to creep in? What's the real question behind your doubt? Get honest about it.

Then take time today to ground yourself—not in your feelings but in the truth of God's Word. Your questions matter, but where you go for answers matters more. Dive into Scripture as if it's water for your soul (because it is). Let His truth remind you of His unshakable faithfulness, so you can walk boldly and live fully in the freedom that comes from trusting Christ.

....

....

....

....

Align: You are what you practice, and you become what you actually follow through on—not just what you intend. Intentions are nice to have, but they're meaningless without action. Action is what builds dreams. So let's take a hot second to rewind the mental tape. Look back on yesterday—did you make that move you said you would? Or did the day escape you?

If you didn't follow through, no shame—but let's get curious. What tripped you up? Was it fear? Distraction? Life? The point isn't to beat yourself up; it's to understand what got in the way, so you can adjust and try again today. Because discipline isn't about perfection; it's about consistency. One bold step at a time, you're becoming the person who lives that dream—not just talks about it.

....

....

....

....

BOLD

Dream Stack: Now let's shake it off and move it forward. What's one thing you can do today to show your dream you're serious? Yes, you can, and yes, you will! Write it down, then live to tell about it.

....

....

....

....

DAY 13

What's Accountability Got to Do With It?

Nothing in all creation is hidden from God's sight.
Everything is uncovered and laid bare before the
eyes of Him to whom we must give account.

—Hebrews 4:13

AS A GROWTH COACH for over a decade, I've heard countless people say, "I just need someone to hold me accountable." Does that resonate with you? Do you find yourself struggling with accountability, looking for someone to help you stay motivated? If so, let's unpack that a bit.

When we rely on others to hold us accountable, we're essentially outsourcing one of our most important assets—our own internal motivation, our "burn." While external accountability can be helpful, relying on it too much can work against us, creating codependency and keeping us from owning our own drive and potential.

True accountability can be defined as *taking personal account* of your own *ability*.

It's not about waiting for someone else to push you forward; it's about taking ownership of what God has already placed inside you. When you depend on external accountability, you're neglecting to develop the endurance and resilience needed to push through on your own. God has already given you everything you need to succeed—but you need to realize it and then take personal responsibility for it.

Here's what I propose: You don't need anyone or anything to do for you what God has already equipped you to do for yourself. Rather you need to learn to take *account* of your own ability and your own dreams, working toward them each day, come rain or shine. Stop waiting for a trainer or a coach or a mentor to jump-start you. You jump-start you. Stop worrying about who's watching or what others think. Care more about what God thinks.

Today's verse from the book of Hebrews addresses this truth head-on. This truth can feel overwhelming at first—knowing that nothing is hidden, that every thought, action, and motive is seen by God. However, this entire chapter of Scripture isn't a call to strive harder in our own strength. It isn't calling us to hustle harder or to live in fear of being found out. It's actually an invitation—an invitation to step out of striving and into faith-rest.

A faith-rest life means we stop living for God's approval and start living from it—resting in what He's already said, already done, and already called us to be. It's the daily decision to trust that His grace is enough, that His presence is constant, and that His Word is true—even when our circumstances feel loud and our hearts feel heavy. It's about being fully known and fully loved. It's not performance-based; it's presence-based.

So instead of letting this truth weigh you down, let it free you. You don't have to hide. You don't have to hustle. You just have to rest—in faith—in the One who already did the work for you.

When we understand that God sees everything, we realize that we don't need to perform or prove ourselves to Him. He knows our weaknesses, our struggles, and our strengths. He knows it all—and still He loves us deeply and unconditionally. The call isn't to work harder or do more to win His approval. It's to lean into His grace, recognizing that our worth isn't based on performance but on His love for us. That being said, His grace doesn't shame us or give us permission to stay stuck—it activates us. It's not passive; it's powerful. Grace empowers us to move forward—not by striving in our own strength but by leaning into His strength, so we can boldly step into what He's called us to do.

God's given you everything you need; that's on Him. Taking account of your ability? Well, that is on you. No one else can do it for you. How far can you go? How deep can you dig? You'll never know if you keep outsourcing your drive to someone else or waiting for someone else to push you. What really matters is the account you will give to God, just as today's Scripture portrays. He wants you to take account of the gifts He's given you, doing what you can do with your whole heart and leaning on Him for the strength to push through life's challenges.

Living with the awareness that we will one day give an account for our lives isn't meant to scare us; it's meant to motivate us to live intentionally, grounded in God's presence. When we truly grasp this, we are free to pursue the call He has on our lives with passion and purpose. The focus is on doing what He has uniquely designed us for—living out our purpose with boldness, knowing His eyes see us fully and His grace covers us completely. The good news is that you don't need anyone else to accomplish this—it's already yours!

Today, I encourage you with this: Do you!

Be true to who God created you to be. If you can push further, push further. If you can do one more, do one more. And if you need rest, rest. Don't rely on others to ignite your fire or fuel your passion—that's on you. Take ownership of your dreams, account for your ability, and trust you're not in this alone. God's with you and directing you every step of the way. He's proud of your fire. He loves your passion. He's watching every part of your journey, cheering you on, and wanting to see you step into all He's created you to be.

He sees you completely, loves you deeply, and understands your every move. Now go *make your move.*

Day 13 What's Accountability Got to Do With It?

Revel: Have you been leaning on others for accountability or relying on someone else to carry the weight of what you're capable of doing yourself? Today, how can you take account of your own abilities?

Pause and reflect. Ask God to reveal the passions He's placed in your heart. Rekindle that inner fire and step boldly into the fullness of His calling on your life. Then use your dream-stacking time to take intentional action and make your move.

_____

_____

_____

_____

Align: Take a moment and rewind—what step did you intend to take toward your dream yesterday? Did you move, even a little? If not, what internal resistance or external barrier got in your way? Was it fear, distraction, doubt, or something deeper? Maybe it was just an honest distraction? Identifying the real obstacle is where transformation begins. Because when you see it clearly, you can surrender it wholly—and move forward not just with intention but also with power. Remember, alignment isn't about perfection—it's about choosing, again and again, to walk in rhythm with God's truth and your divine assignment. So ... what adjustment needs to happen today?

_____

_____

_____

_____

BOLD

Dream Stack: Today, what is one action you can take to move toward your dream? I challenge you to write it down, take that step, and see where it leads.

....

....

....

....

DAY 14

Truth Has a Name

Jesus said, 'If you hold to my teaching, you are really my disciples. Then you will know the truth, and the truth will set you free.'

—John 8:31–32

LIFE CAN HIT HARD. We face unexpected setbacks, detours on our path to our dreams, and trials that seem overwhelming. In those moments, it's easy to let our circumstances shape our understanding of what's true. The pain, disappointment, and confusion we experience often lead us to interpret reality in a way that can distort God's truth.

When life happens, we crave certainty. But because life isn't always certain, we create our own interpretations of each experience, trying to make sense of the uncertainty. These interpretations give us a way to feel in control when our world is spinning and doesn't make sense.

Think about a time in high school when your boyfriend or girlfriend broke up with you and said, "It's not you; it's me." Didn't you immediately wonder, *What's wrong with me?* Of course you did. That experience likely led you to make assumptions about yourself and your own self-worth.

Or remember that business venture that didn't work out and led you to believe, *I'll never be good enough.* Or when your prayers seemed to go unanswered, causing you to think, *God doesn't hear me.* These interpretations not only shape how you view yourself but also impact how you see the world and your relationship with God.

As humans, we seek clarity in our experiences—whether good or bad—and in doing so, we often create stories shaped by personal bias. Over time, we cling to these stories, calling them "my truth." But here's the thing: Just because it's "your truth" doesn't mean it's *the* truth.

What do you cling to when life doesn't go as planned? When things feel uncertain, do you hold tightly to your opinions and biases? Do you lean on your own understanding?

As believers, we're called to cling to something much greater: the truth—Jesus. In today's passage from the book of John, Jesus is clear about this when he says, *If you hold to my teaching, you are really my disciples.*

Did you catch that? If you hold onto what? If you cling to what? Jesus's teachings. Of all the things Jesus could say, have you ever wondered why He says this? Why does He tell us to hold to His teachings? Jesus knew we would crave certainty and clarity, but He also knew that the only way to true freedom in the midst of the uncertainties of life was through His Word.

By holding to His teachings rather than clinging to our own opinions and biases, we demonstrate that we truly are His disciples, His followers. As we hold to His Word—the truth Scripture promises of His truth, not our own—we will know the truth, and the truth will set us free. This wasn't just an intellectual lesson from Jesus; it was an invitation to experience Him, the living truth. He was inviting the disciples to not just know more facts but to *know Him* deeply.

The same invitation is extended to us today. In a world filled with uncertainty, instability, and a whole bunch of "my truths," we desperately need *the* truth. Can you imagine the disciples saying to Jesus, "Yeah, yeah, we hear you Jesus, but *my truth* says …"? Never in a million years. Let's be real: There is no truth without Jesus.

In holding to His teachings, you don't gain just insight—you also encounter Him as your truth. And when you find Him as your truth, you discover true freedom. Therefore, true freedom isn't found in your own understanding or perceptions but in holding tightly to His teachings—His truth—not your own. Only in embracing His truth can you fully experience the freedom He promises.

Yes, your experiences are real, and your interpretations may feel valid, but they don't define what's true. They're simply your perspective on the situation. But as a follower of Jesus, you're called to live by a higher standard—God's truth. This means that your experiences, interpretations, opinions, and biases shouldn't shape your understanding of truth. Instead, God's truth must shape how you understand your experiences. His truth, found in His Word, is what brings real clarity and real freedom.

It's only when you let go of "your truth" and align yourself with His that you'll experience real freedom. So if you're searching for certainty, don't cling to your own interpretations or ideas. Hold onto Him. Cling to truth!

Know the truth and the truth will set you free.

■ ■ ■ ■ ■ ■

Revel: Take a moment to reflect on an experience in your life that you've been holding onto—an event, relationship, or failure that has shaped your perception of truth. How has that experience influenced how you see yourself, others, or God?

Now consider how you can exchange that perception for *His* truth. What does the Bible say about the situation? Spend time with God, bring that experience to Him, and dive into His Word. Seek what His truth declares about your worth, your identity, and His love for you.

Align: Take a deep breath and think back—did you take even the smallest step toward your dream yesterday? Maybe it was a quiet moment of clarity or a brave yes no one else saw. If not, it's OK. This isn't about shame or guilt—it's about awareness. What needs your attention right now to help you realign with the dream in your heart? Grace first then growth.

Dream Stack: Let's cut to it—what's one real action you can take today to bring your dream closer to reality? Not someday. Not soon. Today. Because let's be honest: Your dream doesn't move unless you do. You are what you do, not what you say you will do.

Write it down. Make it happen.

DAY 15

For the Love of "No!"

Now all discipline seems to be painful at the time, yet later it will produce a transformation of character, bringing a harvest of righteousness and peace to those who yield to it.

—Hebrews 12:11 TPT

ONE EVENING, AS I TUCKED my oldest son into bed, he leaned in and whispered, "Can I sleep with you and Daddy? PLEASE?" He continued his pitch, which was strategic, complete with a breakdown of how many nights he had slept with us compared to his siblings. Honestly, he was nearly convincing, but having spent three nights of sharing our bed with one or two other children, I was exhausted, so my answer to him had to be "no."

His reaction wasn't pleasant. He groaned and complained as he argued his case. In that moment, I blurted out, "If you can't handle the no, what makes you think you can handle the yes?" Suddenly, I paused and thought, *Whoa, where else does this show up in my life?*

We all crave the "yes!" We want what we want, when we want it. We long for our problems to be solved today, our dreams to be fulfilled yesterday, and the easier paths to be taken as soon as possible. For us, it's about instant gratification, but that's not how God works.

I've realized that our journey with the Lord is less about the no and more about the preparation for the yes. The goal isn't merely the destination; it's also about who we become on the journey toward it. Our dreams aren't just about reaching that finish line; they're also about the transformation that takes place within us along the way.

As we've learned in prior devotionals, every trial we face, every pressure we endure is building within us our capacity not only to reach our yes but also to have the ability to sustain its blessings. It's not about the destination; it's about the character required to carry the weight of the blessings that come with that yes.

Today's verse reminds us that what we often want is for our prayers to be answered and our dreams to come true, but what we truly need is the transformation of our character.

If we're not careful, we can spend our energy chasing external prizes—success, fulfillment, recognition—thinking they are the goal. But God is after something deeper. His aim isn't just to give us something—it's to make us into someone. Someone who reflects His glory, walks in His love, and can carry the weight of the very dream we're praying for.

And how does He do that? Through His loving, transformative discipline. It's not punishment; it's preparation. Character is built over time, and it's shaped in the places we usually want to rush through—in the waiting, in the disappointment, in the "no" and the "not yet."

When God says "no" or "not yet," it's an invitation to grow. God isn't holding out on you. He's building you. To walk in full alignment with God's will and fulfill the dreams

He has placed on your heart, you'll need to develop the spiritual discipline to sustain your journey through the highs and the lows, the good days and the hard. Spiritual discipline is the ability to control one's behavior and actions to achieve a goal or maintain a standard of conduct, even despite the yes's, the no's, and the not yets. Developing this kind of discipline isn't always convenient or easy, but it's always worth it because you're growing in holiness as God matches your character with His revelation. His discipline is rooted in love and affection as He aligns your heart and mind to His will, training your habits and behavior to match the glory He's revealed to you, so He can give you what He's promised.

The real question is: If you struggle with the no, what makes you think you can handle the yes when it comes? A yes without the character to carry it could lead to pride, selfishness, or a sense of entitlement, but a no or not yet is an opportunity for growth, humility, and trust in the Lord.

I want to encourage you today: Don't let the noes discourage you. Instead, let the training of the Lord prepare you for what's to come. Embrace the character-building process and strive to be just as steady, joyful, and peaceful in the noes as you are in the yeses.

God's timing is perfect. As we've seen, He's not withholding the yes because He's against you—He's preparing you. Stay faithful, stay focused, and trust that the character He's shaping in you today will be the foundation for everything He has for you tomorrow. Remember, God is our yes and amen. He is good and will never give us more than we can handle, nor will He shortcut our character development, because He knows the weight of the blessing. Don't get grumpy; get ready—God's blessings are coming.

Here's to you and every "No!" that is actually preparing you for your "Yes!"

Revel: Where has God said no in your life? Pause and reflect on how this no is paving the way for His greater yes. Check your heart's response to these noes and ask God to reveal how you can align with His perfect timing, preparing you to receive all He has in store when the time is right.

Day 15 For the Love of "No!"

....

....

Align: Did you take the step toward your dream yesterday? If not, what tripped you up? Get real, name it, and then move it. You can't overcome what you won't confront, and you can't align with His truth while cozying up to excuses. Let today be your pivot point.

....

....

....

....

Dream Stack: Today, what's one action—just one—that aligns your external life with the internal vision God has planted in you? Start building on the outside what He's already planted on the inside of you. Put it on paper. Bring it to life.

....

....

....

....

DAY 16

Dare to Dream: Bridge the Gap

Then He said to him, 'I assure you and most solemnly say to you, you will see heaven opened and the angels of God ascending and descending on the Son of Man' [the bridge between heaven and earth].

—John 1:51 AMP

BY NOW, YOU'RE VERY CLEAR on one thing: The day God gives you a dream and the day that dream manifests are two entirely different days. Can I get an "Amen!"? Here you are, sixteen days into your 101-day journey of living your dream on the daily, and you have more than eighty days to go. Maybe now you understand why so many people have a dream but so few live them out—*the gap in between* is no joke!

The journey from having a dream to realizing that dream is often one of the hardest paths we walk—not just because it's challenging (though it is), but also because we're not expecting it to be *that* hard and take *that* long. At a head level, we can anticipate some delays and obstacles that are likely par for the course, but once we set sail, we're hit with the harsh reality that the journey requires more from us and takes more out of us than we could have ever anticipated. Today, my hope is to provide you with deeper insight into *the gap in between* where you are and where you want to be, so you can recognize it and navigate this season with greater boldness and determination.

You may be thinking, *"All right, JG, you've said 'the gap in between' a handful of times. What does it mean?*

The gap in between is that challenging space where your dreams exist but haven't yet materialized. It's the gap in between where you are and where you want to be. It's the distance between what you want and what you have, between your deep desire and your current reality. It's that space between receiving a prophetic word and realizing it. It's where we find ourselves in the tension of waiting—between dreams given and dreams achieved, between heaven's promise and the here and now.

Make no bones about it; the gap in between is hard! It's frustrating and can feel like an eternity, causing you to question yourself, God, and any and every dream you've ever had. This is why many don't start or they quit halfway through, because it can be overwhelming, daunting, and full of discouragements. Therefore, we must understand a few things about the gap.

The first principle is found in today's devotional, in the book of John, when Jesus meets His disciple Nathanael (also known as Bartholomew). This encounter is subtle but powerful—and it reveals something essential about how Jesus sees us. Jesus, as He often did, looked beyond appearances and words. Before Nathanael ever opened his mouth, Jesus saw his heart. He spoke to who Nathanael was, not just what he had done or said.

It's a reminder that Jesus doesn't know just our names—He knows our nature. He knows what we hope for, what we hide from, and what we dream of. And He doesn't just know us from a distance—He loves us, fully and personally, right where we are.

Before we take a single step toward the dream, He's already near—seeing, knowing, and loving us through it all.

The second principle is: Through Jesus's life, death, and resurrection, heaven has been opened to us. He is the ladder connecting heaven and earth, and through Him, we have access to the heavenly realms. Jesus fulfilled all of God's promises, and His Kingdom is both here and still coming. He bridged the gap—He *is* the bridge.

This means, as believers, because of Jesus's sacrifice, we can trust that every step, even the challenging ones, is part of God's plan to bring our dreams to life. Knowing that God created our beginning with the end in mind, we also know He invites us to live our journey from a place of victory in Him. This means we have the unique privilege of approaching the gap in between with a different mindset, because it's not just about bridging the gap between where we are and where we want to be—it's also about embracing the truth that empowers us in the gap itself. The truth is this: The gap in between is where we become the people capable of carrying the weight of the blessings God is preparing for us. Therefore, our role is to have faith in the process and, even more so, faith in Jesus, who has already bridged the ultimate gap.

The final principle, and probably the most practical one, the gap in between is part of the process. It's not a detour, it's not a mistake, and it's certainly not a punishment. The space between where you are and where you're going isn't an indicator of failure—it's par for the course. Think of it like a flight from Oregon to Florida. Halfway there, it'd be ridiculous to think the pilot made a mistake because we're still in midair. Any pilot or flight attendant would kindly assure you that the space between Oregon and Florida is simply part of the journey to your destination and you can't get to where you want to be without it.

Not only is this gap normal and part of the process as we fly in an airplane, but it's also a necessary phase in the pursuit of our dreams, because it's where growth happens, faith is tested, and character is refined. Sure, you can turn back. Sure, you can call it quits halfway through. But if you do, you'll never reach the destination God intended for you. The key to getting from where you are to where you want to be is the commitment to stay the course—to bridge the gap one step at a time, one dream stack at a time. That commitment is what will carry you through.

Your dreams won't materialize overnight, just as a seed planted yesterday isn't harvested tomorrow. Every dream requires time, character development, and the commitment that is forged in the gap in between.

God wants to work through you to bring His will to earth, teaching you how to

Day 16 Dare to Dream: Bridge the Gap

partner with Him in every season, even in the space between. You were made to bridge that gap—not just for yourself but also for others. By fixing your eyes on Him, remembering His sacrifice, and building your dreams on the solid foundation of Christ, your plane will land. Your dreams will come to life. You will bridge the gap.

This is how you bring heaven to earth. This is how your dreams become reality. His Kingdom is both in heaven and here and now. Dare to bridge the gap. Dare to dream.

■ ■ ■ ■ ■ ■

Revel: Pause and reflect on your own *gap in between*. How has this space felt for you? Have you embraced it, or has it been a struggle? Consider how you've shown up during this time between where you are and where you want to be.

Today, view Jesus as your bridge—the solid foundation on which your dreams and life are built. As you partner with Him in the in between, may the journey feel lighter and may you be more bold as you dare to dream with the Lord.

....

....

....

....

Align: Let's be honest—did you actually lean into your dream yesterday, or did life hijack your schedule (again)? No shame here—just awareness. Distractions happen. Detours happen. But staying off-track? That's a choice.

Take a moment: What pulled you away? Was it a full plate, too many tabs open (mentally or literally), or just the weight of the day? Identify it, learn from it, and then shake it off. You're not behind; you're being refined.

If you did show up for your dream yesterday, celebrate that. Write it down. Give yourself some credit—it matters. If you didn't, don't spiral. Just get clear on what needs to shift and make it right today. Maybe even double down. Instead of doing one thing, stretch yourself—do two. Not to punish yourself but to reclaim your momentum.

BOLD

You can do hard things. And better yet, you can do holy things—on purpose, with grit and grace.

....

....

....

....

Dream Stack: All right, let's go! What's one action you can take today to move the needle on your dream? Just one. Come on now—this is your dream! Dig deep, shake off the doubt, and make a move. You weren't made to sit on the sidelines. Write it down, then walk it out.

....

....

....

....

DAY 17

Your Weakness Is Not Overrated

[The Lord said,] 'My grace is always more than enough for you, and my power finds its full expression through your weakness.' So I will celebrate my weaknesses, for when I'm weak I sense more deeply the mighty power of Christ living in me.

—2 Corinthians 12:9 TPT

RAISE YOUR HAND IF you enjoy not being good at something. Raise your hand if you appreciate your own weaknesses. Raise your hand if, in the last month, you've posted the most unflattering picture of yourself on social media. If we're honest, no one loves acknowledging their weaknesses. Yet we all have them—shortcomings, failures, inadequacies. In a world that celebrates strength, success, and victories, our weaknesses are often ignored or even hidden.

How do you view your own weaknesses? What about the weaknesses of others? If we're not careful, we can easily become critical or judgmental, both toward ourselves and others. We might feel ashamed of our flaws, hide them, overcompensate, or cover up what we don't want others to see. Some of us may even pretend our weaknesses don't exist, focusing only on our strengths instead.

Yes, it's important to honor our strengths, walk in our calling, and steward the gifts God has given us. But that doesn't mean we should overlook or be ashamed of our weaknesses. As followers of Christ, we are called to view things differently—a viewpoint that is often the opposite of how the world views things. This includes how we look at words like *strength* and *weakness*.

Today's Scripture makes it clear that in our weakness, God's strength is made perfect. That means our weaknesses are not obstacles to avoid but opportunities for God's power to shine through us. It means your weakness is a divine portal through which God's holy power can be revealed!

Often we spend so much time and energy focused on fixing our weaknesses that we miss the bigger picture. The world tells us to hide our flaws or work harder to overcome them, but God invites us to celebrate them as opportunities for His strength to be revealed.

A real example of this in my life was right before I started writing this devotional. My husband and I were facing overwhelming financial pressures after taking many risks in our businesses. We both knew that God had called us to step into new levels of creating with Him. For me, this included shifting out of a coaching model and into digital content and ministry. I'd love to tell you it worked. It didn't. Or at least not how I thought it would or even close to the ways I envisioned it should. On my own, I felt very weak, discouraged, and unsure of how to move forward. There were days I couldn't even get the strength to get out of bed. Every post, new video, and course I put out there seemed to go unanswered, and the bills kept piling up. No matter what I did, it felt like I was hitting a wall at every turn. Except for one thing—writing.

In this deeply vulnerable place of weakness, I consciously chose to rely on God's grace. Instead of giving in to despair, I spent time in prayer, seeking God's presence, trusting His promise to provide, and doing the thing I knew He had called me to do—write. In this situation, it's clear that my own strength didn't carry me through—it was God's grace. His power was made perfect in my weakness, revealing His ability to provide, strengthen, and guide even when I felt most vulnerable and crazy. The rest is history or, maybe I should say, is in your hands.

If you're not sensing that mighty power in your life, it may be because your focus is on the wrong thing. Wherever your attention goes, your energy flows. Instead of fixating on your weakness, shift your focus to God. His grace is more than enough, and His power works best in your weak spots. When you embrace this truth, God can heal, refine, and empower you in ways you never thought possible. He can reveal His glory through your shortcomings and use them for His purposes.

I encourage you with this; don't run from your weaknesses. Don't cover up or overcompensate for the areas where you feel insecure and incapable. Don't resign yourself to your own flaws by saying, "That's just the way I am." Instead, view your weaknesses as divine opportunities for God to show up and show off in your life. Rather than focusing on your shortcomings, begin to celebrate them, because when you are weak, you will sense the power of Christ more deeply within.

Today, take your eyes off your own insecurity and rest in His security. Take your mind off your own insufficiencies and see that He is everything you need Him to be. You no longer have to be dependent upon your own abilities and fearful of your weaknesses; be completely and totally reliant on *His* power working through you. All you have to do is show up and allow Him to do what only He can do.

Yes, show up in your strengths, using the gifts God has given you. But even more so, embrace your weaknesses, because those are the portals through which heaven can touch earth. Let God's strength shine through you even in your weakest moments.

Day 17 Your Weakness Is Not Overrated

Revel: Take some time to reflect upon what you consider your strengths and weaknesses. Have you evaluated each through the lens of Biblical truth? Have you placed more focus on one while perhaps neglecting or overlooking the other?

Today, ask God for divine revelation regarding both your strengths and weaknesses. How might He be inviting you to use your strengths for His glory? And in your areas of weakness, where might God be calling you to surrender so that His power can work through you?

....

....

....

....

Align: Did you walk with God toward your dream yesterday—or did the noise of life pull you off course? Ask Him gently, "Lord, what got in the way?" His response will always be full of grace and guidance. Remember, this dream is not just yours—it's His too. Today, ask for fresh alignment with His truth and timing. Make sure you trust the Dream Giver more than the dream.

....

....

....

....

BOLD

Dream Stack: Think of your dream as building a cathedral—something beautiful, lasting, and sacred. But how is it built? One brick at a time. So here's the question: What brick can you lay today? Make one intentional move—big or small—that says, *I'm showing up and building with purpose.*

It might feel like just a brick, but over time those bricks become a wall … and over 101 days? A cathedral. So go on—lay your brick. The masterpiece is in the making. Write it. Believe it. Do something about it.

....

....

....

....

DAY 18

Freedom Is a Choice

See, I set before you today life and prosperity, death
and destruction. ... I have set before you life and
death, blessings and curses. Now choose life.

—Deuteronomy 30:15, 19

DID YOU KNOW THAT YOU are free? Right now, at this moment, no matter what is happening in your life—whether things are smooth sailing or crazy challenging—you are free.

But why don't we always *feel* free? I get it. Life can throw so many unexpected difficulties at us—a negative report, personal loss, addiction, political chaos—and these things can make us feel anything but free. Perhaps you can relate.

Here's what I propose today: Maybe we're looking at freedom the wrong way. We tend to think of freedom as the finish line we're trying to cross. But freedom isn't the end; it's the *starting point*. As believers, we have to recognize that freedom was Jesus's end game. He came to this earth, died, and rose again so we could experience true freedom in him. Your freedom in Christ cost you nothing. It cost him everything. AND it means it's not your endpoint; it's your starting point. Therefore, this isn't about you getting free. This is about you learning how to *stay free*. So how do we do that? Through your daily choices.

Many of us think freedom is tied to something external, like when we have more money in the bank or when our circumstances finally line up the way we want. But that's an inaccurate understanding of what true freedom is. If we tie freedom to our circumstances, we'll miss the gift God has given us. Freedom is a gift from God, but it's maintained in the choices we make. That means that the day you get free and the day you stay free are two totally different days. However, they both require the same thing—choice.

Today's verse says, *See, I set before you today*. That's God saying, "Hey, pay attention! I'm giving you an option here!" And what are the options? *Life and prosperity* or *death and destruction, blessings* or *curses*. God gives us the freedom to choose.

Here's the key: Freedom is an ongoing choice. The moment you accepted Jesus as your Lord and Savior, you stepped into the freedom He offers. But maintaining that freedom is a choice you'll need to make every single day of your life.

So that moment in front of you today—the one causing you stress or worry—what if it's not something happening *to* you but instead a freedom moment happening *for* you? What's a freedom moment? It's an opportunity to choose how you will respond.

What will you choose?

Think about it like this: Every moment is a chance to make a choice—it's a freedom moment. When your alarm goes off at 5 a.m. When that conversation with your spouse doesn't go how you hoped. When rejection hits hard or failure knocks again— You're not stuck. You get to choose.

We tell our kids all the time: "You might not get to choose what happens to you, but you always get to choose how you respond." That's the gift. That's true freedom. And God, in His goodness, reminds us: Choose life. Choose freedom.

Choosing life doesn't mean opting for the easy or convenient way. It means making decisions that bring real life—choices aligned with God's purpose for you, ones that nourish your soul and draw you closer to Him. It means making decisions based upon where you're going, not just how you feel in the here and now. It means deciding to stand on the Word of God when everything around you feels shaky. It means choosing the dream God's given you over the fear that you feel.

Freedom isn't a one-time decision; it's daily. It's not about what happens to you—it's about how you choose to respond to what happens to you. It's about recognizing that in every moment, you stand at a Y in the road with the power to choose life or death, to choose freedom (God's way), again and again and again.

So today, remember: You have the choice. You are free. Choose wisely.

Revel: Take a moment to reflect on where you currently stand—the place of choice and opportunity right before you. Even if your circumstances feel challenging, testing your patience, shaking your faith, or causing frustration, ask yourself: How can I intentionally *choose life* today in each of these areas?

Day 18 Freedom Is a Choice

Align: Reflect for a second: Did you create space for both movement and margin yesterday? Movement is the action—the doing, the building, the going. Margin is the breathing room—the space to rest, reflect, and just be. Dreams need fuel—but they also need rest. If something felt off, ask: Where do I need to slow down to speed up? What can I release to restore my rhythm? Remember, sustainable dreams are rooted in rest and built from overflow.

....

....

....

....

Dream Stack: Remember Noah? The guy out there building a massive boat with no sign of rain? People thought he was nuts … until the storm came. That's what faith looks like—it always seems a little crazy, until it rains.

So, what's your "ark move" today? A bold email? A small but powerful yes? That thing you've been putting off but know will move the needle?

You're not just dreaming—you're also building. So grab your hammer, take your step, and trust that the rain is coming. Write down one specific action you can take today to bring that dream of yours one step closer to reality.

....

....

....

....

DAY 19

Trust with a Capital T

Trust in the Lord with all your heart, and do not lean on your own understanding. In all your ways acknowledge him, and he will make straight your paths.

—Proverbs 3:5–6 ESV

TRUST—IT'S A BIG WORD. And I'd like to suggest that your ability to dream boldly is directly connected to how deeply you trust God. It is your foundation as a believer.

But if we're honest, trusting God can sometimes feel like contemplating walking on water. As you know, life has a way of hurting us. We've all been disappointed, let down, or wounded, and it's easy to let those past hurts affect how much we trust God in the present moments. We tend to intellectualize our way out of trusting Him, accumulating reasons based on our experiences, statistics, or fears as to why we *shouldn't* trust again. Even though it can make sense on paper, faith doesn't operate by earthly logic—it operates by divine trust.

When we have a hard time trusting God, it's often because we're shrinking Him down to fit the narrative of our current circumstances. We face a difficult moment and subconsciously believe that God isn't capable. We see a problem and assume He's not in control. But this is backward. Instead of letting our circumstances define our view of God, we need to let God define our circumstances.

My first question to you today is this: Is your trust in the results of God or the character of God?

The truth is, when we only trust the results of God (temporary) and not the character of God (eternal), we're limiting Him. We're lowering our standards of who God is, asking Him to fit inside the box of our current circumstances, pain, and experiences. We focus on the disappointment of the here and now instead of the true character of who God is.

This isn't about trusting situations to work out in our favor. It's about trusting God regardless of the situation. It's not about trusting people to always do the right thing. It's about trusting God with those people even when they do the wrong thing. When you face uncertainty or feel disappointed, you might think, *I can't trust Him; He's hurt me before.* But let me remind you: God is not finished yet. His story for you is still unfolding. As Scripture says, in all things God works for the good of those who love him (Romans 8:28), and He is the *Alpha and the Omega, the Beginning and the End* (Revelation 22:13).

What happens when we lean on only the results of God is that we compartmentalize and intellectualize our understanding of Him instead of trusting Him. Our reasoning becomes our god. Our plans, strategies, and outcomes—things we think we can control—become the objects of our trust. Other people and their actions dictate our sense of security. But Scripture warns us against this. Today's Scripture is all about trust—real trust. The kind that doesn't cling to our own understanding but lets go of the need to have it all figured out. It's a reminder that faith isn't about having all the answers—it's about surrendering what we do understand to God, who sees the full picture. He's bigger than what we see, feel, or know in any moment.

So here's the second question I want you to sit with today: Are you trusting in your own understanding … or are you trusting in Him?

Trusting God when everything makes sense and fits neatly into your own understanding isn't really trust—it's just living in your own reality. True trust shows up when the path feels unclear, when the answers aren't obvious, and when your understanding runs out. That's when trust becomes real—when you lean fully on His reliability, not your own reasoning.

This means we can't serve two masters. We can't ask God to be big and powerful while simultaneously shrinking Him down to fit into our limited understanding when things don't go our way. Trusting God requires us to put Him back where He belongs—above all else. Today's verse goes on to say, *In all your ways acknowledge him, and he will make straight your paths.* This is trust with a capital T. In every decision, every challenge, every frustration—acknowledge Him. Make Him bigger! If you want straighter paths, trust Him more. Surrender the results you want, give Him the plans you desire, let go of your own understanding, and submit to His authority. Then watch what only He can do. *Trust* that He is making your path straight, even when you can't see it—*yet*.

Trust is a process of allowing God to be God—bigger than your pain, wiser than your plans, and faithful through every season. In the midst of whatever you're facing, *Trust* Him and let Him lead the way.

※ ※ ※ ※ ※ ※

Revel: First, do you trust the results of God or the character of God? Second, is your trust in your own understanding or in God?

Take time today to surrender your pain, your plans, and even your dreams at the feet of Jesus. Ask Him to show you any areas where He's calling you to trust Him with a capital T. Then let Him lead you as He makes your paths straight.

Day 19 Trust with a Capital T

Align: Look back on yesterday; did you take a step toward your dream? At this point in the journey, it's easy to let this question become background noise. Maybe you've caught yourself skimming past it … or maybe you're showing up and doing the things but wondering, *Where are the results?*

Let me remind you that the day you plant the seed and the day you see the harvest are two completely different days. And what fills the space in between? Relentless, often boring discipline. If you can't stay faithful here—in the ordinary, unseen, repetitive part—where will you? This is the training ground. This is where you build spiritual grit.

Train yourself in the Lord. Stay focused on the dream. Get bored if you have to. But don't you dare quit. Alignment isn't just something you do—it's who you're becoming. So take a deep breath. Recalibrate. Either recommit or give yourself permission to embrace the mundane, knowing that every small act of obedience is shaping you into someone who can carry the dream God gave you.

Then reflect and realign. Look back on yesterday—did you act in alignment with who God says you are? Did you take a step, no matter how small, toward the dream He's placed in your heart?

If yes, bravo. Keep going. If not, why not? Be honest, then course-correct. Either way—align.

Dream Stack: Today, what is one clear action you can take that will make your dreams a reality? Because let's be honest: Your dream doesn't move unless you do. Write it in faith. Walk it out in boldness.

DAY 20

Live Loved

This is how God showed His love among us: He sent His one and only Son into the world that we might live through Him. This is love: not that we loved God, but that He loved us and sent His Son as an atoning sacrifice for our sins.

—1 John 4:9–10

IF YOU'RE ANYTHING LIKE ME, you've probably spent a good portion of your life afraid of getting it wrong, afraid of failing, afraid of making mistakes. I used to carry this deep-rooted fear of rejection, worried that if I didn't perform perfectly or measure up to others' expectations, I wouldn't be accepted. This fear often led me to play small, prioritizing the opinions of others over God's voice and delaying the dreams He had placed in my heart.

Most of us long to be accepted, to be loved for who we are. But the problem isn't in the desire for love; the problem is where we go to satisfy that desire. Too often, we seek validation from others or strive for worldly achievements in hopes of feeling more valued and loved. The real question isn't whether you have a need to be loved—you do. The real question is: Where are you turning to have that need met?

Here's the truth found in today's passage: You were created in love, from love, and for love. Love isn't something you have to earn or chase—it's woven into the very fabric of who you are. God designed you with a deep, innate need for love because it reflects His own nature. His love is what defines you.

And here's the best part: God's love for you isn't rooted in your actions or performance. It's rooted in who He is—steadfast, unconditional, and complete. His love doesn't change based on what you do; it's anchored in who He always is.

That means you can stop striving *for* love and start living *from* love. Love isn't your destination; it's your origin. Instead of chasing after validation, you can rest in the fact that you are already fully loved by God. It means that you don't have to seek love in accomplishments, relationships, or approval from others because God has already poured His love on you through Jesus.

Because of Jesus, you are free to live from a place of being fully known and fully loved. Your life is not about earning approval or proving your worth; it's about expressing the love that God has already placed inside of you. When we grasp this truth, it changes everything, and your life becomes a beautiful expression of heaven's love, a paintbrush in the hands of the creator.

For example:

In relationships: Imagine you're in a friendship that hits a rough patch. There's tension, misunderstandings, and maybe even a feeling of rejection. In that moment, instead of trying to prove you're right or earn back approval, you choose to respond with love. You forgive, you listen, and you extend grace because you understand that you are already fully loved by God. Your worth isn't dependent on how your friend responds but in how you reflect God's love in that moment.

At work: Maybe you didn't get the promotion or recognition you hoped for. Instead of feeling discouraged or jealous, you remember that your worth isn't tied to your achievements or the approval of others. You continue to show up with excellence, kindness, and integrity, not to earn something from the world, but because you are grounded in the love God has already given you. Your work becomes an expression of that love.

Facing criticism: When someone criticizes you—whether it's constructive or hurtful—it can sting. But instead of letting it define you or diminish your self-worth, you choose to live from the love you have in Christ. You reflect on how much God loves you, not based on your performance or others' opinions, and that helps you respond with grace, humility, and confidence in who you are.

Each of these situations shows that when we grasp the truth of being loved by God, it doesn't affect just how we see ourselves but also how we interact with the world around us. We become conduits of that love in all circumstances, because we no longer live to gain love from the world—we live to give love to the world. Every action, every word, every decision becomes an opportunity to reflect the love of Christ.

Even when life is hard. Even when things don't go as planned. Even when you make mistakes or face rejection—you are still loved. And because you are loved, you can live from that love in every situation. So the next time fear creeps in or doubt starts to whisper lies about who you are, remember who you are: You are loved. You were created in love, and you are called to live out that love. Love is not something you have—it's who you are.

Live loved. Because you are.

■ ■ ■ ■ ■ ■

Revel: What would your life look like if you lived *from* love instead of striving *for* love? How would your choices, interactions, and priorities change if you embraced the truth that you are already fully loved by God? What would you do more of? What would you let go of?

Reflect on these questions, then in your dream stacking time, take conscious steps *from* love.

Day 20 Live Loved

....

....

....

....

Align: Look back on yesterday—did you walk in step with God or did the pace of life pull you out of rhythm? Pause and ask Him, "Lord, where did I drift?" He's not here to shame you—only to lovingly guide you back. This dream belongs to Him as much as it does to you. Invite Him to realign your heart today with His pace, His plan, and His presence.

....

....

....

....

Dream Stack: OK, dreamer—what's your next bold step? Not the perfect one, not the ten-steps-from-now one—just the next one. Write it down. Do it with your whole heart. And celebrate the win tomorrow.

....

....

....

....

DAY 21

Fact vs. Truth

[Jesus said,] 'I have given to them Your word [the message You gave Me]; and the world has hated them because they are not of the world and do not belong to the world, just as I am not of the world and do not belong to it. I do not ask You to take them out of the world, but that You keep them and protect them from the evil one.'

—John 17:14–15 AMP

WE'VE GOT A LOT OF "FACTS" vying for our attention. There are facts that tell us we're doomed as we face a difficult diagnosis, that we're out of money, that the world is chaotic. Our circumstances might say we've failed, that we're not enough, or that things will never change. There are other contradictory expert opinions announced like facts, such as "Sun exposure helps your body produce vitamin D and boosts mood" vs. "Sun exposure increases your risk of skin cancer and premature aging." Or what about "Running strengthens your heart and adds years to your life" vs. "Running wears down your joints and increases injury risk over time."

It's all so confusing.

Here's the simple key (not always the easiest to implement): As believers, we don't live according to facts. We live by the truth of God's Word. And often we make the mistake of lowering the truth of Scripture to match the facts instead of elevating the facts to align with the *truth*.

But what's the difference between facts and truth?

Facts are limited to a specific context, perspective, or happening; truth is a heavenly reality and is eternal. Facts believe in something. Truth believes in someone.

As believers, we don't lean our lives on the facts; we lean our lives on the One who holds the entire world in the palm of His hands —God! You hear it all the time—"The fact of the matter is…"—followed by a string of data, circumstances, and expert opinions. And while those facts may not be false, they're also not necessarily truth. Facts keep us focused on what we can see: the circumstances, the statistics, the research, the odds. None of those are inherently wrong—until we start building our lives on them.

The fact was, Noah had no logical reason to build a boat. There were no forecasts, no evidence that said it would rain enough to flood the earth. By all appearances, it was not likely—not even possible. But the truth? God's word never fails. He said it, and He brought it to pass.

The fact was, Mary couldn't conceive a child without a husband. It defied biology. It broke every natural law. But the truth? Nothing is impossible with God.

The facts may be in—but they don't override the authority of God's word. So yes, know the facts. Acknowledge them. But don't lean your life on them.

In today's Scripture Jesus tells us that, although we live in this world, we are not *of* this world, and though that doesn't automatically make everything easier, it makes it simpler. In the midst of all the crazy facts, Jesus confidently and proudly confirms what he did to support us. He gave us God's Word, which is our daily bread.

God's Word feeds you (Jeremiah 15:16), shields you (Psalm 18:30), and protects you

(Psalm 46:1). It holds you even in the midst of chaos (Colossians 1:17). It's sharper than any two-edged sword (Hebrews 4:12) and will be your guiding light, a lamp for your feet (Psalm 119:105). The facts are temporary. God's truth is eternal. Therefore, when the facts scream at you, run to the Word of God. When the facts seem overwhelming, run to the Word. When you don't know what to believe, run to the Word of the Lord.

Maybe the point of our lives as believers is not to be surprised by the facts anymore, but to be in awe of His truth! Today, may you live to make His truth your reality. Don't live from the limitations of facts—live from the power of truth. Be patient as God's plan unfolds. Be consistent in your faith, even in difficult seasons. Stay focused and steadfast when life gets crazy. And above all, rather than the facts swirling around you, let God's truth define your life.

You do get to choose what you will live by—facts or truth.

What will you choose?

■ ■ ■ ■ ■ ■

Revel: Choose one fact you're facing today—something that feels limiting or discouraging—and bring it into alignment with the Word of God. What does Scripture say about it? How can you live more from God's truth and less from the temporary facts you see around you?

Let that truth guide your perspective and response.

....

....

....

....

Day 21 Fact vs. Truth

Align: Take a moment and think about yesterday. Your actions either helped bridge the gap between where you are and where you want to be—or they didn't. Which was it?

And more important—how are you showing up today? This is your moment to realign, reset, and get back in the game. Don't sit in guilt—shift into gear. The dream hasn't changed; maybe your focus just needs a little tune-up.

....

....

....

....

Dream Stack: Based on the truth that hit home for you today, what's one bold step you can take to move your dream forward?

The facts might say it's impossible. The facts might say you're not ready. But the truth? The truth says you're called and you're equipped, and God is with you. So what's that step? Write it down and defy the facts as you walk in truth.

....

....

....

....

DAY 22

You're So Handy

For we are God's handiwork, created in Christ Jesus to do good works, which God prepared in advance for us to do.

—Ephesians 2:10

ONE OF THE GREATEST LIES Satan tries to convince us of is that we don't have a purpose. He whispers that we are too ordinary, too unqualified, or too broken to make an impact in the world. In the seasons of uncertainty, Satan seeks to fill us with self-doubt and discouragement, trying to blind us to the truth of God's call on our lives. The enemy wants nothing more than for us to believe that our lives are just a series of random events with no greater meaning—nothing more than a waiting game until the next hardship or distraction hits. But this is far from the truth.

God has a purpose for your life—a divine plan designed before the foundation of the world. In Jeremiah 29:11, God speaks directly to His people, telling them that His plans for them are not only for their well-being but also to give them a future full of hope. His purpose for you is not something random or unimportant; it's woven into every moment of your life. Though the enemy tries to convince you otherwise, you must hold fast to the truth of who you are in Christ. This can't be just an intellectual concept, it's one we have to trust and ultimately embody.

When the enemy tries to plant seeds of doubt and despair, remember that your purpose is not defined by your past mistakes or the opinions of others. It's also not defined by your levels of clarity and certainty, job titles, or accomplishments. As today's passage so beautifully reminds us, our purpose was defined by God long before we ever took our first step. He prepared it in advance, on purpose, with purpose, for us to walk in it. Did you catch that? Your purpose, though it may feel like something you're figuring out as you go, is not random to God, nor does any part of your journey catch Him off guard.

When Scripture says, *For we are God's handiwork,* it means His workmanship or His artwork, which comes from the Greek word poiēma. That means you were crafted, with skill and a purpose, by God, for His purposes. Specifically, you were *created in Christ Jesus for good works.* This describes origin, identity, and destiny all wrapped up in one! You were created in Him, by Him, for Him, to do good works. Though good works do not give us salvation, they are absolutely meant to be the result of salvation.

This means your purpose is not something you have to question—it's already been set. Your purpose isn't something you need to strive to find or constantly question—it's already established by God, derived from who He designed you to be. Even before you took your first breath, He had carefully crafted a purpose unique to you, preparing opportunities in advance for you to walk in. The only thing you have to do is walk in it.

Think of the many Biblical figures who were seemingly ordinary, yet God used them for extraordinary purposes: Moses, who doubted his ability to lead the Israelites; Esther, who questioned whether she could make a difference in a foreign land; and even David, who was overlooked as a shepherd boy but called to be a king. These individuals didn't have a perfect understanding of their purpose, but they said yes to God, trusting that He would show them the way.

In the same way, you are called to step into your purpose, not because you have all the answers or feel fully equipped, but because God is the One who equips you. His strength is made perfect in your weakness (2 Corinthians 12:9). When you feel discouraged or tempted to give up, remind yourself of His truth—your purpose is far greater than the lies the enemy tries to feed you.

The challenge is not in discovering your purpose but in embracing it. It's time to stop doubting if God will use you or questioning whether you're equipped. You are *God's handiwork*, which means He has meticulously designed you for the tasks He's called you to. Instead of hesitating, start partnering with His promises. When we stop doubting and start agreeing with the truth of what He's declared over us, we begin to walk in the fullness of our calling. You were created on purpose, for a purpose, and the gifts, talents, and passions He's placed inside you are part of a grand, divine plan that only you can fulfill.

Eat this for breakfast. Marinate in it all day long. Choke on it if you have to. Whatever you need to do, believe it.

You're so handy!

Revel: Take a moment to reflect on God's powerful promise—that you are His masterpiece, created in Christ Jesus to do good works that He has already prepared for you.

Invite the Holy Spirit to make this truth come alive within you so deeply that you can't help but embrace it fully. Then ask the Lord to show you how He wants to guide and direct you toward the specific purpose He has designed for your life. Use your dream stacking time to take intentional steps toward stepping into that divine purpose.

Day 22 You're So Handy

....

....

....

Align: As you marinate in today's truth—knowing that God gave you purpose and prepared it in advance, on purpose, with purpose, for you to walk in—take a moment to look back on yesterday. Did you walk in that purpose? Did your actions reflect movement toward the promise of God over your life? If not, what got in the way? Identify it. Call it out. And ask yourself: How can I move differently today? Because your purpose hasn't changed … but your alignment might need a reset.

....

....

....

Dream Stack: What's one bold move you can make today that aligns with who God says you are and what He's called you to do? Jot it down and make it happen. Let your purpose lead the way and take a step that reflects both your identity and your dream.

....

....

....

DAY 23

Greater Things

[Jesus said,] 'Whoever believes in me will do the works I have been doing, and they will do even greater things than these.'

—John 14:12

DO YOU BELIEVE THAT YOU were born for *more*?

All of us, at some point, have felt this deep, profound call for more—that yearning for something greater than the life we're living. This isn't a call for more material things, achievements, or success (though we may seek such things if we're not careful)—it's a call for more of Jesus within us. As believers, this should be a natural, deep desire to grow in Christ and experience the fullness of His life working in and through our lives.

But here's the thing: It can't stop at desire. It has to become our reality. We're called to live in the fullness of Christ, allowing His power and presence to actively flow through our everyday lives. That's what "greater things" is all about.

If we're not careful, we'll start building our lives around what we can do instead of what He can do through us. We unintentionally box ourselves in with human limits—past outcomes, predictable goals, familiar strategies—when God is inviting us to build based on His ability, not ours.

Imagine if, in every meeting, at every decision point—whether it's in the boardroom, a small group, or even around your dinner table—you didn't base your vision on what happened last year or what seems realistic for this year. What if you paused and asked yourself, *What did Jesus do? And how can we walk in even greater things, just like He said we would?*

In today's verse, Jesus makes a powerful statement: *Whoever believes in me will do the works I have been doing, and they will do even greater things than these.* Have you really thought about that? Jesus isn't downplaying His power—it's a bold reminder of the promise He made to us and an invitation to walk in it. Through His life, His Spirit, and His example, we are empowered to do *greater things*. This is the more you've been longing for.

But what does greater things actually look like in your life? Especially when you've prayed for, sought after, even expected miracles and they didn't happen. Jesus's call to greater things isn't about a one-time answer to prayer. It's a lifestyle. A *lifestyle* of miracles in Him. It's a lifetime of raising the bar for His presence and cultivating an appetite for the miraculous—wherever you are in the world outside the church walls. It's about rising above the here and now and chasing after the realities of His Kingdom as you partner with Him and bring heaven to earth. It's learning to no longer minimize the power of heaven to fit the probabilities of life but to gain a heightened awareness of what He can do and to live your life in such a way that your life becomes marked by greater things.

His invitation is simple: Just believe!

So the next time you're facing a difficult situation at work or in your personal life, and it feels like all the conventional solutions don't seem to make a real difference, instead of relying solely on your own strength, looking to your past to create definition, or using the statistics posted around you to create metrics, remember Jesus's promise: Just believe. Take a step back and pray, asking for His wisdom, guidance, and strength. Then follow the prompt of the Holy Spirit as He leads you to creative solutions that go beyond what you would have considered on your own. This is the more—the greater things.

I propose that your desire for more of the Lord is an appetite given *by* the Lord. Do not dumb it down or minimize it. Do not let delay, disappointment, or any defeat keep you from believing in it. Instead, recognize that the dreams God has placed in your heart have a purpose, and they're meant to be brought to life. Every heartache, every injustice, every broken system has a solution, and those solutions aren't found in the world around us; they are waiting to be unlocked from within us. God's divine answers are placed inside you, locked up in those dreams He's given you. This means the world needs you and your dreams, because they need Jesus who lives in you.

So today, remember that old phrase, "What would Jesus do?" because it not only applies today, but it also points to the idea that greater things are waiting for you! Jesus didn't just set the bar; He told us to rise above it. This wasn't meant to tease us—it was to elevate our belief in what He can do in and through us, so His power might be made evident in our lives.

As you lean into God's presence, believing in the truth of His promise, learning to listen for His voice, you start to see opportunities to bring His Kingdom into your everyday life—whether it's through acts of kindness, speaking life into others, or stepping out to share the Gospel when the moment is right. Each of these moments might seem small, but they are filled with the power of God, demonstrating that greater things are happening through you, because you're partnering with Him in His mission. This partnership with God's will is what empowers you to step into greater things. It's not just about chasing success or fulfilling dreams; it's also about embracing the promise He's given you and walking in the works He's already set before you. You matter. Your dreams matter. And yes, you were made for greater things.

Revel: Take a moment to truly consider what it would look like to step into the more—the greater things—with the Lord today. This isn't about diminishing who He is or questioning His power. Quite the opposite. It's about aligning yourself with the very promise He's eager to fulfill in and through your life.

Day 23 Greater Things

Let your heart burn for more of Him—more of His presence, more of His Kingdom at work in your everyday life. Then pause and reflect: What could that look like right now, in your life today, to walk in greater things?

....

....

....

....

Align: Look back on yesterday—did you take that one step toward your dream? It doesn't have to have been massive. Maybe it was a hard conversation, a sent email, or one written page in your book. If you did take it—pause and celebrate that. Forward is forward. Every step matters.

If not, what got in the way? Be honest. Sometimes the biggest obstacle isn't what's happening around us; it's what's happening within us. Now here's the key: Don't get stuck in the guilt. Use the awareness to grow. Ask yourself: What needs to shift today so I can move forward? Whether it's creating space, setting a boundary, or simply recommitting to the dream, do it.

....

....

....

....

BOLD

Dream Stack: Today, choose to do the greater thing. Not in your own strength, but with the Lord. You're not building this dream alone—He's right there with you. With Him, what's one bold move you can make that brings you closer to what He's called you to? Keep it simple, write it down, and go all-in.

Because let's be real—greater things look good on you.

....

....

....

....

DAY 24

Is "Happy" Your God?

You will show me the path of life; In Your presence is fullness of joy; In Your right hand there are pleasures forevermore.

—Psalm 16:11 AMP

"I JUST WANT EVERYONE TO BE HAPPY!"

We've all found ourselves saying this at least a time or two. We all desire happiness, both for ourselves and for the people we love.

For a long time, I had the same mindset. During the first ten years of my marriage, my main focus was making sure my husband was happy. I had unknowingly made his happiness my mission and, eventually, my idol. My well-being became tied to his contentment; his happiness became my happiness. Truth be told, it was exhausting, and it didn't bring true joy or fulfillment.

The problem with this approach is that it subtly shifts our priorities, making other people's happiness our goal. It's not always obvious; it can show up in small, seemingly harmless ways, like tolerating harsh words, enabling unhealthy habits, justifying poor behavior, or sacrificing our own needs to keep the peace. When we make others' happiness more important than living in alignment with God's will, we begin to suppress our true feelings and desires, compromising our convictions and sometimes even our faith. Over time, this leads to inauthenticity and deep dissatisfaction. It's as if we're trying to keep the peace around us while starting a war within us. This is called resentment.

Perhaps you can relate. Whether it's with a spouse, a child, or a friend, trying to manage someone else's happiness can be overwhelming. The truth is, my husband never asked me to carry that burden, and I didn't realize I had taken it on. It started from a genuine place of love, but somewhere along the way, love turned into a heavy weight. And that's when I learned an important truth: Happiness was never Jesus's goal, and it shouldn't be ours either.

"I just want everyone to be happy"—said Jesus never!

Jesus came with a mission, but that mission wasn't to make everyone happy. His goal was transformation through connection. Jesus sought to bring us into the fullness of who He created us to be, and the truth is, not only do we find ourselves when we find Jesus, but we also find the joy we were looking for. This is the meaning of today's verse.

We know that the goal is not happiness; the goal is maturity, completeness in the Lord. And as He's directing us on the *path of life* with Him, His Word says it's His presence that brings us the *fullness of joy*. Did you notice, it doesn't say happiness? It says joy! So what's the difference between happiness and joy? And why is the difference important for us as believers?

Happiness is a feeling. Joy is a fruit of the Spirit. Happiness depends on external circumstances; joy is an internal, spiritual reality. Happiness is a fleeting emotion—it comes and goes. This is why we often feel happy through gifts, kind words, a promotion, or a beautiful sunny day. However, those feelings can quickly disappear with a harsh word, a setback at work, or a long stretch of bad weather. The good news is, joy is lasting, even eternal, because it's a response to the deeper work God is doing in our hearts. Happiness, or the chase of it, can be exhausting. But true joy, the fullness of joy is found only in the presence of the Lord. All that to say: Happiness is cheap. *Joy is priceless.*

When my goal was no longer my husband's happiness but his maturity and completeness in the Lord, everything changed. It didn't make it easier, but it gave everything meaning. When I stopped focusing on him needing to be happy, I was able to support him in becoming the best version of himself as He walked out His own journey with the Lord. I no longer offered easy outs or said things just to make him feel better. Instead, I started speaking the truth in love, standing with him through hard times and celebrating his growth. Not only that, I committed myself to doing the same. We both dove into finding our true joy, not in the comfort or convenience of this world or happiness of one another, but in the presence of the Lord. This lifted the weight off both of us and allowed us to grow together, becoming more like the people God created us to be, on the path of life, in His presence, which is the *fullness of joy.*

This same truth applies to you. It's not about pursuing fleeting happiness but about striving for maturity and wholeness in Christ. Instead of avoiding challenges or discomfort, we need to embrace the pressures that refine us and find true joy in the fullness of His presence. Your marriage, your relationships, your life, and your character aren't meant for short-lived happiness. They are meant to reflect God's purpose and glory as well as His joy. So instead of chasing happiness, chase the kind of joy that can be found only in His presence.

Choose completeness over comfort. *Joy over happiness.*

Revel: Take a moment today to reflect on happiness versus joy. Are you relying on external moments of fleeting happiness, or are you deeply rooted in the sustaining joy that comes only in God's presence? Are you chasing other people's happiness or finding the fullness of your joy in the Lord?

Consider the ways you can deepen your dependency on Him. Use your aligning time to shift your focus from pursuing temporary satisfaction and comfort to embracing an internal, Spirit-led life of joy that is not tied to circumstances but to your connection with the Lord.

Day 24 Is "Happy" Your God?

....

....

....

....

Align: Keep it simple. Did you move toward your dream yesterday? If not, what got in the way—and how will you shift today to get back on track?

....

....

....

....

Dream Stack: Today, in honor of divine alignment, what's one specific action you can take to move your dream forward? Once you identify it, write it down. There's power in putting vision to paper. Then take the step. One move, in alignment, can shift everything.

....

....

....

....

DAY 25

Forget About It

[The Lord said,] 'Forget the former things; do not dwell on the past. See, I am doing a new thing! Now it springs up; do you not perceive it? I am making a way in the wilderness and streams in the wasteland.'

—Isaiah 43:18–19

HAVE YOU EVER FELT STUCK in your past? Afraid to take risks because of what happened yesterday or even a decade ago? Struggling to dream, love, or live fully in the present moment because of past disappointments and hurts is normal.

But I'm here to remind you: You're not normal!

We all have a history of pain, failure, and unmet expectations. It's a shared human experience, but what we choose to do with that pain is what defines our journey forward. Unprocessed pain can quietly consume our energy, drawing our focus away from what's possible and locking it onto what was. When we live in fear of being hurt again, we stop engaging with life fully. We may not even realize it, but we begin to operate from a place of self-protection; instead of playing to win, we're simply playing not to lose. This mindset can keep us from stepping into the fullness of what God has in store for us.

Beyond being emotional, pain can also be psychological. Our brains have a tendency to look for danger (to avoid it), to focus on the negative (to understand it), and to dwell on what went wrong (in an effort to prevent it from happening again). Over time, this creates a natural response that trains our brains to constantly search for what's wrong.

Beyond being both emotional and psychological, pain is also very spiritual. We do have an enemy who uses our past against us, reminding us of our failures, planting seeds of doubt about the future, and trapping us in strongholds and cycles of regret and fear—all with the sole purpose of us not living out the intended design of the Lord.

By holding onto past pain, of any kind, we inadvertently allow it to shape our future. Instead of being led by faith and hope, our choices are driven by fear and caution. But God invites us to process that pain, to heal, and to be restored, so we can fully embrace the abundant life He has promised. No matter the effects of pain, we must not idolize it. We cannot lower the standard of heaven to accommodate for it, and we cannot throw the happenings of yesterday on the potential of tomorrow. God doesn't live in your past; you won't find Him back there. Yes, He walked with you through it, but He is not dwelling there, and neither should you.

You might be wondering, "But where is God in all of this?"

Today's Scripture offers a powerful reminder—God is in the new things, the fresh, unexpected ways He's moving in your life right now. Even when it's unfamiliar, even when it doesn't look like what you imagined, He's still working.

This verse calls us to shift our focus from what has been to what God is doing right now. It doesn't dismiss the reality of the past or the pain it brought, but it reminds us that God is making a new way forward. In the wilderness and wasteland moments—whether those lie behind us or ahead—God is actively at work, creating new possibilities for renewal. While the new things He's doing might be hard to see at first and change can be challenging, His promise is clear: He is making a way even when we don't fully understand. True healing and restoration come when we release the past, making space for new dreams, opportunities, and a future shaped by His grace instead of our pain.

Miracles are waiting, but we must believe.

Just like the woman in Mark 5:25–34 who for twelve years had suffered with a chronic condition that caused her to bleed continuously—a condition that not only affected her physically but also left her emotionally and spiritually isolated. According to the laws and culture of that time, her bleeding made her "unclean," which meant she was cut off from community, from worship, from physical touch, and from normal life. She had spent everything she had on doctors and remedies, but nothing worked. Can you imagine that kind of pain and hopelessness? But when she believed and reached out in faith to touch the hem of Jesus's garment, she was instantly healed. The miracle had been waiting there all along, but it was her faith that unlocked it.

Or take the story of the paralyzed man in Luke 5:17–26. His friends believed so deeply that Jesus could heal him, they went to extraordinary lengths to lower him through a roof to get him in front of Jesus. Now picture if that man had talked his friends out of it, convinced them it wasn't worth the effort because he'd been paralyzed for so long. If he had let the impossibilities of yesterday dictate that day, he would have stayed paralyzed. Instead, the faith of his friends, paired with his own willingness, moved them to action—and because they believed, the miracle of healing happened.

In these examples, miracles were already within reach waiting to be revealed, but it was belief—faith in Jesus—that made the impossible possible. They didn't dwell on the past, linger in the pain, and minimize the power of Jesus. They stepped forward into the new thing.

If you find yourself slipping back into the familiar pain of the past, take a deep breath and remember God's Word: *Forget the former things*. Truth is, holding onto the past only keeps you stuck there. But here's the good news—you have a choice. You can release what was and fully embrace what is—the new thing God is doing right now.

God isn't found in what has been; He's alive and moving in what's next. He's making a way in the wilderness. He's bringing streams into the wasteland. Look up. Pay attention. He's doing a *new thing!*

Do you see it?

Day 25 Forget About It

Revel: Take time to reflect on the areas where you've been stuck in past pain. What emotions or experiences have kept you from fully trusting God with your future? Identify those areas and bring them before the Lord, asking for His grace to release them.

Then ask God about the *new thing* He is doing in your life. Ask for divine revelation to recognize the streams He's causing to flow in your desert and the path He's creating in the wilderness. Let Him show you how He's bringing restoration and new life, even in places that feel barren.

Finally, make a conscious decision to focus on God's promises. Whenever memories or past fears resurface, remind yourself of Isaiah 43:19. Move forward in faith, trusting in the new things He is calling you into.

....

....

....

....

Align: Take a moment to look back on yesterday. Did you take even one step—big or small—toward your dream? This isn't about hustle or checking a box. It's about intention. It's about alignment.

If you did move forward, pause and celebrate it. That matters. Momentum is built one faithful step at a time. If you didn't, feel no shame, just curiosity. What got in the way? Was it distraction, discouragement, fear, busyness, or maybe a lack of clarity? Be honest with yourself. You can't shift what you won't recognize and name.

Now here's the most important part: How will you respond today? What needs to shift in your mindset, routine, or faith walk so you can realign with the dream God's placed in your heart?

The dream is still there. God's still in it. The next step is yours to take.

....

....

....

....

Dream Stack: Today, what is one thing you can do to move toward the dream God has given you? See that He's doing a new thing—you should do one too! Write it down, make it plain as day, then make it happen.

....

....

....

....

DAY 26

Reigning in Life

Death once held us in its grip, and by the blunder of one man, death reigned as king over humanity. But now, how much more are we held in the grip of grace and continue reigning as kings in life, enjoying our regal freedom through the gift of perfect righteousness in the one and only Jesus, the Messiah!

—Romans 5:17 TPT

ARE YOU REIGNING IN LIFE?

For too many, the answer would be no. Many feel bound by the struggles of this world—trapped by fear, anxiety, depression, addiction, or other negative patterns they've come to accept as normal. And I know some of you are probably thinking, *JG, did you even read yesterday's devotional?! I'm still trying to heal from my past! Slow your roll!*

I hear you, and I'm here to keep it real. We cannot let fear, anxiety, addiction, or negative patterns become our normal. As believers, this is not the life God has for us. These things aren't part of His design, and they don't align with His heavenly work in our lives. Yes, you are allowed to process and heal, but you are not meant to stay "stuck in the Lord"—as though that's a thing; it's not a thing. So buckle up, buttercup, because today you're about to receive heaven's keys to walking in even greater breakthroughs and restoration.

Jesus died to not only save us from eternal damnation but also to free us to live … or shall I say, *reign in life!* That's the truth. He paid the ultimate price—His life—for a reason.

Today's beautiful and powerful reminder conveys the truth that Jesus died to break the power of death, sin, and the enemy's strongholds over our lives. He came to replace those chains with the grip of grace and to *empower* us to *continue reigning as kings in life.* Notice it says "reigning in life," not "reigning in heaven." That means we are called to experience the fullness of that freedom here and now.

Romans goes on to say, *Just as condemnation came upon all people through one transgression, so through one righteous act of Jesus' sacrifice, the perfect righteousness that makes us right with God and leads us to a victorious life is now available to all* (Romans 5:18 TPT).

This verse tells us to understand two things:

1. Through *one righteous act* (Jesus's sacrifice), we are free to reign.
2. Through faith in Jesus (our ongoing surrender), we remain free to reign.

If you were born into a royal family as a prince or princess, you would be the next heir. The next heir receives the right to be king or queen purely by birthright. They don't have to work for it, earn it, or perform to attain it. It's a gift, freely given through the bloodline. However, to remain victorious and secure in their kingdom, that heir must stand firm in their identity and responsibilities or the kingdom could be overtaken by traitors or enemies. The inheritance may be free, but maintaining the freedom of that kingdom is a different story.

The same is true for you. When you declared Jesus as your Lord and Savior, you were made an heir of His Kingdom. The chains of sin were broken, and you were set free from the imprisonment of death and defeat. You no longer live in the grip of sin; you now reside in the *grip of grace*! You did nothing to earn this—it was a gift, given freely because of the sacrifice of Jesus on the cross. The moment you became a believer you received the fullness of that inheritance.

Jesus's sacrifice purchased your freedom to reign in life, but maintaining that freedom, living in its fullness, requires your ongoing choice. Every day, you must choose to step into the freedom He's given you, hold the line, and remember who you are in Him. Therefore, freedom to reign in life is not a one-time event; it's a continual choice. It's a daily decision.

Jesus has done the work to set you free, but it's up to you to embrace and live out that freedom, choosing each day to walk in His victory. As heirs to the throne of God, our role is to maintain that freedom by standing firm in our identity and purpose in Christ, resisting anything that tries to pull us back into bondage. This also means freedom to reign in life is both a gift and a responsibility.

God's freedom to reign does not mean an absence of trials. You will face failures. It doesn't mean you won't be tempted or find yourself in doubt. You will. It doesn't mean sin will be eradicated from the world. It won't be. But it does mean that sin no longer has a hold on you. *Grace* does. It means that grace empowers you to stand firm, to hold the line of your freedom, and to make everything that doesn't align with heaven bow its knee. You're not "stuck in the Lord," you are "free in the Lord." So live like it.

Jesus has given you the gift of freedom—the power to reign in life. But walking in that freedom? That's your choice, your responsibility. So today, choose to receive it fully. Embrace the victorious freedom He paid for and step boldly into the life He's called you to live. You were made to reign—with Him, in Him, and through Him.

Revel: Are there areas in your life where you're not walking in the fullness of freedom God has given you to reign in life? Take a moment to identify one specific area where you've been feeling stuck, limited, or bound—an area where you can honestly say, "I'm not reigning in life." It could be related to fear, doubt, unforgiveness, a habit, or a mindset. Bring this area before the Lord and repent, acknowledging anything that's been keeping you from experiencing His fullness.

Then, as an heir to God's throne, declare freedom over that area. Speak life, victory, and God's promises over it, remembering that you are seated with Christ in heavenly

Day 26 Reigning in Life

places. Claim the freedom and authority you've been given through Christ to reign over this area of your life until you see the fullness of the promise.

....

....

....

....

Align: Before you do anything else, stop and take it in—you're twenty-six days in. That's twenty-six days of showing up, pressing in, and saying yes to the process. If you've been faithfully aligning and dream stacking, that means twenty-six intentional choices, twenty-six daily steps, twenty-six powerful moments where your mind, heart, and actions are aligning more closely with the Lord. That's not a small feat. That's worth celebrating.

You may not be seeing the results yet—but you're likely feeling the shift. You've moved past the awkward beginning and into the rhythm-building phase. Your faith is rising. You're more aware of God's presence in everyday moments. And deep down, you're starting to sense that little voice that says, "This might actually be working."

And if your process has had some ups and downs—or if you haven't quite settled into a daily alignment rhythm yet—give grace. You're human. We all are. But here's the beautiful part: You still have seventy-five days ahead. That's seventy-five opportunities to recalibrate, refocus, and re-engage with intention. It's not too late to align your actions with who God says you are and what He's called you to do. And honestly … aren't you just a little curious what might happen if you went all-in?

So today—no matter where you're at in the process—align. Take a few minutes to pause, reflect, and journal. What progress do you see? Not just around you but within you? That's where the real transformation begins.

....

....

BOLD

....

....

Dream Stack: Today, keep it simple; what is one thing you can do to move toward the reality of the dream God has given you? Write it down and make it happen. You'll thank yourself tomorrow (ask me how I know).

....

....

....

....

DAY 27

The Danger of Comparison: Embracing the Unique You

I praise you because I am fearfully and wonderfully made;
your works are wonderful, I know that full well.

—Psalm 139:14

HAVE YOU EVER FOUND YOURSELF comparing your life to someone else's? It's natural to compare yourself to those around you, to who you used to be, and even to who you think you should be. But here's the truth: Comparison is one of the biggest dream killers.

We live in a world that's hyperconnected, where we are constantly exposed to the lives of others due to digital technology. Social media, the internet, and news sources create an unceasing flow of information, opinions, and images. There's a constant buzz around us, making it easy to feel overwhelmed by what everyone else is doing, saying, or achieving. This constant exposure can lead to a scroll-and-compare culture, leaving most of us with a deep sense of inadequacy as we measure our lives against the curated, often filtered realities of others. This connection, though it can be helpful, makes comparison an easy trap to fall into. If we're not careful, we spend so much time looking at the lives of others, often in microscopic detail, that we lose sight of who we are and what God has uniquely designed us to do.

"They're crushing it in their career … what am I even doing with mine?"

"She's a mom, runs a business, and somehow always looks put together—why can't I manage half of that?"

"I've been working just as hard as they have, so why does it feel like I'm stuck?"

"He's younger than I am and has already bought a house … I can barely pay rent."

"I used to be in such good shape—where did that version of me go?"

"I thought I'd be married by now. Everyone else seems to be living their dream life, and I'm just … waiting."

"They make it look so easy—why does it feel so hard for me?"

Oh, the trap of comparison.

But here's the truth: We weren't created to live in comparison. God didn't place us here to measure ourselves against others—He made each of us with intentionality and purpose. Just like today's verse reminds us, we are *fearfully and wonderfully made*, exactly as He designed. In this context, that phrase *fearfully made*, doesn't mean filled with fear—rather, it speaks to awe and reverence. It's a recognition of the intricate and amazing nature of human creation, which inspires a sense of wonder as we ponder the complexity and individuality of how God made each of us. That means the goal isn't to be like someone else or to measure up to their standard—it's to be the best version of *you*, exactly as God intended. And let's be honest—it's impossible to become the best version of yourself when you're too focused on trying to be like someone else.

When you compare yourself to others, you are forgetting the simple truth about who God is and who He created you to be. When you doubt your worth, you are essentially second-guessing God's perfect design; you're telling God He may not have gotten it right.

Consider the world around you: the mountains (over 1.1 million unique peaks), the oceans (covering over 70 percent of Earth and housing more than a million species), and the trees (over 3 trillion individual trees). God made each one of them, and He knows every single one. The beauty of creation reflects the beauty of God's perfect design. Everything—every creature, every mountain, every tree—has its own unique value. None of it can be compared to another. And that includes you.

This is why we praise Him. We praise Him because we acknowledge that everything He created is wonderful. From the mighty mountains to the roaring water, from the stars in the sky to the trees we see, everything has its place and purpose in His design—including you. Just as no mountain compares to another, no star to another, *you* too are uniquely made. That means you are invaluable, and God has made you exactly as you are for a specific purpose in His Kingdom.

You've been called to shine brightly—exactly as you were designed. Don't tolerate comparison. Don't entertain insecurity. Instead, praise God for how wonderfully He made you. You are a part of His glorious creation, and your uniqueness is something to celebrate and be in awe of, not shrink from.

Today, I encourage you to stop comparing and start praising. You are *wonderfully made*. God knew exactly what He was doing; appreciate and marvel at His work.

■ ■ ■ ■ ■ ■

Revel: How can you embrace and celebrate the unique person God has created you to be rather than comparing yourself to others?

Take some time to list the wonderful qualities God has gifted you. Ask Him to reveal more about who you are and who He designed you to be, then take a moment to celebrate those attributes.

Day 27 The Danger of Comparison: Embracing the Unique You

....

....

....

....

Align: Zoom out for a second. If yesterday were a single puzzle piece in the bigger picture of your dream—did it fit? Did it move things forward even just a little?

If it did, good job. Small pieces lead to a big, bold puzzle. Celebrate the wins along the way. If it didn't, don't stress—but don't ignore it. What pulled you off track? What resistance did you hit? Name it. Then ask: What needs to shift today so that piece locks into place tomorrow?

....

....

....

....

Dream Stack: Today, what is one specific action you can take to bring your dream closer to reality? Write it down. Now go do that, you wonderful human, you!

....

....

....

....

DAY 28

What's in a Name?

> With my whole heart, with my whole life, and with my innermost being, I bow in wonder and love before you, the holy God! Yahweh, you are my soul's celebration.
>
> —Psalm 103:1–2 TPT

THERE IS PROFOUND POWER IN A NAME.

I've always believed that. So much so that my husband and I spent a great deal of time choosing names for our children because we believed that speaking their names—thousands of times each day—was speaking into existence the very character God had given each of them.

As we reflect upon the Creation story, we see how God, with purpose and intention, spoke everything into existence. Then, as we study the Old Testament, we see that a name wasn't just a label; it reflected a person's character and identity. My, oh my, there is power in a name.

The same is true for God. In fact, the Bible reveals nearly a thousand names for God, each reflecting a different aspect of His character. Every one of these names affirms the truth that God is everything we could ever need, and He has given us these names to build our lives upon, to trust in, and to celebrate.

Jehovah Jireh means "the Lord will provide," emphasizing that God is our provision. *Jehovah Rapha* means "the Lord who heals," highlighting God's power to heal both physically and spiritually. *El Shaddai* means "God Almighty," representing His all-sufficient power and authority. *Jehovah Shalom,* which means "the Lord is peace," reveals God's ability to bring peace amid chaos. I could go on and on. But, of all these names, one stands above the rest—*Yahweh*. It seems to encapsulate the fullness of who God is to us. It is *the name* that reminds us that God is *everything* we need—our soul's deepest source of strength and celebration.

I remember a moment when my sweet Aslan heard the name Yahweh for the first time and asked, "Mom, what does that mean?" At first, I felt shocked that I hadn't taught her this name sooner, but then I felt a sense of awe, knowing I had the privilege of explaining such a profound truth.

I paused for a moment, knowing that while it's a simple question, the answer is incredibly deep. I explained, "Yahweh means 'I AM' or 'He who is.' It means that whatever you need, He is that. If you need answers, He says, 'I AM your answer.' If you need healing, He says, 'I AM your healer.' If you need peace, He says, 'I AM your peace.'" I went on and on, and finally, Aslan smiled and said, "I get it, Mom. He is *all the things!*"

I laughed because "all the things" is a phrase I use all the time. But she was right—*He is all the things!*

At that moment, a truth settled in my heart: If I truly embrace that God is the great I AM, the One who is everything and anything I need, what else could I want? My soul not only can breathe deeply in His presence but even can celebrate this incredible reality, just as today's Scripture declares.

I believe that when we truly grasp the meaning of His name—Yahweh—our souls will naturally celebrate, and we can rest confidently in who He is, no matter what comes our way. Everything else in life—people, circumstances, opinions—may shift, but God is constant. This is the foundation where our trust and hope should rest because He is unchanging, *the same yesterday and today and forever* (Hebrews 13:8).

So who do you need God to be for you today? The only thing standing between your need and His ability to fulfill it is your awareness and invitation. He is already everything He promises to be—He is the great I AM. But the question is, will you take the time to recognize your need? Then will you call upon Him and allow Him to meet it?

The challenge is never in God's ability to be what you need; it lies in your efforts to figure out what you need, in your understanding of who He really is, and in your willingness to let Him in. To experience the fullness of His name, take these steps:

1. **Identify your need.** Who do you need God to be in your life today? Is it your provider, your protector, your healer, your comfort?
2. **Dive into Scripture.** Explore His Word to discover how He reveals Himself in that role. If you need provision, meditate on Philippians 4:19: *And my God will meet all your needs according to the riches of His glory in Christ Jesus.* If you need shelter, reflect on Psalm 46:1: *God is our refuge and strength, an ever-present help in trouble.* These Scriptures confirm that God is who He says He is.

Once you've found the Scripture that speaks to your need, ask God for a personal encounter. Don't just stop at knowledge—invite Him to reveal Himself in a deeper way. Seek an experience with God, where His name becomes a living, transforming reality in your life. Then, like Aslan, when you do this, you open the door for Him to be all the things—everything you could ever need or desire.

I pray that you grow in the knowledge and revelation of who God is. As you identify your needs, explore His Word, and encounter His presence, may you experience the power of His name—Yahweh—the great I AM.

Day 28 What's in a Name?

Revel: Who do you need God to be for you today? What Scripture speaks to His character in this way? How can you actively seek to experience Him as this in your life today?

Take time to reflect on who God is, how His character is unchanging, and what that means for your daily walk with Him.

....

....

....

....

Align: If yesterday were a seed, did you tend to your dream? Did you plant and water it or leave it untouched? Whatever you did, learn from it. And today? Plant with purpose. Water with faith. Show up as if you matter, as if your dreams matter—because they do.

....

....

....

....

Dream Stack: Sticking with that same theme, think of your dream like a seed today. Here's the question: What's one thing you can do today to nurture that seed? Maybe it's making a phone call, writing the first paragraph, mapping out a process map or strategic plan for your team, or simply showing up in faith.

So go ahead—write it down and sow something today. The harvest begins with this moment.

....

....

....

....

DAY 29

Contagious Generosity

Each of you should give what you have decided in your heart to give, not reluctantly or under compulsion, for God loves a cheerful giver.

—2 Corinthians 9:7

HAVE YOU EVER WITNESSED someone laughing so hard it made you laugh even if you didn't get the joke? That's the contagious nature of joy—once it starts, it spreads. The more you laugh, the more others around you will start laughing too. It's infectious, and it lifts everyone up.

On the flip side, we also know how easily illnesses can spread. The world has seen how fast a cold—or a pandemic virus—can be passed from person to person, demonstrating the power of contagion. But what if I told you there's something more powerful than a contagious illness, and it should be spread farther and wider than even laughter?

Generosity.

In a world that constantly pushes for greater fulfillment through acquiring more—more stuff, more recognition, more wealth—one realizes there has to be a better way because even with all we have, we can still feel like something is missing. That's because we are looking for true fulfillment in the wrong places.

In God's Kingdom, true fulfillment comes from giving, not from gaining. It's not about what we accumulate but about what we share. The real reward isn't in what we keep—it's in what we give away.

Whether it's time, encouragement, resources, or simply the act of being present for someone else—when we give from a place of faith and love, we're participating in something eternal. And in that space, we discover a kind of joy that gaining alone could never offer. Therefore, generosity is not only a blessing to others; it's also a blessing to us. When we give with joy, it not only brings joy to others, but it also multiplies joy in our own hearts. Just like laughter, true generosity is contagious. It spreads, touching lives far beyond our own.

We see this kind of contagious generosity in Jesus as He modeled a life of selfless love and open-handed living, and we see it in the early church. In Acts 4:32–35, we read of a community of believers who were united in heart and mind. They shared everything they had, and because of their supernatural generosity, no one had a need. Imagine a world like that—a world where we live in unity, sharing everything we have and meeting each other's needs without hesitation. Sounds impossible, right? But with God's grace, anything is possible.

God's generosity through us can create a ripple effect of meeting needs and bringing heaven to earth. If we lived out this generosity, we would reflect God's Kingdom on earth—bold, joyful, and overflowing with love. Today's Scripture affirms this truth and goes on to say: *Now he who supplies seed to the sower and bread for food will also supply and increase your store of seed and will enlarge the harvest of your righteousness. You will be enriched in every way so that you can be generous on every occasion, and through us your generosity will result in thanksgiving to God* (2 Corinthians 9:10–11).

Here's the framework for understanding God's provision and generosity:

1. **He multiplies our seed as we sow it.** Scripture doesn't say that He supplies seed so you would be able to sow; He supplies it *to the sower*. This implies you're already doing it. We often wait for God to multiply before we give, but God's Kingdom operates differently. He asks us to give first, trusting that He will multiply what we sow. Whether you have a lot or a little, let Him catch you in the act of sowing.
2. **God supplies our needs.** He sees the seeds you are sowing and Scripture tells us that He knows what you need *and* provides for you. As you sow, He will supply your needs, because He is your source. We cannot forget that.
3. **He gives us more than enough.** God isn't just a God of enough—He's a God of overflow. As you give, He gives you more. He will *increase your store of seed*.
4. **When you give, you will receive.** God not only blesses how much seed you will sow, He blesses *the harvest of your righteousness*. Your giving enriches your life in every way so that you can be generous on every occasion. God can give more to you because He can trust you with what He's given, and He's not only giving you more to sow, but He's also giving you more of a harvest to reap.
5. **Your generosity is contagious.** The greatest result of your generosity is that it results in others thanking God! We don't want people to thank us as we give to them; we want them to see what we did as God's answer to their prayers. We don't want the credit; we want God to get the credit. When we give freely, it creates space for others to experience God's goodness and provision through our acts of kindness.

Inevitably, we are all sharing something each and every day. What are you sharing today? Are you spreading fear and doubt, or are you impacting those around you with the contagious generosity that flows from a heart full of God's love?

This isn't about the amount you have or what you give—it's about the posture of your heart. It's about recognizing that your true source is God, not money or stuff. True joy comes from giving, no matter the size of the gift. If you have time, share it. If you have extra income, bless others with it. If you have a skill, offer your expertise. We all have something to give. With a pure heart and sincere motives, give freely. Your generosity brings glory to God.

Day 29 Contagious Generosity

May your giving flow freely and abundantly until it's both cheerful and contagious.

■ ■ ■ ■ ■ ■

Revel: How would you rate your generosity? Is it minimal, casual, or *hilarious*? How can you exemplify the spirit of generosity by seeking to give rather than gain?

Allow God to examine your heart and reveal your motives. Ask Him who He wants you to bless today and how you can share with others, whether through your finances, time, or talents.

....

....

....

....

Align: Let's evaluate: Did yesterday's actions align with the vision of your dream? If not, feel no guilt; this is just data. What needs to shift today so your calendar reflects your calling?

....

....

....

....

Dream Stack: Today, think intentionally—what's one specific thing you can do to move your dream forward? Not something that feels merely productive, but something that truly aligns with the vision God placed in your heart.

Whatever it is, name it, own it, and do it. Momentum is built one choice at a time. So what's your move today?

....

....

....

....

DAY 30

Lost for Words: Praying When You Don't Know How

God, the searcher of the heart, knows fully our longings, yet he also understands the desires of the Spirit, because the Holy Spirit passionately pleads before God for us, his holy ones, in perfect harmony with God's plan and our destiny. So we are convinced that every detail of our lives is continually woven together for good.

—Romans 8:27–28 TPT

HAVE YOU EVER BEEN AT A LOSS for words, and not in a good way? Often life can leave us speechless. Even as I write this, I am in a season where I just can't make sense of the here and now. Blow after blow, attack after attack, setback after setback. Some days it feels comical because I just can't make this up; other days, I feel hopeless and drained because I'm not quite sure where the light at the end of the tunnel is. To make matters worse, I have had three close friends lose loved ones—to suicide, cancer, and a bizarre accident.

If we're not careful, life's toughest challenges can be hard to navigate, often becoming a major roadblock that diverts many of us from pursuing our God-given dreams. Life can hurt—deeply. Unanswered prayers and unexpected losses leave us with questions like, "Why, God?" and "Where are you in this, Lord?" or worse, render us completely speechless.

If this is where you are today, hear me clearly: I see you, and more important, God sees you. The pain is real, and sometimes there are no easy answers on this side of eternity. However, even in the midst of heartache, there is hope, and today's Scripture provides us with a profound truth to hold onto.

The first thing we must remember is that God is the *searcher of the heart*. He fully knows our longings, our dreams, and even our deepest disappointments. This is foundational because, in the middle of hardship, it's easy to forget that God sees us and knows how we feel. If we fail to understand His nearness, we start to question His character.

That being said, though God is in charge, He is not controlling every detail of a broken world. Free will brought sin into our world, and the consequences of that sin continue to affect our lives today. Yet even in the midst of chaos, God is sovereign, still working, and He is victorious. God's Word tells us that *every detail of our lives is continually woven together for good*. We must be convinced of this, certain, even *decided*.

By definition, the word decide means to come to a resolution in the mind as a result of consideration. But let's break it down even more. The word "decide" comes from the Latin word decidere, which is a combination of two root words:

"De" meaning off
"Caedere" meaning to cut
Put them together, and to decide literally means "to cut off."

So when you make a decision, you're not just choosing one thing—you're cutting off everything else that doesn't align.

Life may bring unexpected challenges and deep pain, but our lives must be marked by a firm decision for the Lord. He is good—period. He is making a way—period. He is working all things for our good—decided. This decision kills all other doubts and ways of thinking, anchoring us back where we belong—in the hands of the Father.

This doesn't mean that once we've made this decision, we'll always know what to pray for. And that's OK. Today's passage reminds us that the Holy Spirit is constantly interceding for us, praying in perfect harmony with God's plan for our lives, even when we can't find the words. How incredible is that? Even when we're too hurt or confused to pray, the Spirit is advocating for us, aligning us with God's eternal purposes. All we have to do is agree with Him.

Not knowing what to pray doesn't mean you shouldn't pray at all. When words escape you, pray in the Spirit. This gives you direct access to God's will beyond your understanding, especially in moments when your heart is heavy and your circumstances feel overwhelming. Build up your spirit by allowing the Holy Spirit to rise within you (Jude 1:20). In doing so, align yourself with God's perfect will and trust that He is guiding your prayers in divine alignment (Romans 8:26-27).

Don't avoid prayer. Pray in the Spirit. In fact, today, I encourage you to find yourself before the Lord *without* words. Though the Lord loves every prayer you pray, hearing every one of them, allow the Spirit to intercede on your behalf. You don't need the perfect words; just align yourself with His perfect will. Spend time praying in your prayer language today, and if you haven't received this yet, ask God for this powerful gift—He will give it to you.

Bottom line is God is not done. He is weaving your story together for good. He's holding the pieces, and He's asking you to trust Him with the process. You can rest assured that the victory is secure, so even when you can't see how things will work out, you can trust that the Holy Spirit is working behind the scenes, connecting the dots in ways you cannot even understand.

Day 30 Lost for Words: Praying When You Don't Know How

Revel: How's your prayer life? Is it just a list of requests, or do you sometimes struggle to find the right words? Maybe the weight of your circumstances has led you to doubt God's goodness, and as a result, your prayer life feels weakened. Take a moment to reflect.

Today, I encourage you to find yourself without words before the Lord. Pray in the Spirit trusting that He knows! Partner with Him in this and allow Him to transform your story into a testimony of His goodness.

....

....

....

....

Align: Keep it simple. Did what you did yesterday move you closer to the purpose God has placed in your heart? If not, what obstacles got in your way, and how can you overcome them moving forward?

....

....

....

....

BOLD

Dream Stack: Today, what's one step—just one—you can take that brings you closer to the bold dream God has placed in your heart? It doesn't have to be big. It just has to be aligned. Write it down and make it happen.

Remember, bold dreams require bold faith. So move forward today, not in your own strength but with full confidence that God goes before you. Let your actions be led by prayer. Move with bold confidence, knowing the Spirit is already ahead of you—passionately pleading your case and making a way before you even get there.

Allow your movement to be soaked in presence, not pressure. You were never meant to chase the dream alone. You were called to partner with the Lord as you build heaven on earth.

....

....

....

....

DAY 31

Go Deeper, not Further

At each place they went, they strengthened the lives of the believers and encouraged them to go deeper in their faith.

—Acts 14:22 TPT

IN TODAY'S FAST-PACED WORLD, success is often measured by how much we accomplish and how quickly we do it. We're pushed to move faster and do more in less time, and though it's practical to measure progress in some areas of our lives, this relentless chase for more often leaves us burned out, empty, and wondering why we feel so drained.

Could it be that our burnout comes from focusing on the wrong things? Our focus on speed and quantity is shallow—and so is our fulfillment. What if the answer isn't about doing more, faster but going deeper for longer?

In today's verse, we see Paul and Barnabas traveling and spreading the good news of Jesus. It's important to note that a few verses earlier, Paul was literally stoned and left for dead (Acts 14:19). This wasn't just a hardship; it was brutal, life-threatening opposition.

Yet Paul got up. And not only did he stand up, but he also went back into the very city where people tried to kill him. He faced the very place that had brought him pain and kept moving forward preaching the gospel. Paul didn't just rise physically; he rose spiritually too. He faced fear, death, and opposition head-on and declared they had no hold on him.

This is a powerful lesson for all of us. Paul's example shows that to truly move forward, we often need to confront our past experiences—our pain, our struggles, our disappointments—not to be defeated by them but to be strengthened through them. The things meant to break us can be used by God to make us. And when we go back to those places of hurt, declaring God's power and victory, we override the enemy's plan to keep us down.

But there's more to Paul's journey. Verse 22 tells us that Paul and Barnabas *strengthened the lives of the believers and encouraged them to go deeper in their faith*. This is key. They weren't focused just on doing more or reaching more people. They were focused on depth—on strengthening and deepening the believers' faith. They didn't say, "Do more for God"; they said, "Believe more in God," and they said this after they were stoned and left for dead.

What does that mean for us? It means that if we want to go further in life, despite the pain we've experienced, we need to go deeper with the Lord. If you want to overcome your past, go deeper. If you want to endure the trials you're facing, go deeper. If you want to experience true success, go deeper. If you want to live a life that counts, go deeper. If you want to dream bolder with God, *go deeper*.

The real answer is not in how fast or far we go, but in how deep we go with Christ. The deeper we go in our relationship with Him, the stronger we become and the more we are able to endure. Therefore, going further with the Lord is always a by-product of first going deeper with Him. Your growth is a reflection of your depth. To go higher, you must go deeper.

Today, I encourage you to stop chasing the world's version of success and start pursuing true depth with the Lord. Go deeper in your faith. Go deeper in your understanding of His love and His plan for your life. That's where we find the strength to keep going, the power to overcome, and the fulfillment you're searching for.

Revel: Where in your life are you focusing on speed or quantity rather than depth with the Lord?

Take time today to shift your goal from merely going further in life to seeking a deeper, more intimate relationship with God. Spend extra time in prayer, asking God to help you grow in faith, wisdom, and closeness with Him instead of running faster after the things of this world.

....

....

....

....

Align: Yesterday is behind you—did you show up for your dream? Even if it was just one small step, celebrate it. Because those small, faithful steps? They lead to the biggest gains over time.

Take a moment to reflect: Were your thoughts aligned with God's truth? Was your heart postured toward His promises? Did your actions reflect the dream He's placed in you?

Day 31 Go Deeper, not Further

Pause. Breathe. Reflect.

....

....

....

....

Dream Stack: What would it look like to show up boldly for my dream today, even if yesterday wasn't perfect? First, go deeper, then … go further! Do one more. Write it down. Do it. Count it.

....

....

....

....

DAY 32

Rooted in the Lord

The righteous shall flourish like a palm tree: he shall grow like a cedar in Lebanon. Those that be planted in the house of the Lord shall flourish in the courts of our God. They shall still bear fruit in old age; they shall be fat and flourishing.

—Psalm 92:12–14 King James Version

YESTERDAY, WE EXPLORED THE IMPORTANCE of depth in our relationship with God. Today, we'll go even deeper by focusing on what it means to be rooted in Him.

As we discussed, your growth is a reflection of your depth. To go higher, you must go deeper. But let's be clear—the goal of going deeper with God isn't merely for outward success or to "go further." We root ourselves in God because He is our source of life, our daily bread, our everything. If we want to make a lasting impact in this world, withstand life's trials, and thrive, we must understand the necessity of being deeply rooted in Him.

Today's Scripture paints a powerful picture using the image of a palm tree. A palm tree stands tall and strong even during hurricanes. While houses and cars are tossed around, the palm tree bends but doesn't break. Its root system is what gives it such resilience. Unlike many trees, the palm tree has thousands of roots spreading out in all directions, anchoring it firmly in the ground. These roots form a dense network that allows the tree to withstand storms, droughts, and floods. Even when it bends in high winds, the bending itself strengthens the tree, making it even more resilient.

This image offers a profound spiritual lesson. Like the palm tree, when we are deeply rooted in God, we won't break when the storms of life might cause us to bend. The very challenges we face can strengthen our faith and deepen our reliance on God.

Psalm 92 says: *Those that be planted in the house of the Lord shall flourish in the courts of our God.* When David wrote about dwelling in the house of the Lord, he meant that he wanted to abide in the presence of God, firmly established in Him and flourishing because of Him. It means:

- **Being fed:** The house of the Lord—His very presence nourishes us. In Him we receive the sustenance we need to grow spiritually.
- **Being protected:** God's presence offers us safety and stability during life's storms. It's where we can find shelter when the winds of adversity blow.
- **Being challenged:** In the house of the Lord, we are challenged to grow in our faith, to stretch, and to be held accountable in our spiritual journey.
- **Being connected:** God's house, His presence, is where we deepen our relationship not only with Him but also with other believers. We are not meant to do life alone; we grow stronger when we are connected to others in the body of Christ.
- **Being fruitful:** When we are planted in God's house, in His presence and in a community of other believers, we are able to bear fruit even in the most challenging seasons.

- **Being a blessing:** Being planted in God's house isn't just about receiving blessings—it's also about being a blessing to others. When we are rooted in Him, we overflow with His goodness and can pour into the lives of those around us. It's divine capacity!

Living in the house of the Lord isn't a one-time decision; it's a daily, sometimes minute-by-minute choice to remain rooted in God, to seek our safety, security, stability, and purpose in Him rather than being moved by the shifting circumstances of the world.

You are only as strong as where you are planted. When you are deeply rooted in God—planted in His house, nourished by His Word, and grounded in His love—nothing can uproot you.

Get rooted in him, today and every day.

Revel: Where are you planted? Are your roots deep in God, or are you feeling unstable in the shifting sands of life? What can you do today to deepen your roots in Him?

Take some time to reflect on the foundation of your faith. Perhaps you need to commit to daily time in God's Word beyond these devotionals. Maybe it's time to get connected with a local church and surround yourself with fellow believers who can encourage and support you. Ask God to reveal what you need to strengthen your roots in Him.

Day 32 Rooted in the Lord

Align: Where did you lean into the dream yesterday—and where did you pull back? What mindset or habit helped you gain momentum, and what might have held you up?

Take a moment to realign—mentally, emotionally, spiritually, and practically—so you can move forward today with intention. Stay in motion, walk in step with the Spirit, and flow with what God is doing in and through you.

....

....

....

....

Dream Stack: Today, what is one intentional thing you can do to manifest—to show, display, or act on—the dream God has placed in your heart?

Remember, this isn't about forcing something to happen through your own strength. It's about partnering with what God has already spoken over your life. Manifesting your dream means living in alignment with it—letting your choices, your habits, and even your attitude reflect the truth of what He's called you to do. So what does that look like for you today? Maybe it's having a courageous conversation. Maybe it's sending the email, writing the plan, or simply showing up with renewed faith.

Whatever it is—do it boldly. Because when you act in faith, even in small ways, you make the invisible dream visible—to yourself, to others, and to the world around you. Write it. Claim it. Move on it.

....

....

....

....

DAY 33

What's Your MO?

Examine your motives to make sure you're not showing off when you do your good deeds, only to be admired by others; otherwise, you will lose the reward of your heavenly Father.

—Matthew 6:1 TPT

WHAT DRIVES YOU? What gets you out of bed in the morning? What keeps you going through the day?

We all have a driving force behind our actions whether we realize it or not. The term *MO* (modus operandi) means "mode of operating." It's our reason for doing things, the motivation behind our actions. Motivation is powerful. It can help us reach goals, like losing weight, starting a business, or mending a relationship. Motivation isn't about the *what*—it's about the *why*.

If you find yourself stuck in the mud or repeating cycles of unhealthy patterns, it may not be what you're doing that needs to change but the motivation behind *why* you're doing it.

Think about it:

- If your motivation is to be right, you might find yourself in constant arguments.
- If your motivation is security, you might stay in a job you hate.
- If your motivation is to be loved or valued, you might stay in toxic relationships.
- If your motivation is to hide, you might play small or turn to unhealthy vices.

Today's Scripture tells us to examine our motives. Your motives determine your actions—whether you're showing off or holding back. What you're doing (or not doing) is driven by a deeper motivation, and identifying that is key as we mature in the Lord.

Your motives matter.

Let's be real—the Lord absolutely wants to bless you. He delights in giving good gifts to His children, and He has an amazing plan filled with purpose and blessings for your life. But more than pouring out those blessings, what He longs for most is a relationship where He is at the center of your desires.

God is a jealous God—He doesn't want you looking around for validation or being driven by the world's motivations. He wants to be your focus, the One you turn to with your dreams, your struggles, your hopes, and your fears. Yes, you'll face fears, but He doesn't want you to be driven by them. Yes, you'll have bold dreams, but those dreams shouldn't have you. And yes, you'll have people who influence your life, but He doesn't want them to be your ultimate source of motivation. Above all, He longs for an intimate relationship with you. *He wants to be your motivation; He wants to be your MO.*

So today, here's your heart check: Are you doing whatever you're doing *for* the Lord? Or are you doing it for approval, validation, or recognition? When you shift your motivation to be solely on the Lord, doing everything you do for an audience of one, you find true freedom. You're no longer striving to please others or meet worldly standards; you're operating from a place of deep desire to please God.

Take a moment to reflect on what's in front of you today—your career goals, health goals, relationships, your career path, parenting, dreams—all of it. Now set those aside for just a minute. Close your eyes and picture Jesus standing right in front of you. Focus on Him until everything else fades into the background and it's just you and Him.

This is eternity. One day, you'll stand before Him face-to-face, and He will be all that matters. In that moment, it won't be about what others thought of you but about how you lived for Him. Now imagine that moment is happening now as you go about your day—working out, building your business, raising your children, working toward your dreams—whatever you're doing, do it *for Him*. Motivated *by Him* with a heart centered *on Him*.

This is pure motivation.

This is the best sort of MO. This is the kind of heart God desires—one that beats for Him alone. When fear, doubt, or insecurity pop up, or even when the need to succeed, impress, or validate yourself arises, return to this place of purity. Let your motivation be rooted in the One who is within you, not the world around you.

Let your heart burn with a passion for Him. Let *Him* be your motivation, today and always.

Revel: Take a moment to consider what's truly driving you. Where is your motivation rooted? Is it grounded in God or influenced by external pressures?

To realign your focus, I encourage you to close your eyes and imagine Jesus walking into your space. As He observes your actions and your heart, ask yourself: Why am I doing what I'm doing? Let this exercise draw you into a deeper connection with Him, transforming your heart and intentions toward purity.

Day 33 What's Your MO?

Align: It's time to pause and check in on your mindset, heartset, and dreamset. Were your thoughts yesterday rooted in truth—or were they shaped by fear, doubt, or comparison? Did you invite God into the process, or were you trying to carry it all on your own? Think about the choices you made: Did they reflect the person God is shaping you to be? Did you take any steps—even small ones—toward the dream He's placed in your heart?

Take it all in. No guilt—just honest feedback. Breathe deep. Let the Holy Spirit realign your character with His truth, His grace, and His glory.

....

....

....

....

Dream Stack: What's one thing you can do today to keep it real, keep it aligned, and move you one step closer to turning that God-given dream into reality? Make it plain. Make it real. Make it happen.

....

....

....

....

DAY 34

What's in Your Hand?

Then the Lord said to him, 'What is that in your hand?' 'A staff,' he replied. The Lord said, 'Throw it on the ground.' Moses threw it on the ground and it became a snake, and he ran from it. Then the Lord said to him, 'Reach out your hand and take it by the tail.' So Moses reached out and took hold of the snake and it turned back into a staff in his hand. 'This,' said the Lord, 'is so that they may believe that the Lord, the God of their fathers—the God of Abraham, the God of Isaac and the God of Jacob—has appeared to you.'

—Exodus 4:2–5

IN OUR JOURNEY TOWARD GROWTH and becoming all God has created us to be in any and every area of life, there are pivotal moments where we must release what's in our hands so He can give us something even greater. That means that whatever got you to where you are won't necessarily be what takes you to where you've never been. That doesn't necessarily mean what you've been doing is wrong; it just means it's no longer right.

In today's Scripture we see Moses at this pivotal moment. God asks Moses a simple but profound question: *"What is that in your hand?"* And Moses replies, *"A staff."*.

It seems ordinary—a tool of his trade as a shepherd—but God is about to transform this ordinary object into a symbol of divine power and authority. God tells Moses to throw the staff down, and it miraculously becomes a serpent. In this moment, God isn't just performing a miracle; He is also shifting Moses's identity and calling.

Up to that point, the staff in Moses's hand represented his role as a shepherd, caring for sheep in the wilderness. It was a symbol of compassion, authority, and defense for his flock. But God had a much larger purpose for Moses. What was once a shepherd's staff would soon become the tool through which God would use Moses to lead an entire nation out of bondage, but first Moses had to let it go. God wanted to take the simple tool in Moses's hand and use it to accomplish something miraculous.

When Moses laid down what God had placed in his hand, he realized that God wasn't calling him to herd sheep anymore—God was calling him to lead an entire nation from slavery to freedom. This wasn't simply about God exchanging what Moses had for something greater (Moses's ordinary for God's extraordinary); it was also about God transforming how Moses saw himself—this was a shift in identity.

My question to you is this: What's in your hand?

As you ponder what God might be asking you to release in this season, consider this: If you hold on too tightly to the old, you risk missing out on the new. The blessings God gives us in one season are meant to be surrendered when He calls us to the next. If Moses had refused to throw down his staff because it was the only thing he knew, he would have never experienced the miracles that followed. He would have continued herding sheep when God had freeing a nation in mind. Though it can be difficult to let go of what's comfortable and familiar, we must trust that when God asks us to surrender something, it's always because He has something greater in store.

Don't downgrade God's extraordinary because of your ordinary. Often we let our own fears, failures, or feelings of inadequacy stop us from stepping into what God has for us. We minimize what God has placed in our hands. We think, *It's just a staff. It's not enough.*

Like Moses, who saw himself as a stuttering, insecure shepherd, we allow our internal narratives about ourselves to drown out God's truth about us. We define ourselves by our past mistakes or present limitations rather than by God's calling. But God doesn't see us as we see ourselves—He sees us through the lens of who He created us to be.

God isn't asking for what you don't have—He's asking for what you *do* have, so He can transform it and lead you to where you've never been. It might seem like something small—a skill, a talent, a resource—but God sees it differently. He wants to use whatever you have, no matter how insignificant it seems, to accomplish His greater purpose. It's not about how big or impressive your offering is but about your obedience in surrendering it to Him. Will you trust God with your ordinary and allow Him to work his extraordinary power within you to move you into your next season?

Whatever is in your hand, God wants to use it. He wants to transform it. But even more, He wants to transform YOU—into the person He created you to be. He wants to reveal His power through your life. The question is, are you willing? Will you give Him what's in your hand?

What got you to where you are won't take you to where you were destined to be. Give God what's in your hand and let Him be responsible for the miracle. May your ordinary become His extraordinary.

Revel: What's in your hand? What is God asking you to release so He can move you into your next season in miraculous ways? Acknowledge anything you're holding onto and surrender what you have to the Lord today.

Next, what skills, talents, or resources have you been downgrading, thinking they are too small for God to use? Identify one area in your life where you can allow God to take your ordinary and do something extraordinary.

....

....

....

....

Day 34 What's in Your Hand?

Align: As you reflect on yesterday, ask yourself: Did my choices reflect the future I'm believing in? If not, what got in the way, externally or internally? Was it fear? Distraction? Doubt? And more important, what needs to shift today so your actions align with the dream God has placed in your heart?

Remember, reflection isn't about guilt or shame—it's about growth.

....

....

....

....

Dream Stack: What is one thing you can do to move closer to your dreams? Remember, when you dare to dream, you're not just chasing goals—you're aligning yourself with God's purpose. So don't just dream it—live it.

Write down one bold step you can take today as a commitment to yourself—and to the calling God has placed within you.

....

....

....

....

DAY 35

Sit Still

'Be still, and know that I am God.'

—Psalm 46:10

THESE DAYS, IT CAN FEEL like we are constantly on the move, always searching for answers. We look to Google, coaches, courses, and self-help resources for clarity. Yet even with all this information, we often remain unsettled and worry about the unknown. It's as though the more we google, the less we know.

What about you? Are you still searching for answers today? Despite all the wisdom and advice available, do you still find yourself weighed down by worry, fearing the future and unsure of what lies ahead? It's normal to feel this way, but there's a better way to navigate the busyness of life—stillness.

In the book of Psalms, David faced a similar reality to what we experience today. Despite living thousands of years ago, he dealt with significant challenges too. He vividly describes the chaos around him as the earth giving way, mountains falling and quaking, and waters roaring (Psalm 46:1–3). Here David acknowledges the turmoil of life—the overwhelming noise, chaos, and uncertainty. He doesn't deny its reality. But in the midst of this turmoil, David redirects his focus to a greater truth: *The Lord Almighty is with us; the God of Jacob is our fortress* (Psalm 46:7).

Then comes the powerful, transformative message from the Lord to David, and I believe to us as well: *Be still, and know that I am God.* In the midst of the noise and uncertainty of life, God reminds us that our response shouldn't be more striving but stillness.

Why stillness?

Stillness leads to knowing. We often think that peace comes from the absence of problems. But true peace comes from the Lord. When we're moving a thousand miles an hour, it's hard to see this. But when we slow down, it becomes clear as day.

Be still means to stop striving, fighting, and pushing. It's derived from the Hebrew word *rapha*, which means "to be weak, to let go, to release." In essence, when God invites us to be still, He's asking us to surrender to Him. It's not about giving up and waving the white flag; it's about giving in and raising your hands in worship as you release control and trust only in Him. Through this act of surrender, you encounter Him. In this place of stillness, you come to truly *know* Him.

The Hebrew word for *know* in this verse is *yada*, which means to know by experience—an intimate, personal knowledge. Stillness is not about just silence or meditation; it's about experiencing the presence of God. We don't get quiet just to follow a process; we get quiet to encounter the creator of the universe. In stillness we move from seeking answers to experiencing the One who holds all the answers. It's here you encounter the Lord.

One encounter with the Lord shifts the atmosphere both around you and within you. When you pause in His presence, you make space for His peace to fill your heart.

This isn't just in your quiet time or in worship; it's available to you at any time of the day. All you need to do is be still, then know.

Instead of searching harder trying to manufacture peace, *be still*. Let the stillness become a space where you first surrender to Him—your will, your way, your plans, and yes, your dreams. Then expect to encounter God's presence. Begin to *know* Him in a deeper, more profound way.

Today, instead of striving for answers, take a moment to rest in the presence of God. Stop seeking solutions outside of Him—let *Him* be the answer you're looking for. Let stillness become a space where you pause in His presence and experience His goodness, where your heart aligns with His truth, and where you come to know Him on a deeper level. He is the answer you're searching for.

Be still, and know…

Revel: How has the busyness of life kept you from being still? Even in your quiet time, are you seeking a process or an encounter? Are you searching for answers, or are you seeking intimacy with the Lord?

Today, take time to be still, to surrender, and reflect on Him—let this be a moment of genuine encounter with the Lord.

Day 35 Sit Still

Align: Look back on yesterday. Ask yourself: Was I thinking like someone who trusts God's promises—or someone trying to control the outcome? Am I trusting God's timing—or becoming impatient and discouraged?

Take a moment to realign—mentally, emotionally, spiritually, practically—so you can move forward today with intention.

....

....

....

....

Dream Stack: What's one thing you can do today to move toward your dream—to take real, aligned action—while remaining in a mindset and heartset of stillness before the Lord?

It's not about hustle. It's about harmony. Let your movement come from a place of rest, not rush. Write down one intentional step that reflects both faith and stillness.

....

....

....

....

DAY 36

Gratitude

Taste and see that the Lord is good; blessed
is the one who takes refuge in Him.

—Psalm 34:8

TO BE HONEST, keeping a gratitude journal has never been my strong suit. We hear it all the time: "Write down what you're thankful for; count your blessings." I even had a journal once that my mom gave me with the title, *Fine, I'm Grateful—A Journal to Catapult Me from My Default Position of Complaining to Counting My Blessings*. I tried it for a few days, and that's the end of that story.

What about you? How's your gratitude practice? Many people admit they're too busy to have one, some overlook its importance, and others struggle to stay grateful during tough seasons of life—times of loss, disappointment, or heartache.

We often think gratitude is about thanking God for what He's done, and when things are going well, that's easy. When the sun is shining, your health is good, your bank account is full, your relationships are thriving, and everything's falling into place, saying thank you feels natural, even effortless. We toss up a quick thanks to God as we move through our day, yet we barely stop to reflect.

But what about the hard days? What about the seasons of loss, sickness, or unanswered prayers? It's much more challenging to practice gratitude when nothing seems to be going right. During those times, it's easy to let our disappointments and struggles overshadow our thankfulness.

I have learned this key truth: Gratitude isn't just about thanking God for what He does—it's about honoring Him for who He is. Gratitude isn't based on results or circumstances. It's about acknowledging God's goodness, no matter what's happening around us. His goodness doesn't change even when our situations do. We don't thank God only because He gives us good things; we thank Him because He is good. Period.

In Psalm 34, we see David practicing this kind of gratitude. He first declares: *I will extol the Lord at all times; His praise will always be on my lips. I will glory in the Lord; let the afflicted hear and rejoice. Glorify the Lord with me; let us exalt His name together* (Psalm 34:1–3). David's focus is entirely on God's character, not on his own circumstances.

Then we see David recount God's goodness: *I sought the Lord, and He answered me; He delivered me from all my fears. Those who look to Him are radiant; their faces are never covered with shame. This poor man called, and the Lord heard him; He saved him out of all his troubles. The angel of the Lord encamps around those who fear Him, and He delivers them* (Psalm 34:4–7). David first praises God for who He is then thanks Him for what He's done.

Then he ends with the beautiful declaration that is today's verse: *Taste and see that the Lord is good; blessed is the one who takes refuge in Him*. David has experienced God's presence and goodness firsthand, and his gratitude overflows.

Here's my encouragement to you today: Live gratefully for who God is, not just what

He does. Yes, it's important to remember what God has done in your life—recounting answered prayers, fulfilled dreams, and moments of provision. But true gratitude comes when you recognize who He is in all seasons, both good and hard, when life makes sense and when it doesn't. If life feels overwhelming right now, I encourage you to meditate on who God is—His faithfulness, His love, His provision. As you do, you'll find your spirit lifted, your heart encouraged, and your strength renewed. If this chapter of your life is a beautiful one, I encourage you to do the same: Focus not just on what God is doing but also on who He is. Continue to meditate on His character. May you experience and know His goodness, not just in this season but always!

Begin your gratitude practice by first honoring God for who He is. Take time to reflect on His goodness regardless of the season you're in or how your day is going. Then thank Him for what He has done—recall His mercies, the blessings you've received, and the prayers He's answered. He is truly worthy of praise! Last, taste and see that He is good—today and always.

Remember this: God is good, no matter what. That's something you can always be grateful for.

■ ■ ■ ■ ■ ■

Revel: How grateful are you? Whether you've been intentional about a gratitude practice or not, take a moment to reflect: Are you focused more on what God has done *for* you or on who He is *to* you?

Take a moment to examine your heart. Then begin today—whether through singing, journaling, or praying—praise Him for who He is.

....

....

....

....

Day 36 Gratitude

Align: Take a moment to consider yesterday. Was your heart postured toward surrender—or were you striving to make things happen in your own strength? Did you invite the Holy Spirit to lead, or were you carrying it all on your shoulders? And let's be real—did you actually take that step you said you would?

Wherever you landed, today is a new opportunity. Lay down whatever didn't serve you and open your hands to receive everything the Lord is longing to give—peace, clarity, strength, and direction.

....

....

....

....

Dream Stack: Let's rock and roll—it's a new day and another chance to bring heaven to earth! What's one thing you can do today to move closer to your dream? Remember, it's not about excuses or even good reasons—it's about priorities. Today, make your dream a priority. Write it down and make it happen.

....

....

....

....

DAY 37

Perpetual Perfectionism

[Jesus said,] 'Be perfect, therefore, as your heavenly Father is perfect.'
—Matthew 5:48

YIKES. CAN WE ALL JUST ADMIT that perfectionism is hard? Or better yet—impossible. So why would Jesus tell us to be perfect, just as our Heavenly Father is perfect? That feels like a pretty unreachable standard.

Let's be real: no one wakes up saying, "Today, I'm going to be perfect—just like God." Not you, not me. And yet, somehow, we still find ourselves chasing perfection. Not in the way Jesus meant it, but in a way driven by something else—approval. We strive to be perfect to earn validation, acceptance, and love from others, not from a place of divine surrender, but from human pressure. And that's where the real problem begins. This perpetual cycle of perfectionism will wear you out because it's fueled by fear, not love. Social media and the modern culture we live in can amplify the facade we all aim to perfect, making us feel like we have to look flawless to win. Nobody wins for being perfect, yet we all try *and* fail, which only feeds our fear. Though we strive for it as if there's a prize waiting for us at the end, in all reality, it's a race with no finish line or trophy. That being said, if perfectionism is impossible, why does Jesus call us to *be perfect*? The answer lies in understanding the deeper meaning of *perfection* in this context.

When we aim for perfectionism, it's often about self-validation, about proving we're worthy. It's a fear-driven pursuit—one that will leave us drained and disconnected from God's purpose. But Jesus's call to perfection is not about performance; it's about love. It's about a relationship with Him.

If you read the verses leading up to today's verse, you'll notice Jesus is talking about love, not flawlessness. He says, *"You have heard that it was said, 'Love your neighbor and hate your enemy.' But I tell you, love your enemies and pray for those who persecute you, that you may be children of your Father in heaven. He causes his sun to rise on the evil and the good, and sends rain on the righteous and the unrighteous. If you love those who love you, what reward will you get? Are not even the tax collectors doing that? And if you greet only your own people, what are you doing more than others? Do not even pagans do that?"* (Matthew 5:43–47) Then we see Him go on to say something that is life-changing for all of us: *"Be perfect, therefore, as your heavenly Father is perfect."*

Jesus did not come to shame or condemn; he came to show us a better way. He did not come to abolish the law but to fulfill it, giving us the grace we needed to walk as he walked. His life redefined the new, greatest commandment: LOVE!

In this passage of Scripture, Jesus isn't asking us to live without mistakes. He's calling us to reflect the perfect love of the Father—a love that goes beyond what's easy, what's comfortable, or what feels good. This is not easy love, but the kind that causes us to love even our enemies. To love the unlovable, the difficult, and even those who hurt us. That's the perfection Jesus is talking about. It's not about how we perform but about how we love others—especially when it's hard. This perfection is about embodying God's heart of love, a love that overflows from a heart fully connected to God.

If you're caught in the trap of perfectionism, chances are you've lost sight of God's love. You've traded His grace for performance, striving to meet standards He never set for you. And if you're struggling to love others, especially those who are hard to love, it's a sign that you're living your life based upon the world's standard of love, which is conditional at best.

The truth is that perpetual perfectionism is unsustainable. But perpetual love—God's love flowing through us—is a lifestyle that transforms us and others. Jesus loved us perfectly, not when we had it all together, but when we were still messy, broken, and far from perfect. He loved us when we made mistakes, when we took wrong turns, and when we didn't do things the right way. Even now, as you live a life serving Him, He doesn't love you more. Likewise, when you fall back into sinful patterns, He doesn't love you less. He loves you because He loves you because He loves you. This is perfect love, which casts out all fear.

When we reflect on the depth of God's love for us, it empowers us to extend that same love to others. It's not about being perfect; it's about loving like Him.

Today, I encourage you in this: Instead of chasing perpetual perfectionism, pursue perpetual love. Perfectionism is overrated. Perpetual love is not.

Choose love.

Revel: Today, what would it look like to love as Jesus does? Picture yourself letting go of the heavy burden of perfectionism and resting in the grace of His perfect love. Reflect on how this exchange might transform you, creating more space for unconditional love, connection, and peace in your relationship with others, yourself, and even God.

If you're struggling to love someone today, ask God to show you His heart for that person. Pray for His abundant, unrelenting, perpetual love to fill you so deeply that it overflows, allowing you to love others freely as He loves you (and yes, that includes even those who are hardest to love).

Day 37 Perpetual Perfectionism

Align: Keep it simple as you look back on yesterday. Did you take even one step toward your dream? If not, what got in the way? What obstacle tripped you up or slowed you down?

Today, regardless of what happened yesterday, take some time to realign with heaven's realities.

Dream Stack: What's one step you can take to make your dream a reality? Remember, progress isn't about perfection—it's about staying in motion. Momentum is built one choice at a time, one step at a time. So stay focused, stay grounded, and take the step. Your future is shaped by what you do today. Put it on paper. Bring it to life.

DAY 38

Sense and Reason

Now the mind of the flesh [which is sense and reason without the Holy Spirit] is death [death that comprises all the miseries arising from sin, both here and hereafter]. But the mind of the [Holy] Spirit is life and [soul] peace [both now and forever].

—Romans 8:6 Amplified Bible, Classic Edition

SENSE AND REASON—We tend to place so much value on these two word. We often say things like, "That makes sense" or "My reason for doing that was …." Logical. Practical. Grounded in common sense. And though that can be fair, it doesn't always align with what God is calling us to do.

Sense: A logical or reasonable way of thinking.
Reason: The ability to form judgments, draw conclusions, and provide explanations for our actions.

In my book *DREAM—I Dare You*, I talk a lot about the brain and how it functions. In short, you have a brain, and that's a good thing—use it! But we need to understand what part of the brain is designed to do. It's a survival mechanism, wired to keep us safe and avoid pain. It analyzes the experiences of the past in order to inform our current actions. Ultimately, it takes what happened yesterday and throws it on our tomorrow.

This makes it nearly impossible to step out of our comfort zone, trying something new or, heaven forbid, daring to dream the impossible (even with God). Why? Because why on earth would I try something that didn't work before? Why on earth would I do something that would cause me pain again? Do you see the sense in that? Or the reason behind it?!

Over time, the experiences you have impact how you think, and how you think ultimately shapes the way your brain is wired. Every time you have a thought, it creates a pathway in your brain. The more you think a thought, the wider the path gets. The wider the path gets, the more you think the thought. It's a vicious cycle.

This is how we develop our sense of logic and reason. But here's the catch—without the guidance of the Holy Spirit, sense and reason often trap us in the familiar, the safe, the "known." We start believing every thought we have, reinforcing patterns of behavior and living in a world shaped by our past, not the potential or power of God. And then we wonder why we're not bringing heaven to earth. Sure, the Lord calls us to walk in faith, but let's be honest—our brain seems to have a different plan, and it does everything it can to convince us its plan is the right one.

Here's the truth: Jesus didn't always make sense. In fact, he was far from reasonable. Many of the things He did in His lifetime did not make sense to human reason or logic. However, I'd like to propose that He showed us a better way. In today's verse in Romans, we see a clear distinction between living by sense and reason (our own understanding) and being led by the Spirit. It says: *The mind of the flesh [sense and reason without the Holy Spirit] is death. … But the mind of the [Holy] Spirit is life and [soul] peace.*

This verse teaches us that relying on sense and reason alone leads to spiritual death, but when our mind is guided by the Holy Spirit, it brings life and peace. It's a shift from self-reliance to Spirit-dependence. And that shift changes everything.

It's what I like to call Holy Spirit pace. Holy Spirit pace is the rhythm of life that comes from walking in step with the Spirit of God—not rushing ahead in self-effort and not falling behind in fear or hesitation. It's not rushed, anxious, or performance-driven; rather, it's steady and intentional, listening before leaping, surrendering before striving. We're trading burnout for peace, pressure for presence, and control for confidence in the One who knows the way. It's less about speed—and more about alignment as we trust that God's timing isn't just right—it's perfect.

Einstein once said, "The intuitive mind is a sacred gift, and the rational mind is a faithful servant." Sadly, we have honored the servant (sense and reason) and forgotten the gift of the Spirit-led life. As believers, we have the very presence of the Holy Spirit within us. But too often, we drown it out because it doesn't fit into our neat boxes of logic and practicality.

The Holy Spirit doesn't always make sense. He's not bound by human reasoning. He moves in ways that challenge our understanding because His goal isn't our understanding; it's to renew our hearts *and* transform our minds. A Spirit-led, renewed mind is anchored in heavenly truth, and that's where true peace and life are found.

The next time you feel the pull of your sense or reason, pause. Begin to cultivate a Holy Spirit mindset by asking Him to guide your thoughts and actions as you boldly chase after the dreams He's given you. Surrender the need to understand everything and allow His peace to lead you every step of the way.

Remember, faith defies all logic.

※ ※ ※ ※ ※ ※

Revel: Where have you let sense and reason hold you back from fully trusting God's guidance? Take a moment to reflect on an area of your life where the Holy Spirit may be asking you to trust Him beyond logic or reasoning. Then use your dream stacking time to follow His lead throughout your day.

Day 38 Sense and Reason

Align: Look back on yesterday. Were you pacing with the Lord? Instead of racing through your to-do list or trying to figure everything out on your own, did you pause and invite the Lord into your process?

Today, ask the Holy Spirit to set the pace. Align with His rhythm—where peace takes priority over pressure, presence outweighs performance, and trust replaces the need for control. Then breathe, trust, and walk in step with Him.

Dream Stack: Holy Spirit pace, y'all. What's one intentional step you can take today toward your dream—not rushing ahead but walking in sync with the Spirit as He leads you? Write it down and let His peace set the pace and your feet make the move.

DAY 39

Mental Health God's Way

We demolish arguments and every pretension that sets itself up against the knowledge of God, and we take captive every thought to make it obedient to Christ.

—2 Corinthians 10:5

HAVE YOU EVER STRUGGLED with negative thoughts? Maybe a better way to phrase that is: What do you do with your negative thoughts?

We all have negative thoughts—you know the ones vying for the space called "truth" in your mind that ought to be reserved only for the Word of God?! Yeah, those. For the sake of keeping it real, keeping our minds fixed on God's Word can feel much harder than it should. Can I get an amen!? I am here to tell you that if you've ever wrestled with negative thoughts, you're not crazy, you're human.

However, perpetual negative thoughts have led to what many call a mental health crisis. For the past four years, *anxiety* and *depression* have consistently been among the most searched terms online. Anxiety disorders alone affect over 40 million adults in the United States every year, and that doesn't even account for a significant global health challenge as it pertains to mental health, with many people still lacking access to proper treatment. Though various interventions have been developed to address this issue, the results have been less than ideal.

As believers, though we recognize the value of professional studies and statistics, we must first turn to the Word of God for the ultimate definition and guidance on mental health. We cannot allow our lives to be conformed to statistics; rather, they should be conformed to the likeness of Christ. That means our job is to look like Him, and the only way we can look more like Him is by thinking like him.

Consider the negative thoughts you've been having. The ones that feel true even though they're not. Would you say that at times you feel imprisoned by them? Held captive by them? Truth be told, negative thoughts can be overwhelming, as if you're in a roller coaster of emotions that takes you up one minute and pulls you down the next. The dark thoughts are frightening, the anxious ones exhausting, and the self-critical ones chip away at your soul. If left unchecked, they become so frequent that they start feeling normal, and when we start mistaking that normal for truth, we're in trouble.

Because that "truth" starts coloring the way we see everything—our own life, our relationships, our purpose on earth, our view of God, and ultimately, our mental health. But today's Scripture reminds us that we're not meant to let our thoughts run the show. We're called to *take captive every thought to make it obedient to Christ*. This Scripture reveals this battle isn't just about mental health—it's also about spiritual warfare. And the battle in our minds is one we're equipped to fight with the truth of God's Word.

Mental warfare is real, and it's something we need to pay attention to. Most people let their thoughts define their reality, but as believers, the foundation of our reality is not our thoughts—it's the Word of God. Too often we assume our thoughts are accurate just because they *feel* real, but truth isn't based on feelings. It's based on what God says. Let me tell you something important: You have thoughts, but you are not your thoughts.

Satan wants nothing more than for you to believe the lies in your head, because as long as you do, you'll never live in the freedom of God's truth. But here's God's truth: You are not captive to your thoughts—you are called to take your thoughts captive. You are not captive to them; make them captive to you.

If your thoughts are causing anxiety, fear, doubt, or worry, you are believing a lie. The Bible tells us that the truth sets us free. Anything less than freedom is not God's truth, no matter how "true" it feels at the moment. The key is to stop accepting every thought that comes to your mind as fact and start doing what Scripture commands—taking your thoughts captive and making them obedient to Christ. That means it's not about what you think; it's about what *He* thinks.

Though the world tries to define mental health in a myriad of ways, Biblical mental health is a mind dominated by heaven's realities. It's a mind able to manage someone's decisions in the midst of the tension between what is and what God says. This is beyond coping; it's thriving!

Biblical mental health is not merely the absence of distress in your life but an proactive process of taking your thoughts and causing them to be obedient to Christ. It's renewing your mind so much with Biblical truth that heaven's realities become your focal point, giving you the capacity to deal with your current reality. It's about learning how to manage your thoughts, emotions, and actions by trusting in God's divine, eternal promises in the midst of life's challenges. Taking your thoughts captive is not just a mental exercise—it's also a spiritual practice that shapes your identity, builds your dreams, and aligns your life with God's truth.

I encourage you today to become relentless about your mental health. You're not a prisoner to your thoughts. They don't define you. Take those thoughts captive and make them obey what God says. Care less about what *you* think and more about what *God* thinks.

Day 39 Mental Health God's Way

Revel: What thoughts have been dominating your mind lately? Identify one negative thought that's been weighing on you. Then look up Scripture that speaks truth against that lie and declare it over your life this week. Make every thought you think today become obedient to God's Word.

....

....

....

....

Align: Look back on yesterday. Did you take a step toward your dream? If not, what obstacles got in your way? What can you do to overcome them today and move forward? Don't rush through this moment, making it just another task to complete. Let it be about realigning your heart with His. Don't just picture yourself doing for the Lord—see yourself becoming who He has called you to be, walking fully in His grace.

    Pause. Reflect. Realign.

....

....

....

Dream Stack: What's one specific action you can take today to bring your dream closer to reality?

As you've learned, we don't just think our way into a new way of living—we act our way to a new way of thinking. So take those thoughts captive and make them obedient to the dream God has placed in you. Now go on … write it down and do the thing! You've got this, because God's got you.

....

....

....

....

DAY 40

On Mission

As the time approached for him to be taken up to heaven, Jesus resolutely set out for Jerusalem.

—Luke 9:51

RESOLUTE IS A WORD WE DON'T OFTEN USE, but perhaps we should. To be resolute means to be admirably purposeful, determined, and unwavering. It describes someone with a clear goal, living intentionally and *on mission*.

Does that word describe how you live each day? We'd all like to think so, but the reality is, it's easy to get distracted. We live in a world full of things competing for our attention. Even with the best intentions to pursue a specific goal or mission for the day, how often do you find yourself at the end of the day thinking, *I meant to do x, y, and z but got so distracted*? One day of distraction turns into five, then a hundred, and for some, even a lifetime. The truth is, the greatest obstacle to living resolutely and staying on mission is distraction.

Distractions are anything that divert or pull your attention away from what God has called you to do and from the things that matter most. The problem with distractions is that they often come disguised as ordinary responsibilities—laundry, email, technology, never-ending to-do lists, and one more activity our kids play in. None of these things is inherently wrong, but when they keep you from your mission, they become distractions.

So how do we stay resolute and on mission when life seems to constantly pull us in different directions?

If we look at Jesus, He modeled this perfectly. Today's Scripture shows us Jesus, knowing the challenges that were ahead—the pain, the sacrifice, the cross. And yet, He still set His face toward Jerusalem. He was unwavering in His commitment to the mission—and that mission was you.

Jesus lived with one goal in mind: to give His life so *you* could have eternal life. Despite knowing the pain and sacrifice ahead, nothing could detour Him. Often it's easy to overlook His sacrifice and minimize what Jesus went through because the things we face seem so monumental. But consider this: He left the glory of heaven to come to earth; He was born in a manger (of all places) to a poor family; He had to face every kind of temptation; He was rejected by his own people; He was misunderstood, criticized, and even despised by religious leaders (who should have recognized and honored Him). He was betrayed for thirty pieces of silver, was falsely accused, subjected to an illegal and unjust trial, and His closest disciple, Peter, denied knowing Him (can you say, "pain of abandonment!?"). He was beaten, spat on, mocked, and severely whipped by Roman soldiers, who then placed a crown of thorns on His head, causing further pain and humiliation as He was forced to carry His heavy wooden cross through the streets of Jerusalem. He was nailed to the cross, experiencing one of the most excruciating forms of execution, and was forsaken by God, who literally had to turn His back on

Him because He became sin. And yet, through it all, He remained resolute because His mission was clear—He came to save you. No distraction, no obstacle, not even betrayal or suffering could shake His resolve.

So while your challenges and even distractions may seem monumental, they pale in comparison to those of Jesus and the eternal mission He came to fulfill. Hear me—I don't say this to minimize your struggles but to maximize the love and power behind Jesus's sacrifice and the example He set for us.

Now it's time to live even more resolute, more on mission than you ever have. It's time we follow in the footsteps of Jesus and begin living our lives on mission, and I know just how we're going to do it. Every day, we must recognize that we face the tension between *the tyranny of the urgent* and *the priorities of the important.* The tyranny of the urgent is filled with things that demand immediate attention—bills, emails, chores, you name it; we all have them. These things know how to come find you and, generally, you will naturally react to them. At face value, that isn't wrong, but if they dominate your day, they can keep you from pursuing the things that really matter, the priorities of the important.

The priorities of the important are things like pursuing your God-given dreams, writing that book, learning a new skill, building your business, or investing in others, but unlike those urgent things, they will require intentional focus to accomplish them. They won't come and find you. They won't scream for your attention. They won't beg for you to notice, and in fact, they will kindly wait for you until you decide to consciously put them first. You must make the choice to be resolute about them.

Distractions will always compete for your attention, no matter who you are or how many dreams you have. The tension between them and your goals is inevitable. However, having a clear understanding of what matters most and intentionally aligning your daily schedule with those priorities will enable you to live with purpose, just as Jesus did, staying focused and on mission.

The good news is that over the past few weeks, you've been training yourself to focus on what truly matters—learning to prioritize what you want most over what seems urgent. Don't lose heart. This is a daily practice, and like Jesus, you must stay resolute in your mission, continually seeking God's heart and making room for His guidance. I encourage you to carry this practice beyond the first thirty minutes of your day. Set aside an hour or two to prioritize the important. Today, move your dreams to the top of your to-do list and focus on what matters most.

The choice is yours. Will you stay resolute? Will you live on mission with God? You'll be glad you did.

Day 40 On Mission

Revel: What would it look like to live *on mission* resolutely? Today, follow Jesus's example and stay focused on your God-given mission!

Take a moment to make two lists: one, the tyranny of the urgent—those distractions that tend to pull you off course; and two, the priorities of the important—those things that align with God's bigger purpose for your life. Begin restructuring your day (not just your mornings) to prioritize the important things.

....

....

....

....

Align: Today's word is a powerful reminder of why prioritization matters—and why your daily alignment time cannot be optional. It sets the tone. It grounds you. It keeps you centered on heaven's reality, not the chaos around you.

Yes, the reflection may feel repetitive—but that's where the power is. Daily alignment isn't about checking a box; it's about shaping a mindset and heartset. When you pause to focus on God's truth over your life, everything within you and around you begins to shift.

So pause. Savor God's truth. Embrace it. Become it. Then ask yourself: Did I walk in true alignment yesterday? If not, there's no shame—just space for realignment. Adjust where you need to and move forward with grace and intention.

....

....

....

....

Dream Stack: What's one action from your list of important priorities you can integrate into your day today? Make a note and stack your win. You'll be glad you did.

....

....

....

....

DAY 41

Hungry?

'My food,' said Jesus, 'is to do the will of him who sent me and to finish his work.'

—John 4:34

HAVE YOU EVER BEEN REALLY HUNGRY? The kind of hunger where you're so starved you'll eat just about anything?

They say it's the worst time to go grocery shopping when you're *that* hungry. My dad used to say it's also the worst time to make decisions. He'd remind me, "HALT! Don't make decisions when you're Hungry, Angry, Lonely, or Tired." It's a lesson that has stuck with me.

We often see hunger as a bad thing—something uncomfortable and negative. Messages everywhere tell us, "Eat every two hours" and "Don't let yourself get hangry." But who said hunger is bad? What if, instead of resisting it, we began to see hunger as a signal informing us of a deeper need?

Here's a bold thought: Maybe we aren't hungry enough—spiritually, that is.

I believe many of us are too full—like after a big Thanksgiving meal—on the busyness of life. We're up to our eyeballs in all the things, but we're discontented, disconnected, and left wondering why we're not feeling alive or on mission. It's because we've lost the drive, the hunger, to be fully consumed by God's purpose for us.

Yesterday, we talked about how Jesus was on a mission. He had one target: YOU. He came to do the will of the Father, which was ultimately to save humanity, to save you. His mission was so central to His life that it sustained Him, just as food would, and we see that in today's passage.

Can you say the same? Can you honestly say that your deepest hunger is to do the will of the Father? That you are driven, consumed, and satisfied only by living out His purpose for your life? For most of us, the answer is probably no. And that's why so many are distracted by worldly desires, clinging to things that will never truly satisfy, and why we feel bored, anxious, or unfulfilled. We are seeking fulfillment in things that can never fill the spiritual hunger within us.

Yet Jesus shows us where true nourishment comes from: *My food is to do the will of him who sent me.* This means that His hunger, His passion, His focus—everything He craved—was to do God's will and finish the work He was sent to do. This is the kind of hunger Jesus modeled for us. This is where we ought to find our breath, our purpose, and the very life we're searching for. It's not in waiting for someone else to step up; it's in taking action ourselves and aligning our lives with what God is doing in heaven and then doing it on earth.

I've done a lot of things in my life, but there's something undeniably life-giving about doing the will of the Father. It's not just about accomplishing tasks for God—it's about the journey *with* Him, the closeness and connection that deepen as we partner together. And I guess that's the real gift: The more I do with Him, the more I crave His presence. And the more I crave His presence, the more time I spend with Him. The more time I spend with Him, the more I desire to serve Him. It's a divine cycle—and quite contagious!

When we walk in step with God, partnering with Him in His plans, it's as if our soul comes alive in a way nothing else can replicate. The things we once thought would satisfy us pale in comparison to the deep fulfillment that comes from aligning ourselves with God's heart and purposes.

So if you feel spiritually hungry today, GOOD! Your hunger isn't bad. It just needs to be directed to the right source—God—doing everything He's called you to do. Yes, you need real food, water, safety, and secure relationships, but those things can't fill the spiritual void you're looking for. Only God can do that.

Ask God to awaken your hunger today. Let him stir up the passion for the things He's placed in your heart. If it's for children, awaken that. If it's for education, awaken it. If you have a heart for single moms, for the Church, for business—whatever it is, awaken that hunger. Feast on God's Word and His purposes. Ask for revelation that stirs your heart for what's possible, so you're moved to action.

We need people who are spiritually hungry. Will that be you?

Revel: How's your spiritual hunger? Take a moment to ask the Lord to reveal what it would look like to hunger for Him in deeper, more authentic ways. If your hunger has been misplaced—focused on worldly things—repent and seek to develop a taste for His truth and His will.

Then spend some time reflecting on the passions that ignite your heart and stir your spirit. Let these be the guideposts for where God is calling you to direct your focus today.

....

....

....

....

Day 41 Hungry?

Align: Reflect on yesterday—did you take any steps toward your dream? If not, get curious. What held you back? Name it. Then decide how you're going to move through that today, staying in greater alignment than you did yesterday.

You can't win 'em all, but you can get better with practice. Remember, practice makes permanent.

....
....
....
....

Dream Stack: Get hungry today. Not just motivated, hungry. The kind of hungry that drives you to chase after the will of the Father, where nothing else will satisfy. Let that hunger drive you to pursue what He's called you to do—with focus, with urgency, and with unwavering obedience.

Now decide: What's one action you can take today that brings you closer to the dream He's placed in your heart? Put it at the top of your to-do list—and don't let anything or anyone pull you off course. Stay locked in. Stay hungry. Heaven moves when you do.

....
....
....
....

DAY 42

Journey Well

Let us throw off everything that hinders and the sin that so easily entangles. And let us run with perseverance the race marked out for us, fixing our eyes on Jesus, the pioneer and perfecter of faith. For the joy set before him he endured the cross, scorning its shame, and sat down at the right hand of the throne of God. Consider him who endured such opposition from sinners, so that you will not grow weary and lose heart.

—Hebrews 12:1–3

SOME OF THE GREATEST WORDS of encouragement I've received came from a friend. Today, I share them because I will echo these same words of encouragement to *you*: "You, my friend, are doing the hard work! You are running toward what you want most, and because of this, hundreds and even thousands of lives have been and will be transformed because of your bravery, because you keep saying YES to God. Everyone loves the destination, but you're showing people how to love and value the journey and find God in every moment. You are showing people how to *journey well*."

As I write this, tears stream down my face because I believe with my whole heart that God is using and will continue to use your dreams to change the world, and I pray you see the full manifestation of that in your lifetime. AND maybe even more important, I also pray that you *journey well*.

Perhaps you're asking yourself, *What does it mean to journey* well *with the Lord?*

I'm glad you asked.

As you settle into a lifestyle of dreaming with the Lord, you realize that the goal is not just reaching the goal; the dream is not just about the fulfillment of the dream. It's not just about reaching the destination or journeying to get "there." It's about *journeying well*, which is walking faithfully, with purpose and joy, as God leads you toward His promises.

The last thing I want for any of us is to fall into the pattern of the Israelites who, despite witnessing God's miracles, spent years grumbling and complaining as they wandered in circles because of their doubt and lack of trust. God gave them a promise. He told them they would experience the Promised Land, yet they did not make it because they did not *journey well*. Instead, may we be like Joshua, someone who saw the giants but also saw the promise. He believed in the power and faithfulness of God, and he didn't let fear stop him from moving forward. He trusted in the Lord's plans and kept his eyes on the promise ahead, even when the obstacles seemed overwhelming. He *journeyed well*.

So how do we become more like Joshua? How do we break free from old ways of thinking and step into God's plans with confidence? Today's Scripture provides an answer and gives us a powerful road map to help us journey well.

1. **Throw off everything that hinders.** Scripture tells us to throw off *everything* that is holding you back—not just some things. What is hindering you? Is it a mindset that doesn't serve your future? A routine that no longer aligns with the goodness of God? It could be the way you start your day, the people you surround yourself with, your job, or the way you talk to yourself. If it's not aligned with what God is doing in your life, it's time to throw it off.

2. **Run the race with perseverance.** The next instruction is to *run with perseverance*. We're called to run—not walk, not crawl, not overthink—but run! Sometimes we hesitate because we overanalyze or question ourselves. But God is telling us to get moving. Step into what He's calling you to and don't overcomplicate it.

    At the same time, this race isn't a sprint; it's a marathon. Others of us are sprinting, trying to get there fast, but that only leaves us exhausted and burnt out. Marathon runners know they have to pace themselves to endure the whole race. Likewise, we must learn to *pace with the Holy Spirit*. Perseverance is about sticking with it through the highs and lows, the uphill battles, and the lonely stretches, and trusting that God is with us every step of the way.

3. **Fix your eyes on Jesus.** As you run, fix your eyes on Jesus, not the destination. Have a goal, yes. Be clear on your dream, for sure. But keep your eyes on Jesus as He is your greatest prize. He's the One who gave you the dream in the first place, and He's the One who will see it through. Yes, having a dream is important, but more important than the dream itself is the One who holds it all.

4. **Endure with joy.** Jesus endured the cross for the joy set before Him. He saw beyond the suffering and pain, knowing the joy of fulfilling God's will. In the same way, there will be challenges on your journey. But don't endure for the sake of endurance—find *joy* in the process. Embrace the good, the hard, and the difficult as part of God's refining work in your life.

5. **Do not grow weary.** We all get tired. We all want to give up at times. But God calls us to lean on Him for strength. Remember that Jesus has gone before you. He's already paved the way, and because He overcame, you too will overcome. So when you feel weary, dig deep. Maybe repeat the first four steps and anchor back in. Keep running your race knowing that you've got this because *He's got you*.

Let today be a reminder that you are not running alone. You are running the race marked out for you with Jesus as your guide, your strength, and your greatest reward. Keep pressing on!

Day 42 Journey Well

Revel: Using Hebrews 12:1–3 as your guide, consider which step God is highlighting for you today. Do you need to throw off hindering mindsets, run with perseverance, fix your eyes more on Jesus, find joy in the process, or guard yourself from growing weary?

Ask the Holy Spirit to reveal where you need to focus and spend time in prayer, inviting Him to help you align with His will. Remember, the goal isn't just to arrive—it's to journey well with the Lord, trusting Him every step of the way.

....

....

....

....

Align: Take a moment to reflect on yesterday—did you take a step, even a small one, toward your dream? The truth is: You are what you consistently do. So choose alignment. Choose intention. Choose to keep showing up.

....

....

....

....

Dream Stack: Today, journey well. Don't just check the box—become. This isn't about just reaching the dream—it's about letting God reach you in the process.

Think about the thing you know you need to do today. Now ask yourself: Who do I need to become so that doing that thing becomes a natural overflow of who I am?

Write it down. Get clear. Then carve out the time to be that person—and do that thing. This is transformation at its finest.

DAY 43

Faithful Love

[Jesus said,] 'My child, don't underestimate the value of the discipline and training of the Lord God, or get depressed when he has to correct you. For the Lord's training of your life is the evidence of his faithful love.'

—Hebrews 12:5–6 TPT

OUR RELATIONSHIP WITH GOD'S LOVE is often influenced by how *we* experienced love—or lack of it—through our earthly fathers. The reality is that our understanding of God the Father is not based on how our human fathers treated us, no matter how great or flawed they may have been. God is *not* like any earthly father. But because of our human filters, we often compare His ways to those of our earthly parents. This can lead to misconceptions about God's love for us.

I grew up with a father who was very results-driven. He was a good dad, but the narrative I internalized was this: *Do the right thing, and I will love you. Do the wrong thing, and I will reject you.* As a result, I carried a lot of stress around doing the right thing. I felt like my identity was tied to my performance, learning was high stakes, creating something new was too risky due to the fear of rejection, and love, well, it felt anything but free. It felt conditional, to say the least. Maybe you can relate to that in some way. If so, today's passage offers us a radically different way of understanding God's love for us.

First, Jesus acknowledges that we will not always get it right. We will stumble. We will fail. And that's where God's love comes in to correct and train us, not to shame us or guilt us. Second, Jesus urges us to not *underestimate* God's discipline. This discipline is not about punishment but about training. God's discipline is for our *good*. Did you hear that? *The Lord's training of your life is the evidence of his faithful love.* It's not a rejection of us but an invitation into His holiness, into a deeper relationship with Him.

Here's the truth we need to embrace: God's love is not dependent on our perfection. His love is relentless, unconditional, and redemptive. He loves us so much that He meets us right where we are, yet he *does not leave us where we are*. If God's love only met us where we are and left us the way we are, it would be codependency, not love. See, codependency coddles dysfunction. It enables cycles. It does encourage empathy but neglects the truth that grace also corrects and redirects. But God's love? It's different. He loves us too much to let us stay the same. That's the difference. His love doesn't just comfort us—it transforms us. It lifts, refines, and empowers us to be everything He designed us to be. That's real love. Love that both embraces you and calls you higher. Love that heals and stretches.

This is the kind of love that changes everything. This is the love of the Father.

Therefore, God's discipline and correction are evidence of His faithful love. They prove that He loves us enough to refine us, to lead us away from sin, and to shape us into the image of Christ. God draws us to Himself, not out of condemnation but out of a deep, unwavering love. He doesn't push us away when we fail. Instead, He draws us closer. He says, *"Come to me."*

This is what love does. It draws us in. We are no longer motivated by fear of rejection or guilt; we are motivated by His love. His love is pure, perfect, and holy, and it invites us to become more like Him.

If you desire to see God more fully, to experience deeper revelation, and touch heaven here on earth, it starts with receiving His invitation to be loved by Him. It's in His pure love we are refined to see God more clearly and recognize His work in our lives. When we surrender to His love, we allow His correction to heal our hearts, our minds, and our lives.

Today, allow God's love to draw you in, refine you, heal you, and transform you into the person He has always called you to be.

Revel: How has the love (or lack thereof) from your earthly father influenced the way you view your heavenly Father? Are there areas where you have projected past pain or misconceptions onto God's perfect love for you?

Take a moment to invite the Holy Spirit into those spaces. Receive His love today, knowing that it is not based on performance or perfection but on His deep, unconditional love for you. Let His love be an open invitation to discipline, correct, and refine you as He brings healing and transformation into your life.

Day 43 Faithful Love

Align: It's Day 43—which means you're just about to take your forty-third intentional step toward the purposes and promises of God for your life! That's no small thing. That deserves a celebration, a high five, and a serious pat on the back!

But here's the shift: This isn't just about doing the thing. It's about becoming the person. It's not just a habit—it's your identity. You're not just aligning as an action … you're becoming aligned as a way of life. From verb to noun.

So as you reflect on yesterday, ask yourself: Where did alignment feel natural? Where did it still feel a little awkward or off? Remember, awkward until awesome.

Pay attention. Those small shifts matter. Keep highlighting what works, keep refining what doesn't, and allow today to be another day where you consciously commit (or recommit) to living a lifestyle of alignment with the Lord.

Dream Stack: Today, what is one action you can take to move you toward your dream? If not you, who? If not now, when? Keep it simple, make it plain, and get 'er done!

DAY 44

Control Is Boring

The Lord is my rock, my fortress and my deliverer;
my God is my rock, in whom I take refuge, my shield
and the horn of my salvation, my stronghold.

—Psalm 18:2

WHERE ARE ALL my control freaks today?

If you're like, "What's that?" you're not who I'm talking to, but you might know someone who needs to hear this. For those of you who know *exactly* what I'm talking about, this is for you.

Control. Oh, how we love it. How often do we find ourselves saying, "I've got it under control"? We think control is sexy, don't we? It gives us power, invincibility, and the illusion that we can keep everything in order, perfectly as planned.

Truth be told, control is a fear-based protection mechanism. And it's not something someone is born with. Control is not who you are; it's something you learn to do. For those who struggle with control, it's because they grew up in an environment that was very out of control, so they sought a way to protect themselves. And guess what? It worked. Control has a way of making you feel like you can protect yourself from the pain, chaos, and hurt of it all. We control to avoid discomfort, to stay ahead of the problem, to ensure nothing surprises us or catches us off guard. But here's the thing—control comes with a heavy price. It's like picking up a shield for a battle we were never meant to fight. And it works until it doesn't.

Ask me how I know.

You might get the results you want when you control the situation, but it often leads to a deeper feeling of emptiness. Obsessive control has a way of making our soul feel tired, drained, and worn out. You're not tired—you're bored.

Bored?!

Yes, bored. Though you've got a lot on your plate and you're doing all the things, you're controlling everything, and that is boring. You know you were created for more— more than just doing the things you can control. You were made for adventure, creating with the Lord, uninhibitedly and unencumbered, to experience the power, goodness, and mercy of God through your life. But to truly experience His presence in your life, you need to surrender your need to control.

Today's Scripture reminds us of this. I encourage you to take a moment and meditate on the passage, and as you do, notice it doesn't say, "I am my rock." It doesn't say, "I am my own shield." It reminds us control freaks that there is a God and we are not Him. Ultimately, He is everything we need, and when we stop relying on our own strength, when we let go of our need to control, He is able to fully step in and be what we need Him to be. He's there as our constant helper, guiding us, protecting us, and delivering us from the situations we're trying to fix on our own. But we've got to get out of the way.

The reality is *we don't have it all under control.* The sooner we realize this, the sooner we can embrace the peace that comes with surrendering. It's in letting go of our need to control that we step into a new level of freedom. A freedom that says, *I trust You, Lord. I trust that You will lead me, protect me, and provide for me in ways I cannot do for myself. You are my strength.* This is the heart of surrender. It's not giving up; it's giving in, fully relying on God—especially when it doesn't make sense and when we can't see the full picture.

Freedom happens when we make the decision to stop resisting, to stop trying to manage every aspect of our lives and to control everything and everyone. Today, surrender. Trust. Let go of insecurity, fear, and the need to control and allow God to be God. You'll have way more fun, I promise.

Revel: Ask yourself today: What is one area where I need to surrender control and trust God more fully?

Take a moment to release your grip on that situation and choose to let God take the lead. You'll find that when you stop trying to control the outcome, you start living with a peace that surpasses all understanding and have more fun in the process.

....

....

....

....

Align: Reflect on yesterday—did you take a step toward your dream? Remember, you are who God says you are, but you're also shaped by what you consistently practice. Take some time to explore: What parts of your day reflected who you're becoming? What habits or patterns do you need to release that are not in alignment with who God says you are and what He's called you to do?

Day 44 Control Is Boring

Get honest. Then rinse, reset, and repeat. Let your reflections guide and fuel your dream stacking time today—because alignment isn't just about awareness, it's also about action.

....

....

....

....

Dream Stack: Today, what is one action you can take to move you toward your dream? Write it down, make it a priority, and don't stop until you're proud.

....

....

....

....

DAY 45

Show Me Your Glory

It is the glory of God to conceal a matter; to search out a matter is the glory of kings.

—Proverbs 25:2

HAVE YOU EVER ASKED GOD a question and felt like you received no clear answer? You've prayed, fasted, sought counsel, and still nothing seems to be revealed?

It's natural to ask questions, especially when life feels overwhelming, and you're searching for clarity or direction. In moments of confusion, pain, or uncertainty, we instinctively want to know why. However, though it's human to seek answers, constantly asking why can unintentionally open the door to doubt. Instead of grounding us in God's promises, it can leave us wrestling with uncertainty. Though it's normal to desire answers, as believers, it should be abnormal to allow that desire to cause us to doubt God's faithfulness in providing them.

Today's verse reveals a powerful truth—one that might feel a little frustrating at first, because why would God hide the answers we're so desperate to find? Why make us search? But what if God isn't withholding answers *from* you—what if He's hiding them *for* you? What if His intention isn't to make you wait passively but to invite you into an active pursuit—not just of answers but of *Him*? This verse reminds us that God isn't hiding answers *from* us but *for* us—in the richness of His glory.

God conceals revelation within His glory.

Proverbs 25 describes seeking not as an arduous hunt for answers but as the *"glory of kings."* As sons and daughters of *the* King, we are invited to live in this royal identity, pursuing the depths of God's heart. This pursuit requires humility and trust, a willingness to surrender our desire for quick fixes in exchange for the richness of His presence.

Consider this: Where God hides the answers is just as important as the answers themselves. God places what we need in His presence—in His glory—because the process of seeking Him transforms us. It draws us closer to His heart and further from the temporary distractions of this world. It teaches us to look not just for an answer but also to look for Him. We don't need more answers; we need more of Him.

This shift in awareness moves you from demanding answers to seeking His presence. When you encounter God's glory, your questions fade into the background, because His glory satisfies the deepest parts of you in ways that human answers never could. Instead of looking for answers, begin seeking Him.

Imagine this: I'm playing a game of sardines with my kids. You know, it's like hide-and-seek but in reverse. One person hides, and everyone else spreads out, searching high and low to find them. But here's the twist—once you find the person hiding, you don't shout and give them away; you quietly join in, squeezing yourself, like a sardine, into the hiding place.

In the same way, we seek the glory of God in the hidden spaces of our lives. God often invites us into places where His glory isn't obvious at first. Like playing sardines, it requires perseverance, moving through the darkness of doubt, uncertainty, or even difficulty. But once we find His presence, His glory, we don't just walk away—we dwell in it. Then just like in sardines, we become part of this bigger movement of people as we pull people into His glory!

He is after our hearts, drawing us closer to Him and teaching us to trust and rest in His perfect will. He cares more about our eternal character than our need for immediate relief or answers. God's goal isn't to make us comfortable but to transform us into the image of Christ, and he does that through His glory. When you step deeper into His glory, you root yourself in the truth of His goodness. You discover His love, His faithfulness, and His perfect will. This allows you to make peace through the pressing, to trust Him more in the midst of the tension, and to endure, faithfully, despite the challenges and the unknowns.

The next time you find yourself overwhelmed with questions or answers you can't find, pause and realize that they are an invitation into His glory. Allow yourself to shift into a posture of faith, trust, and discovery. As you seek Him, you will begin to see the fullness of His glory. And when you encounter His glory, you'll realize that the peace, joy, and revelation found in His presence are far greater than any answers you thought you needed.

Don't seek just for answers; *be transformed by His glory*. Heck, go play a game of sardines. You'll be glad you did.

Revel: What answers are you seeking right now? Rather than focusing solely on the questions you have and the answers you desire, consider shifting your perspective to seek His glory first.

Through prayer, worship, or quiet reflection, ask God to reveal Himself to you in real ways. Simply pray, "Show me Your glory, Lord." Let this posture bring peace to your heart and draw you closer to Him.

Day 45 Show Me Your Glory

Align: Let's rewind for a sec—how did you show up yesterday? Did you lean in, take a step, even a small one, toward your God-given dream? Take inventory of what worked and what didn't. Double down on what worked and forget the rest.

Greater alignment always begins with greater awareness. Take time today to invite the Holy Spirit to reveal what you need to see and know as you move through your day.

Dream Stack: Today, what is the next bold step you can take to make your dream a reality? You get what you work for, not just what you wish for. Write it down; make it happen!

DAY 46

Vulnerability

Bear one another's burdens, and so fulfill the law of Christ.

—Galatians 6:2 ESV

VULNERABILITY. HOW DO YOU FEEL about that word? Do you welcome it or avoid it? Do you live it out in your day-to-day life, or is it simply a good idea? For many of us, vulnerability is a touchy subject—we're comfortable talking about it, but living it out is another story.

When we think of vulnerability, it's often associated with extremes. Maybe you think of the person who overshares on social media or that one friend who tells everything to everyone. On the other hand, maybe you see vulnerability as a sign of weakness, something to avoid in order to protect yourself, so you build walls around your heart, creating distance between yourself and others. This was my perspective for years. Vulnerability felt unsafe, unpredictable, and far too risky. I avoided it at all costs.

But recently, I had a conversation with my husband on a podcast about this very topic. Because vulnerability has become somewhat of a buzzword these days, I was curious to get his take on it. I asked him, "What does vulnerability mean to you?"

There was a long pause—about ten seconds—which felt awkward in the middle of a recording. But his response was worth the silence: "Vulnerability is letting someone into your process exactly where you're at."

That simple yet profound statement changed how I view vulnerability. It's not about oversharing or putting yourself on display. True vulnerability, especially in the context of Christian love, is about letting someone see you exactly for who you are, how you feel, smack dab in the middle of your journey—allowing them to meet you in your process, without having to pretend like you have it all figured out.

Today's verse from Galatians reminds us of this. When we bear one another's burdens, we fulfill the law of Christ—the command to love one another deeply. Talk about vulnerability! Vulnerability, therefore, is an essential part of living in community the way God intended. But this kind of love isn't one-sided. It requires mutual openness and trust, where both people put down their defenses and allow real connection to take place.

Often, we avoid being vulnerable because we fear judgment, rejection, betrayal, or disappointment. But what if, instead of guarding ourselves, we invited trusted friends and family into our process? What if we allowed them to help carry our burdens, speak into our struggles, and support us in our journey? Rather than rushing to judgment, we can choose to step into someone else's shoes. My husband and I have started using the phrase, "Can I invite you into my process?" It's our way of saying, "I'm feeling vulnerable, and instead of shutting you out, I'm asking you to come in. Please be gentle."

We also recognize when one of us seems guarded or distant, and we ask, "Can you invite me into your process?" It's a gentle way of saying, "I see something's off. Will you let me in so I can support you?" Only through vulnerability can true healing, restoration, and growth begin.

As believers, we are called to love one another in ways that protect, uplift, and gently restore. Vulnerability is our response to that calling—not a sign of weakness but an opportunity to build genuine relationships that both give and receive the love and support God intends for us to share. It's an act of trust—trusting in God and in the people He has placed in our lives.

Maybe today, God is asking you to take a step toward vulnerability. Perhaps you need to allow someone into your process, or maybe you need to ask for permission to join someone else in theirs. Either way, bearing one another's burdens with love is not just a suggestion—it's how we fulfill the greatest commandment of Christ.

Revel: Vulnerability builds bridges and strengthens bonds rooted in Christ-like love. Consider these questions today:

- Who is someone you can trust to walk with you in your process? How can you invite them into your life today?
- Who around you may need your support? How can you offer to be part of their journey and help carry their burden?

Take a moment to ask God for the courage to be vulnerable and for the wisdom to know whom to trust.

Day 46 Vulnerability

Align: Reflect on yesterday—did you take any steps toward your dream? If not, identify what held you back and why. Then, from the overflow of your alignment time, identify a God-centered way to overcome that obstacle today.

....
....
....
....

Dream Stack: What's one action you can take today that brings you closer to the dream God has placed in your heart? Write it down.

Then maybe—just maybe—you get bold and a little vulnerable. You reach out and ask that certain someone from your reveling time to support you as you take your next step. Because here's the truth: A dreamer was never meant to dream alone.

There's power in partnership, in community, in being seen. So don't just take the step—invite someone into it. Ask them to pray with you, walk alongside you, and dream alongside you. Your courage might be the spark someone else needs to say yes to their own dream too.

....
....
....
....

DAY 47

Revival

Everyone look! Come and see the breathtaking wonders of our God. For He brings both ruin and revival. He's the one who makes conflicts end.

—Psalm 46:8–9 TPT

REVIVAL. IT'S A WORD WE ALL LOVE, RIGHT? We picture stadiums filled with people on fire for God and entire towns transformed through week after week of passionate worship. We long for that next big moment—from Kathryn Kuhlman to the Brownsville Revival—when the world experiences a powerful move of God.

Or maybe you're on the other end of the spectrum. Maybe just hearing the word *revival* makes you cringe. Perhaps you've been caught up in the hype of one of these events, only to be left with a broken heart and more questions about who God is and what He's really about.

What if we need to unlearn and relearn what revival truly means in order to experience it the way God intends—purely, intimately, individually? Who said revival has to be about massive crowds in stadiums that last only a brief moment in time? What if revival is meant to be a lifestyle, not an event? A continuous transformation of the heart rather than a one-time experience?

I propose that revival is meant to start within us, you and me, day by day, as we seek God's presence and let Him renew us from the inside out. Revival is a lifestyle that begins with a whole heart.

As we learned yesterday, vulnerability and heart healing are not signs of failure—they're vital and ongoing steps in becoming who God created you to be. When we allow ourselves to break, the layers we've built up—of pride, fear, and self-sufficiency—begin to fall away. And in that place of vulnerability, we find the beauty of who we truly are. The pieces of our lives may feel shattered, but in God's hands, those broken pieces become the foundation for something new, something more authentic and whole.

We see this in today's Scripture. At first glance, it can feel a bit jarring—on one hand, we're in awe of the breathtaking wonders of our God ... and on the other, we see Him allowing both ruin and revival to unfold. Why would God allow ruin? But if we consider the bigger picture, we see a powerful perspective of God's role in both ruin and revival. Though God doesn't cause pain, He does use it. I'd even suggest that He allows the ruin to make room for the revival.

When we are pressed, when we experience tension and hardship, there's an opportunity to lean into God as never before. In that desperation, we find a deeper relationship with God—a true encounter that transforms us from the inside out. Ultimately, I've come to learn that breaking and healing are a holy invitation to experience the greatest expression of heaven—*revival*.

Pain brings breaking, breaking leads to healing, and healing sparks revival.

Revival is often overspiritualized, but at its core, it's simply an improvement in the condition or strength of something. Historically speaking, revival occurs as a result of renewed strength. It's an outward expression of an internal renewal, a burst of life that follows from deep healing. Revival isn't some mystical event—it's a healed soul set free.

If you desire revival, pursue healing. If you want healing, embrace the breaking.

Revival doesn't come without ruin, and healing doesn't happen without first being broken. It's in the hard, pressing places that we are refined, and God's glory shines through us. When we encounter God in our brokenness and experience His faithfulness, something ignites within us that can't be denied.

We all want something new—but are we willing to embrace the breaking? We all long for revival—but are we willing to heal?

If you're in a season of breaking, remember that God is with you. He doesn't just bring revival; He lovingly walks with you through the ruin and leads you to healing. Trust Him in the breaking, because it's the path to transformation. Let the walls fall, let the layers come off, and invite Him into the process. Revival is waiting on the other side.

■ ■ ■ ■ ■ ■

Revel: How can you surrender into the loving arms of Jesus today and experience true revival within your soul? Are you fully open to receiving the deep healing He offers? If so, are there areas in your life where you need to break or let go?

Don't resist the process—invite His healing presence into every corner of your heart. Allow the healing balm of heaven to touch the deepest wounds, bringing true freedom and fullness of life. Revival starts here, with a soul set free.

Align: Take a moment and look back on yesterday. What step did you take (or not take) toward your dream? What got in the way and why? How can you posture your heart and mind even more today to align your actions with the vision God has given you?

....

....

....

....

Dream Stack: What's one action today that will bring you closer to your dream? May your actions reflect your dreams, not your fears. Dream it, draft it, and do it. (Seriously— write it down. You're way more likely to make it happen when you do.)

....

....

....

....

DAY 48

Maturing in the Lord

> The mature children of God are those who are moved by the impulses of the Holy Spirit. And you did not receive the 'spirit of religious duty,' leading you back into the fear of never being good enough. But you have received the 'Spirit of full acceptance,' enfolding you into the family of God. ... For the Holy Spirit makes God's fatherhood real to us as he whispers into our innermost being, 'You are God's beloved child!'
>
> —Romans 8:14–16 TPT

ARE YOU MATURE IN THE LORD?

Note that I didn't ask if you were old or young, a child or adult. I asked if you were *mature*.

Too often, we find ourselves getting older without truly growing up, adulting without maturing. Many pride themselves on aging, but that doesn't necessarily mean they're becoming wiser.

Today, I invite you to join me on a journey—stop adulting and start *maturing* in the Lord.

To be mature is more than being fully grown. Though the world may offer various definitions, for believers, true maturity is defined by God's Word. It means being spiritually rooted and growing in His truth. The book of Romans guides us in understanding this, so we can live it out in our daily lives.

Today's verse tells us: *The mature children of God are those who are moved by the impulses of the Holy Spirit.* You know you're mature in the Lord when you're moved by the Holy Spirit, not your own impulses.

Let's be honest—many of us are impulsive. We react when someone cuts us off in traffic or when plans don't go our way. We feel triggered so we react. We *feel* so we *do*. But spiritual maturity means that instead of reacting to circumstances or responding based upon how we feel, we are moved based only upon the impulses of the Holy Spirit. This is divine alignment. If He moves, I move. If He's speaking, I'm speaking. Being connected to Him changes how we respond to life. Though we won't get this right every time, it raises a new standard—one that causes us to stop making excuses and start responding from a place of peace and wisdom. Let me suggest this: The way you respond says a lot about your level of maturity.

The verse continues: *You did not receive the 'spirit of religious duty,' leading you back into the fear of never being good enough.* You know you're mature in the Lord when you believe the truth and no longer return to the lies of the enemy.

The enemy is the father of lies, and his goal is to keep you from the destiny God has for you. Too often, we go back to the lie that we're not enough—not good enough, not worthy enough, or will never have enough. But maturity in the Lord means we stop believing these lies. Even though they may feel real, they're not. As you grow, you'll learn to see lies for what they are—lies! You know you're mature in the Lord when you don't buy into the lies as you used to; rather, you choose to walk in the fullness of the truth of who God says you are.

Then we read: *You have received the 'Spirit of full acceptance,' enfolding you into the family of God. ... 'You are God's beloved child!'* You know you're mature in the Lord when you embrace your identity in Christ and you know you're fully accepted.

Your behavior does not define your identity—God's Word does. Too many of us allow our actions to shape how we see ourselves, but God calls us to align our behavior with the identity He's given us. You are His beloved child, and as you grow in Him, you'll start living out that truth in every area of your life. You no longer strive for acceptance; you surrender to it. You no longer let your behavior define who you are; you allow your God-given identity to direct your behavior. As a mature child of God, you will allow yourself to be fully accepted and enfolded into the family of God.

Romans 8:17 (TPT) goes on to tell us that *we qualify to share all His treasures ... and we also inherit all that He is and all that He has. We will experience being co-glorified with Him provided that we accept His sufferings as our own.* You know you're mature in the Lord when you accept both the good and the hard as from the Lord.

This verse reveals two important keys to our spiritual maturity. First, we share in His treasures! Scripture tells us we inherit *all* that He is and *all* that He has. This is the promise of abundance. As we continue to align our lives with His, we receive all that He desires to give. What an incredible gift.

But it doesn't stop there. True maturity is also marked by our ability to embrace His sufferings as our own. It's easy to trust God when everything is going well, but true spiritual growth happens when we worship Him in the midst of hardship. The mature believer understands that it's not about the circumstances—it's about His presence with us through it all. Both the good and the hard moments are opportunities to grow deeper in Him. An adult may not always see this, but a maturing child of God does.

I encourage you to embrace this framework with a heart of grace, not guilt. If you're not yet seeing signs of spiritual maturity, don't fall into shame or blame. Instead, be thankful that Scripture lays out a clear path for growth. Start studying it and allow it to guide your journey of becoming more like Christ.

It's time to stop adulting—going through the motions of life without true growth—and start *maturing* in the Lord. Let's allow the Holy Spirit to guide our impulses, align our hearts with God's truth, and step into the abundance He has for us.

Day 48 Maturing in the Lord

Revel: What would it look like to move beyond simply adulting and intentionally deepen your walk with God, to mature in Him? Instead of striving for outward results, make spiritual growth a priority.

Today, take some time to reflect upon spiritual maturity. Use Romans 8:14–16 TPT as your guide: Follow the lead of the Holy Spirit, reject the lies, embrace your identity as God's beloved child, and see both the joys and challenges as opportunities for growth.

....

....

....

....

Align: Take a moment to pause and do a quick self-audit—how did you show up yesterday?

Did your thoughts, words, and actions move you even one step closer to the dream God placed on your heart? Did you lean in with intention—or did something hold you back?

Whatever it was, name it. Then ask yourself: What needs to shift today to make even more room for alignment? Because here's the truth: Alignment is built one choice at a time. So check in, reset if needed, and step forward—on purpose, with purpose.

....

....

....

....

BOLD

Dream Stack: Today, what is one action you can take that will bring you closer to your dream? Write it here and then make your move. Remember: Your dreams don't move unless you do. May today's choices reflect your maturity in the Lord.

....

....

....

....

DAY 49

Don't Just GO to Church, BE the Church.

[Jesus said,] 'And I tell you that you are Peter, and on this rock I will build my church, and the gates of Hades will not overcome it.'

—Matthew 16:18

ACCORDING TO THE JOSHUA PROJECT, about 3.49 billion people in the world have never heard the name of Jesus. That's about 43 percent of the global population. The organization estimates that's 7,248 distinct people groups who haven't rejected the Gospel but simply haven't been reached to hear His name. This staggering reality should awaken something in our hearts.

When we hear statistics like this, our minds often jump to terms like *evangelism* or *The Great Commission*. Yet shockingly, a study from Barna Research also found fewer than 1 in 5 believers surveyed (17 percent) understand what The Great Commission means to the point where they could explain it. Too many of us think, *I'm not a pastor or an evangelist*, and dismiss the responsibility. But here's the truth: Ministry isn't a title; it's a calling, a purpose, an identity we all share as followers of Christ. It's not something we do; it's who we are. You've been commissioned—this is God's plan for you.

Being commissioned isn't for a select few. It's heaven's plan, and *you* are a vital part of it. Jesus called us to be His body, His hands, and His feet, taking the Gospel to the ends of the earth. So what does that look like for you and me? How do we step into this responsibility and embrace our role in God's mission?

In Matthew 16:13–16, we see a profound exchange between Jesus and His disciples: *When Jesus came to the region of Caesarea Philippi, He asked His disciples, 'Who do people say the Son of Man is?' They replied, 'Some say John the Baptist; others say Elijah; and still others, Jeremiah or one of the prophets.' 'But what about you?' he asked. 'Who do you say I am?' Simon Peter answered, 'You are the Messiah, the Son of the living God.'* Jesus affirmed Peter's declaration in today's verse and said, *And I tell you that you are Peter, and on this rock, I will build my church, and the gates of Hades will not overcome it.*

A couple of things to note here. First, Peter, in this moment, boldly proclaims who Jesus is. He doesn't minimize who He is by saying He's a friend or a prophet; he declares Jesus is the Savior of the world, the Son of God. Then we immediately see Jesus speak identity right back at Peter. He says, *You are Peter,* which literally means "rock." What's ironic is that we know Peter later denies Christ, yet Jesus chose him to be the foundation of the Church. This should be a comfort to anyone who feels inadequate or unqualified or as if they don't measure up—you *are* a part of God's plan, no matter your past.

Then Jesus says, *On this rock, I will build my church.* The word *church* here does not mean, nor has it ever meant, four walls. In fact, the word He uses is *ekklesia*, which comes from the Greek words *ek*, meaning "out," and *kaleo*, meaning "to call." The word refers to a gathering or assembly of people who are *called out*. In ancient Greece, it was used for citizens called out of their homes to gather publicly. I propose that Jesus was then calling his disciples and is now calling *us* out of our comfort zones, the four walls, and even our own homes to be witnesses in the world, to testify about His saving grace.

If we're not careful, as a Westernized church body, we become more accustomed to *going* to church than *being* the Church. The Church isn't a building—it's *people*. It's you and me! We are part of the ekklesia, God's called-out assembly, purposed to stand boldly in public, in our workplace, our community, and our family, sharing the truth of the Gospel, using words when necessary. This isn't for some of us, it's for all of us. Including you.

So what does that look like? Where do you start? The first step in living out your commission is answering Jesus's question: "Who do you say I am?" Your understanding of Jesus as the Messiah, the Son of the living God, is foundational to everything. It's not just about knowing about Him; it's also truly knowing Him and allowing that revelation to birth a deep passion for Him.

Second, you must recognize that you are God's church. The rock Jesus speaks of is not just Peter but all of us who confess that Jesus is Lord. The church isn't a building with four walls—it's *people*. It's you and me. It can't be something we go to; it must be how we see ourselves. We are God's ekklesia; we are God's called-out assembly.

Third, you are called. Period. You don't need a title to be commissioned—you're already called by God. Therefore, being part of God's mission shouldn't be optional or even vocational. It's a call, one you responded to when you became a believer. Whether you're in ministry or the marketplace, you are part of God's plan to reach the world. He's called you, and He will equip you—all he needs is your "Yes!"

Finally, this isn't a passive mission. The work of spreading the Gospel and being part of God's commission is active and intentional, and it requires us to step outside of our comfort zones on the daily.

It's time to stop sitting on the sidelines waiting for your pastor to do the heavy lifting. That means, buckle up, buttercup, and let's embrace our calling and be the hands and feet of Jesus to the world. It's time to be *commissioned*—the world is waiting.

■ ■ ■ ■ ■ ■

Revel: Now is the time to rise up and embrace your identity as God's ekklesia, His chosen people. How can you embrace this calling even more today? What are a few practical steps you can take to live as the Church, without walls, being the hands and feet of Jesus in the world around you?

Day 49 Don't Just GO to Church, BE the Church.

....

....

....

....

Align: Take a moment to reflect on yesterday—what steps did you take, no matter how big or small, that moved you closer to your dream? Celebrate them. Write them down. Own your progress.

If there were moments you felt stuck or pulled off track, gently name what held you back. What can you shift today to move forward with clarity and intention?

Your dreams are built one choice at a time. Yesterday, you stacked your wins—let those wins fuel today.

....

....

....

....

Dream Stack: What is one action step you can take today that will bring you closer to your dream while living out the Lord's Great Commission? Get ready, get set, *go*. Write it down and put feet on that dream.

....

....

....

....

DAY 50

You Are Who God Says

Do you not know that your bodies are temples of the Holy Spirit, who is in you, whom you have received from God? You are not your own; you were bought at a price. Therefore honor God with your bodies.

—1 Corinthians 6:19–20

FOOD IS AN INTERESTING TOPIC for most people—one that's often tiptoed around or avoided altogether. And honestly, it makes sense. Conversations around food can feel personal, loaded, or even shame-inducing. It's a sensitive subject that touches on identity, control, and comfort—areas we often keep hidden. Yet as His church, as a body of believers, we have to talk about *all the things* while ensuring we are using the Word of God as our standard. This includes food.

We often underestimate the importance of living a healthy life, or we fail to recognize the direct connection between our health and the ability to pursue and achieve our dreams. But ask anyone who has struggled with a disease or health complication—the minute they're not healthy or receive a negative report, nothing else seems to matter. No health, no dreams.

I realize there are issues we cannot avoid. Even the healthiest of people receive the most devastating reports. Yet I fear this is less about fate and more about personal responsibility and living fully into what Scripture says. So today, we are going to do that.

Let's be clear about one thing: You are who God says you are—and yes, you are also what you eat. Today's Scripture says it plain and simple—we are God's temple. We are a reflection of who He is. And because of that, we're called to honor our bodies—not just in some ways but in every way. How you care for your body matters. Not for image. Not for performance. But because you carry His presence. And that changes everything. This means it's time to get healthy, Church. This can't be just a nice idea or something for someone else. It's not a should or an "I'll do it when I have time." Anyone with a calling on their life needs to know this.

This isn't a truth we choose when it's convenient or one based upon how we feel from one day to the next. It doesn't have to do with what the scale says or signing up for the next trending diet plan. It's about learning how to align yourself with God's truth in every area of your life, including your health. Living healthy must be a choice. It must be a responsibility. It must be a commitment. A resolve. A conviction. And as God's church, we must be the leaders in this, not because it's easy, but because it's true.

The Bible says your body is a temple. So the question today is: Are you treating your body like one? Are you treating your body as if the Holy Spirit lives inside you? If not, why not?

We all want to hear from God, feel His presence, and receive His revelation, but how can we when we cloud our minds and dull our senses with unhealthy habits? Whether it's food, alcohol, or other distractions, we're making choices that can lead us away from the clarity and vitality we need to pursue His calling on our lives.

We must recognize that though everything is permissible, not everything is beneficial. God has given us free will, the ability to choose. That includes our habits. The food we eat (or don't eat) is no different—we get to choose and that choice directly impacts how we feel and how we function.

If you want to pursue the dreams God has placed in your heart, hear from Him more clearly, and have the strength to fulfill His calling on your life, it begins with the choices you make today. It starts with how you honor your body—the temple He has given you. Instead of chasing another short-term diet or program, focus on the deeper truth that your body is the temple of the Lord. Let this truth guide every decision you make. Ask yourself: As God's temple, does this choice nourish or deplete me? Does this food reflect the care I'm called to give to God's dwelling place?

We can't hide behind food, distractions, or the "I'll do it later" mindset anymore. We are the example. Your dreams need you alive and well. Start today.

You are who He says you are. You are also what you eat.

※ ※ ※ ※ ※ ※

Revel: Have you been avoiding the conversation about healthy habits? Today, take a moment to view your body as the temple of God. Don't align your habits with what the media and world say—rather, focus on what the Word of God says.

If your body truly is a temple of the Most High God, what are two or three things you could stop doing to honor that truth? What are two or three things you could start doing to better care for this temple? Write them down and commit to taking action!

....

....

....

....

Day 50 You Are Who God Says

Align: Pause for a moment. Write down one or two things you did yesterday that were in alignment with who you are and what God has called you to do. Then take a few deep breaths and allow your mind, body, and spirit to rejoice in the beauty of that moment.

So often we rush past this part—glossing over the miracle of becoming. But with every intentional choice you make, you're stepping deeper into alignment. You're becoming who He designed you to be. And that is worth pausing for.

(And hey, if you're thinking, *I didn't do anything yesterday*, grace is yours. You are still covered, still called, and still becoming. So close your eyes and receive His perspective over you. Then realign.)

....

....

....

....

Dream Stack: Today, write down one bold action step you will take to move toward your dream. Then make it happen. Yes, you can!

....

....

....

....

DAY 51

Temptation vs. Sin

For we do not have a high priest who is unable to empathize with our weaknesses, but we have one who has been tempted in every way, just as we are—yet he did not sin. Let us then approach God's throne of grace with confidence, so that we may receive mercy and find grace to help us in our time of need.

—Hebrews 4:15–16

THERE'S A CRUCIAL DIFFERENCE between temptation and sin, and, as believers, understanding this distinction is key to our spiritual growth.

Temptation is an invitation to sin, the lure from the enemy to make the wrong choice. Sin is the acceptance of that invitation, the agreement to participate.

If we're not careful, we can easily fall into a cycle of shame and guilt when we face temptation. Feeling ashamed for being tempted or guilty for almost giving in can weigh us down. Over time, this shame and guilt can actually make it easier for us to sin because we start identifying more with the temptation rather than recognizing it for what it is—a momentary challenge, not a defeat.

Here's what often happens: We first *feel* tempted. Then we begin to identify with our temptation, because the more we feel the temptation, the more familiar we become with it. The more familiar we become, the easier it is to fall into sin. It's our identification with our sin that can actually be the thing that leads us into sin, but Biblically speaking, we are not our sin! In fact, we are more than just sinners—we are overcomers. We are forgiven, redeemed, and through Christ, we have the strength to resist.

The powerful truth is this: Jesus was tempted too. Which means you are not alone in your struggle. The enemy would love nothing more than to isolate you, to make you feel like you're the only person on the planet battling what you're battling, being tempted by what is tempting you. But that's a lie. You're not alone. You're not the only one.

In fact, today's Scripture reminds us that Jesus is able to empathize with our weakness. He gets it—not from a distance but from experience. He's felt it. He's walked through it. He knows what it's like. And not only did He experience it, but He's also with you in it now. Even when you feel like you're riding the struggle bus, He's right there sitting next to you. You are never alone. He is with you!

Too often, as believers, we want to identify with the perfect Jesus, and though He is and though that should be something we aim for, it's not the only way He wanted to identify with you and me. Jesus was tempted in every way so that you—yes, you—could identify with Him—yes, Him—in the weakest of moments. He did this so that even in your frailty and weakness you would find Him!

The hope found in temptation is this: Even in those moments, Jesus did not sin and because He is our perfect example, we have a way out. In His perfection, we find a different choice to make. We can come boldly to *God's throne of grace* and *receive mercy and find grace* when we need it most. Temptation doesn't get the final word. Jesus does.

Though we know logically that we are sinners, Biblically speaking, we are also overcomers, forgiven, bought with a price, and able to overcome if we recognize the steps we need to take. Temptation is a part of life. But we don't have to succumb to the pressure of it. We do not have to let sin rule our lives *if* we approach the throne of grace with confidence, receiving everything we need from Him in our time of need.

1. **Recognize your moments of temptation.** Sin is a real thing and should not be minimized. Yet it's also not who you are. You have a propensity to sin, yes. But it's not your identity. That being said, you need to recognize your moment of temptation before you actually sin. Don't overlook it or ignore it. Don't become your temptation. Instead, say to yourself, *I am not my temptation. I feel tempted at this moment, but I will not sin. I am who God says I am. I walk like Jesus!* Declare your authority.
2. **Approach God with confidence.** In your moments of weakness, pause and consider this—Jesus wants to meet you right there. Scripture tells us to approach *God's throne of grace with confidence, so that we may receive mercy and find grace to help us in our time of need.* Don't shy away from Him; instead, run to Him with your heart wide open. Allow Him to surround you with the very grace and mercy that will help you overcome the temptation.

    Remember—Jesus didn't come to shame you in your weakness; He came to save you! Those moments of temptation? Those are the very moments Jesus died for. He didn't come to make you perfect; he came to save you from your sin, again and again and again.
3. **Model Jesus.** As you encounter grace, may it move you to model Jesus rather than sin. Instead of falling into sinful behavior or modeling yesterday's attitudes, begin to speak to your soul with Biblical truth. Remind yourself of who you are because of who Jesus is. Allow His standard to become your standard. Get clear on what Jesus would do, then do that because of His grace.

Perhaps the goal isn't just to avoid sin. Maybe the goal is to confidently run to Jesus when you're tempted and let not sinning become the by-product of your deepening relationship with Him. A relationship with Jesus shouldn't cause stress or anxiety over your imperfections. Instead, as you model the heart of Jesus, it should transform you, draw you closer to Him, and allow His grace to lead you away from sin.

I'm here to remind you that your temptation isn't sin—but what you do with your moments of temptation matter. In your moments of weakness, run to Jesus and receive the grace and mercy only He can offer.

Day 51 Temptation vs. Sin

Revel: What temptation have you been facing lately that might actually be an opportunity—not to run *from* Jesus, but to run *to* Him? What if, instead of hiding, you let His grace meet you right where you are and let it fully cover you? Because He's not afraid of your struggle. He's ready to meet you in it.

What about your sin? Is there sin you have been hiding or holding onto that's keeping you from fully embracing the grace of Jesus? Today, confess your sin, for He is faithful and will forgive you. Let His mercy renew and restore you!

....

....

....

....

Align: All right, dreamer, let's rewind—did you take any steps toward that big God-size dream of yours yesterday? Even a tiny one counts. If so, write it down and celebrate the win.

If not, feel no guilt—just get curious. What tripped you up? What threw you off your game? And how can you shake it off and move forward today like the child of God you are?

Let's tweak, adjust, and keep moving. Your dream's waiting, and it's not going to build itself.

....

....

....

....

Dream Stack: What's one step you can take today that will bring you closer to your dream? You know the drill—don't just think about it; write it down and make it a reality.

....

....

....

....

DAY 52

Victory Is Found in Surrender

Surrender to God! Resist the devil, and he will run from you.

—James 4:7 Contemporary English Version

HAVE YOU EVER FELT LIKE you're under constant attack? Like you're hit from all sides over and over again? If you're alive and breathing, you've probably experienced this, and though Scripture tells us the enemy will run from us, it can often feel like we are running from him. The truth is, we have an enemy, and we know that his purpose is to steal, kill, and destroy everything good in our lives (John 10:10). Yes, Satan is real and his attacks are real, but let's not give him more credit than he deserves. We can't ignore his schemes, but we also can't forget the truth: God is far greater. The real problem comes when we lose sight of that.

When the enemy's attacks hit hard—whether through failed plans, broken relationships, or unexpected setbacks—we tend to focus more on the pain than on God's power. It's easy to feel overwhelmed, throw our hands up, and feel as though God has forgotten us in those situations. In these moments, we often find ourselves surrendering—not to God but to fear, doubt, and discouragement.

Surrendering to fear is dangerous. When we focus on what's going wrong and forget God's goodness, we begin to resist His leading. We hesitate to step out in faith, hold back from giving or serving, and delay the dreams God has placed in our hearts. Slowly but surely we find ourselves resisting God and surrendering to the enemy—whoops.

But here's the thing: God has already given us a strategy for victory. And it's not just about resisting the enemy. In fact, the key to resisting the enemy starts with surrendering to God.

Most of us jump straight to the part about resisting the devil, but we skip over the first and most important step—surrendering to God. Surrendering doesn't mean giving up. It means giving in. It means fully trusting God's will and His way, even when things aren't going as we expected. It means laying down our doubts, fears, and disappointments at His feet. It's about resting in His presence and trusting Him completely.

Here's the truth found in today's Scripture: Your victory is found in surrender. Victory doesn't come from fighting the enemy with your own strength. It comes when you surrender fully to God and let Him fight for you.

When you surrender to God, aligning your will with His, resisting the enemy becomes much easier. Resistance using your own strength is exhausting—hit after hit can feel overwhelming. But when you're anchored in God's strength, resistance comes naturally. You're not fighting alone anymore; you're standing firm in the power of the Almighty.

So if you're facing an attack from the enemy today, your first step is to get closer to God. Your job isn't to chase after or run away from the enemy—it's to stay rooted in God's presence, fully surrendered to His will. When you remain close to Him, trusting in His power, you allow God to be the One who fights on your behalf. It's not about what you can do; it's about who God is and what He has already done. Surrender every fear, every worry, and every plan to Him. Trust Him fully, then watch what happens. As you surrender, you put God back in the ultimate authority. As He takes His rightful place within your heart, you find renewed strength to resist the enemy who will flee from you —not because of your strength but because of God's. The enemy isn't afraid of you, but he is terrified of the God who fights for you.

Victory isn't won by our efforts but by surrender. The Lord doesn't need you to fight; He needs you to trust Him and walk in the authority He's already given you. It's about standing firm in the presence of God, knowing He's already won the war.

Today, hold the line by purposefully staying at the feet of Jesus. Surrender to Him, resist the enemy, and watch the power of God move in and through your life.

Revel: Consider where in your life you've been resisting God's voice and surrendering to the enemy's lies instead. Are there areas where fear, doubt, or frustration have taken over? Take a moment to lay those burdens at His feet.

Then consider the areas you need to surrender even more to God. Remember, surrendering to God isn't about giving up; it's about giving into Him. Spend time today in His presence, fully available and open to Him. Let your surrender become your source of strength.

Day 52 Victory Is Found in Surrender

Align: Let's be real—how often do we catch ourselves holding our breath while trying to do all the things for God? With tense shoulders and anxious thoughts, praying that the hard stuff just disappears? But alignment isn't about striving; it's about sitting back. It's about surrender.

Now I'm inviting you to sit back, take a deep breath (for real—inhale, exhale), and let God do what only He can do through your yes.

As you reflect on yesterday, ask yourself: Did I move toward my dream holding my breath or with open hands? Was it all on me or was I postured to allow God to do in and through me what only He can do?

Pause. Reflect. Then teach your soul how to sit back, relax, and let God be God. You do you. Let Him do Him.

....

....

....

....

Dream Stack: Today, what is one bold yet surrendered step you will take to move toward your dream? Write it down, then make it happen.

....

....

....

....

DAY 53

Raising Royalty: Seeing the King or Queen in Your Child

Children are an inheritance from the Lord.
They are a reward from him.

—Psalm 127:3 GOD'S WORD Translation

PARENTING CAN BE TOUGH. Some days are long, frustrating, and exhausting. It can feel like a thankless job, and it can become easy to lose sight of the blessing children truly are. The Bible tells us children are a *reward* from the Lord, but when you're in the middle of tantrums, sleepless nights, teenage rebellion, or even the "leave and cleave" stage, that can be hard to remember.

But here's something that changed everything for me as a parent, and I hope it encourages you: You're raising royalty!

Today's Scripture reminds us that children are God's gift, a reward from Him! Think about that. Really take it in. How would you parent differently if you truly believed the child (even an adult child) before you was a king or queen destined for greatness? Because here's the truth—they are. As parents, we are raising the next generation of leaders, innovators, and world-changers. The little people in your home today will grow up to run our cities, businesses, schools, and churches. They will be the builders of tomorrow. That's not just an inspiring thought—it's reality.

This perspective shift demands that we become more intentional and thoughtful in how we parent and/or support the children around us (even if they're not yours). Yes, it's hard when they throw tantrums or defy us, but the key is to look beyond their behavior and see their God-given potential. We must start seeing our children through God's eyes—not just how they act but also as He has called them to be.

Our role as parents is not just to correct behavior but also to call our children into their God-given destiny. We must not just call them out; we also must call them higher. We must not see them only as they behave; we must also see them through the eyes of our Father in heaven and who He says they are. Rather than judging them by their mistakes, we need to call out the greatness within them, acknowledging when their behavior doesn't align with their true identity in Christ, then pointing them to the Word of God. Remind them who they are according to His truth, not just how they are acting in the moment. Encourage them to reflect on their actions and ask them to realign what they do with who God says they are. Our job is not to shame them for their wrong choices but to point them to their identity and purpose in Christ, speaking life over them as they learn to become everything God created them to be.

When we parent with this perspective, something amazing happens. We stop reacting to their behavior or misguided attitudes and start proactively shaping their character and vision in those challenging moments or seasons. We become a proactive voice in their life that reminds them, even in the messiest moments, that they are royalty in God's Kingdom.

No matter how old your children are, it's never too late to start this process. Begin by asking God to give you fresh insight into who He has created them to be then speaking those truths proactively into their life. Trust that He's equipping you with everything you need to raise them up into their full potential.

If you're not a parent, this message still applies to you. Ask God to give you a heart for the next generation. They will inherit the world, and it's up to all of us to support and nurture them in the ways of the Lord. Don't overlook the fact that the support you give to the little lives around you today will shape the leaders of tomorrow.

So whether you're a parent, mentor, or simply someone who cares for the next generation, remember: You're raising royalty. If you remind them they are kings and queens destined for greatness, they will rise to that level. When they understand who they are, they will begin to act accordingly.

Keep that in mind the next time you interact with a child. God's vision for them is bigger than we can imagine, and our role is to help guide them into it. Let's raise kings and queens for God's Kingdom—one child at a time.

※ ※ ※ ※ ※ ※

Revel: If you're a parent, spend some time asking God about the identity and purpose He's given to your child or children. Ask Him to clearly show you who they are and what He's called them to. Reflect on how you can parent from a place of revelation, calling them higher each and every day. Then consider a few things you can do each day to proactively raise the Lord's royalty.

If you're not a parent, ask God to work on your heart for the next generation. Identify if there is a young person you can mentor or a group of children or teens you can sow your love into. Consider one or two things you can do to impact the next generation.

Day 53 Raising Royalty: Seeing the King or Queen in Your Child

Align: Let's keep it simple. Reflect on yesterday—did you make your move? Did you stay aligned, postured in surrender? Did you do what you said you would do? If not, identify what held you back, and from a place of true alignment, find a way to overcome that obstacle today.

....

....

....

....

Dream Stack: All right, let's give heaven something to talk about—what's one thing you can do today to bring that dream of yours to life?

Got it? Good. Now take a deep breath, channel that faith, write it down, and go make it happen.

....

....

....

....

DAY 54

Dream Together

When Elizabeth heard Mary's greeting, the baby leaped in her womb, and Elizabeth was filled with the Holy Spirit.

—Luke 1:41

YOUR DREAMS ARE POWERFUL. They do something powerful not only within you but also around you. They stir your heart, ignite your fire, and bring heaven to earth. AND not everyone will understand or believe in the dream God has placed in your heart, and that's OK. Dreams are personal, and often the vision God gives you may not be fully understood by everyone around you. In fact, some people may doubt, question, or even discourage your dream. But don't be disheartened by that. Though not everyone will believe in your dream, God will bring the right people into your life who *will* recognize it, celebrate it, and even leap for joy because of it.

Take today's Scripture as an example. When Mary visited Elizabeth, both women were carrying miraculous promises from God that most people did not understand, many even criticized. But the moment these two women came together, something divine happened. This wasn't a regular meeting between relatives—this was a divine connection. Elizabeth understood the magnitude of what God was doing in Mary's life, and she celebrated it with her.

Mary didn't need the approval or validation of everyone around her, but having someone who recognized the divine nature of her calling and stood by her in faith surely made a difference. Sometimes God will send a few key people—like Elizabeth—into your life who will see the dream, feel the excitement, and affirm the calling that God has placed in you. Don't overlook these people because you're too focused on unsupportive ones. Too often it's easy to focus on the people who don't believe in our dreams, who speak negatively about our choices to boldly chase after God, or who convince us to get back in the boat of comfortability. Truth be told: Those aren't your people for the next season God's bringing you into. Don't make them wrong in order to make yourself feel right; simply acknowledge that they're not your Elizabeths.

You need people around you who will not only believe in your dream but will also encourage you, pray for you, and stir your faith. These are your Elizabeths—those people who, when they hear about what God is doing in your life, their spirit leaps within them, and they respond with joy and affirmation. They will call out the greatness God has placed in you, and they will remind you of His faithfulness when the road gets tough.

Dreaming was never meant to be a solo journey. The Bible teaches us that we are better together and shows us that there is divine strength in partnership. Think about the dreamers in the Bible—Moses had Aaron, David had Jonathan, and Paul had Barnabas. None of these leaders pursued their God-given dreams on their own, and neither should you.

The journey to fulfilling a God-given dream is the best kind of life to live, *and* it can be long, challenging, and at times lonely. But with the right people by your side—those who believe in God's dreams for you—the path becomes clearer, your faith is strengthened, and your joy is multiplied. When we walk alongside others, we have someone to lift us up when we stumble, to cheer us on when we feel discouraged, and to celebrate with us when victory comes.

Don't be discouraged by those who don't understand. Not everyone will see what God has shown you. But God will always bring people into your life who will affirm and nurture the dream He has given you. Look for the people whose "baby" jumps when you speak about your dream, who speak truth when you need it most, who affirm God's Word over your life when you forget, and who walk with you in your journey.

Shared dreams create shared strength. Dream together.

■ ■ ■ ■ ■ ■

Revel: Are there any relationships where you need to gently distance yourself because they're hindering your dream—their "baby" is not jumping when you walk in the room? Ask God to give you discernment on the best next steps to take.

Next pray and ask God to reveal the Elizabeths in your life—those who can walk alongside you and believe in your dream. Then reach out to one of these people and share what God is doing in your heart. Invite them to pray and dream with you.

Day 54 Dream Together

Align: Let's do a quick heart check—how did you show up yesterday? Were you moving in the direction of your God-given dream, or did something throw you off course? Whatever it was—name it. Then ask yourself: What needs to shift today so my steps match my call?

Every day is a chance to realign, refocus, and walk it out as if you mean it.

....

....

....

....

Dream Stack: Today, what's one bold action you can take to bring your dream to life? Just one step full of faith, full of fire.

And don't do it alone. Who can you call, text, or bring alongside you to pray, encourage, or even take that step with you? Big dreams were never meant to be a solo mission. So take the step—and take someone with you. It's worth it. Your dream is worth it. Let's go!

....

....

....

....

DAY 55

I Don't Got This

Then [the angel] said to me, 'This is the word of the Lord to Zerubbabel: Not by might, nor by power, but by my Spirit, says the Lord of hosts.'

—Zechariah 4:6 ESV

DO YOUR DREAMS FEEL BIGGER than you? Or do the obstacles standing in your way seem far greater than your ability to overcome them? Either way, take heart—because though your dreams, and yes, even those obstacles, may feel big, your God is bigger than them all.

We live in a world that rewards pushing harder, going faster, and doing more. The message is clear: The strongest, the best, and the busiest are the ones who win. But that's not the truth God teaches us. In His Kingdom, success isn't measured by our strength or effort but by His.

In reality, even the most successful people would admit that behind closed doors, they often feel like they have no idea what they're doing. In fact, many top leaders fear being exposed as impostors. So let's drop the facade—none of us has it all together. And the good news? We don't need to. We're not called to fake our way through life. We're called to overcome, and God has given us the way to do it.

Let's look at Zerubbabel's story in the book of Ezra, which comes after today's Scripture. Zerubbabel was chosen to rebuild the temple after it was destroyed during the Babylonian exile. He had everything he needed—resources, permission, blueprints—and after two years of progress, he completed the foundation of the temple. But then opposition struck. Ever been there? You obey God, make great progress, then suddenly, you hit a wall. Doubts creep in: *Did I hear God wrong? Am I off track?*

For Zerubbabel, the opposition lasted seventeen years! Think about that—seventeen years of stalled progress, unmet expectations, and unfulfilled promise. Now let me ask you: What do *you* do when you face opposition? Do you withdraw, abandoning the dream or vision God gave you? What do you believe when the going gets tough? Do you continue to trust God when obstacles block your way?

Opposition often tests our faith, our resolve, and our trust in God. When things don't go as planned, it can be tempting to walk away—to leave unfinished what God originally called you to complete. But just because the process stalls doesn't mean the promise has failed. The question is: Will you let the delay define the outcome?

When Zerubbabel faced opposition, it wasn't the end of the story. God sent a prophetic word to stir him back into action. The game-changing message from God was today's Scripture: *'Not by might, nor by power, but by my Spirit.'* The Hebrew word for *might* here means force, ability, efficiency. It's associated with human strength, wealth, and resources. *Power* refers to willpower, determination, and inner resolve. But here's the catch: Any God-given dream or calling will always be bigger than your own force, willpower, abilities, and even personal resources. The more you try to do, the more exhausted you'll become.

Sometimes all it takes is a fresh word from God to reignite the vision and remind you that it's not by your strength but by His Spirit that the work will be accomplished. God was telling Zerubbabel that his own strength and resources wouldn't be enough to complete the work; he needed something new and different. Zerubbabel's effort could take him only so far. Instead, God offered a better way—His Spirit.

In this context, God's Spirit is *ruah*—the same Spirit that created the world and parted the Red Sea. It's the same spirit behind everything He calls us to do. God's ruah is the key to unlocking the impossible. When you surrender your might and power, that's when God's Spirit takes over and does the impossible—we move from striving to thriving. The breakthrough won't come through your own human effort but through God's power. How encouraging is that?

Maybe today you're feeling like "I don't got this." Guess what? You're not supposed to. God never intended for you to rely on your own strength. He wants you to depend on Him—on His ruah, His Spirit. You don't got this, but He does! Your job isn't to figure it all out but to surrender your might and let God take over. Let His Spirit work through your yes, so your weakness is an opportunity for His strength to shine.

Let God's ruah breathe life into what feels dead, stalled, or impossible. You're not in this alone, and you never were. You don't have to be strong enough, wealthy enough, or wise enough. You just need to be surrendered enough.

You got this, because God's got you.

Revel: Take a moment to ask God to show you where you've been carrying the false burden of doing it all. Acknowledge the places in your life where you've relied on your own strength instead of His. Repent and surrender that false responsibility to Him. Release the need to strive and invite God to take over.

Now close your eyes and picture yourself receiving from God. Let go of the pressure to have all the answers. Allow His ruah—the breath of life—to fill you. Pause, breathe, and simply receive His peace and provision.

Day 55 | Don't Got This

Align: It's Day 55—can we just pause and celebrate that for a second?! That means you're about to take your fifty-fifth bold, intentional step toward the dream God's placed inside of you. That's no small thing.

So before you jump into what's next, take a breath. Flip back through the pages of this journey. Remember the prayers you've prayed, the bold steps you've taken, and the moments you said yes when it would've been easier to shrink back. You're bringing heaven to earth!

Give yourself the gift of reflection. Let it fuel your faith. Let it remind you that the same God who brought you this far is still leading you forward. Then—and only then—go do the next thing. But do it from a place of remembrance, not rushing.

Dream Stack: Today, name one more bold step you're going to take toward your dream. Write it down. Commit to it. Then go make it happen. Keep stacking those dreams. You're building something powerful!

DAY 56

Sort of Saved

So if the Son sets you free, you are truly free.
—John 8:36 NLT

WHEN YOU HEAR THE WORD *salvation*, what comes to mind? Forgiveness? Justification? Eternal life?

For believers, our lives are defined by this word. It's the key that sets us apart from those who don't believe and determines where we will spend eternity. But here's the problem: Though most of us understand salvation's *power*, few of us grasp its full *reality*. And because of that, we struggle to live in the victory and freedom it's meant to give us.

So, what do salvation and freedom have to do with each other? Everything.

Most of us know that salvation means deliverance from sin and its consequences. When we accept Jesus as Lord and Savior, we are saved from hell and are no longer defined by our sins. This is the power of salvation—freedom from the eternal penalty of sin. But salvation is more than just a ticket out of hell. If we limit it to that, we might end up seeing ourselves as "sinners saved by grace"—a powerful truth, but often we focus on the sinner part and forget that grace changes everything.

Salvation doesn't just save you from sin; it redefines who you are. You are no longer a sinner barely scraping by—you are a new creation walking in union with God. You now have the identity of Christ and are empowered to live like Him here and now. Salvation is not just a moment of repentance; it's a lifestyle of freedom. Jesus didn't die just to save you—He died to set you free. That's the power of today's Scripture, which declares, *If the Son sets you free, you are truly free.*

Freedom in Christ is not something you have to strive for. It's the gift of salvation— the power to live without being imprisoned by fear, guilt, or shame. It means living without restraint, being who God made you to be, and bringing heaven to earth boldly and unapologetically. This is the reality of it.

When we walk in the reality of salvation, we are walking in the freedom Jesus bought for us. This freedom isn't just about getting free—it's about staying free and living from that place of true liberty in Him. True freedom is the recognition that Jesus died for our sins so that we don't have to, and it's the awareness that He died for our freedom so that we can live fully in Him. We're not meant to struggle from a place of bondage but to live *from* a place of victory.

Jesus's mission was freedom. He came to Earth, died, and rose again, so that we could experience *true* freedom in Him. This cost Him everything and cost us nothing. And because our freedom was His victory, it's now our starting point. I encourage you to not just live as a sinner saved by grace but as a child of God living in the fullness of His victory! That means the next time you find yourself circling the same sin and getting less than ideal results, blaming, shaming, guilting yourself or someone else, *make your move*! Remind yourself of who you are in Christ. Envision your sin dying on the cross with Jesus, then walk in the new victory He called you to! You're not defined by your past mistakes or present struggles; you're defined by the victory Jesus won for you on the cross.

In case you forget, you were *called to be free*! (Galatians 5:13). You are meant to walk in the fullness of salvation—to create, live, and serve without limits, beyond sin. Let this truth sink in today, not just as head knowledge but as your identity. Picture yourself completely and totally free. Let that freedom shape your decisions and thoughts and how you approach life.

Start declaring it today: "I am free in the Lord." Let that freedom guide everything you do.

It's time to make your move. Stop living like you're *almost* free and step into the fullness of what Jesus died to give you. You—yes, *you*—are called to live in freedom!

Revel: Are you truly living free? Are you walking in the fullness of what Christ died to give you?

Take a moment to reflect on the power of salvation and, even more so, on the reality of it—the freedom and empowerment that come with it. Ask God for divine insight into what a life of complete freedom in Him would look like for you. Then take a bold step and live it out!

....

....

....

....

Day 56 Sort of Saved

Align: Reflect on yesterday—did you take any steps toward your dream? If not, take time to identify what held you back. Then realign today, choosing to live more like Jesus in your thoughts, your attitude, and your actions.

....

....

....

....

Dream Stack: Let's build something beautiful—again. What's one action you can take today to stack a win on top of your dream?

Remember, if God puts it in you, it's not just a possibility—it's a promise waiting for your participation. So write it down, take the step, and keep stacking. You're closer than you think.

....

....

....

....

DAY 57
Create Uninhibitedly

Go ahead—sing your brand-new song to the Lord! He is famous for his miracles and marvels, for he is victorious through his mighty power and holy strength. So go ahead, everyone, and shout out your praises with joy! Break out of the box and let loose with the most joyous sound of praise! Sing your melody of praise to the Lord and make music like never before! Blow those trumpets and shofars! Shout with joyous triumph before King Yahweh! Let the ocean's waves join in the chorus with their roaring praise until everyone everywhere shouts out in unison, 'Glory to the Lord!'

—Psalms 98:1, 4–7 TPT

SAINT IRENAEUS OF LYONS SAID, "The glory of God is man fully alive." But how often do we truly live that way? As we learned in our devotion yesterday, true freedom is a gift we have through Jesus Christ. We aren't just saved from hell; we are also released to walk fully alive in Him! I don't know about you, but I feel the reality of that kind of freedom should cause us to dance, sing, and create with joy.

Shouldn't the Church be the one leading in creativity, innovation, and trailblazing ideas? Why not? We have every reason to celebrate and express our joy. Our God wins! This reality should shift how we approach everything we do—from how we build businesses to how we worship. When we embrace the freedom that comes with salvation, creativity naturally flows from us.

Today's verse shows what it looks like to create uninhibitedly with the Lord.

Truth be told, as believers, our lives should be marked by creativity. We should be the ones breaking out of the box and lifting new songs of praise to the point that even nature joins in our worship, as the oceans roar and nations shout in unison to the glory of God! Can you imagine?!

Most of you would say you can't. But that's only because you've convinced yourself that "I'm not creative" or "I'm too analytical." Those are common mindsets, yet they're simply incomplete. Creativity isn't limited to art or music—it's not limited to how we think, nor does it have to do with a vocation. It's actually who we are.

Creative means having or showing the ability to make new things or think new ideas. Another definition says it's marked by the ability or power to create. That word *create* means to bring into existence. The Bible says, *In the beginning, God created the heavens and the earth* (Genesis 1:1) and *God created mankind in his own image* (Genesis 1:27). Have we forgotten that we come from the creator Himself? I am here to remind you that you are called to be like Him—to create *as* He does and to create *with* Him. Creativity is not what you do but who you are. It is in your DNA because you were created in the image of God, the ultimate creator.

Stepping into our true identity as children of God unlocks a wellspring of creativity that flows uninhibitedly from our connection with Him. When we grasp the depth of who we are in Christ and the freedom He has given us, we no longer feel the need to hold back or conform to the expectations of others. Instead, we live with the confidence that we are free to create, innovate, and lead boldly in every area of our lives.

This kind of freedom means we no longer feel the need to follow the trends in our industries or fields—we lead them. With access to God's divine wisdom and insight, we're empowered to see beyond the ordinary and discover solutions to problems others may not even notice. Whether in business, education, the arts, or the home, we are called to be pioneers, introducing new ways of thinking and living that showcase the creativity and excellence of our heavenly Father.

If you're a teacher, for example, understanding your identity in Christ will inspire you to teach in a way that nurtures the heart and soul of each child, going beyond the standard methods of education. If you're an entrepreneur, you'll find yourself ahead of the curve, seeing new business opportunities and solving problems with innovation and vision. If you're a worship leader, you'll sing new songs, pulling down heaven's realities to lead others into deeper encounters with God. If you stay at home with your children, your creativity will flow into how you structure your days, bringing life, joy, and peace into your home in ways that uniquely reflect God's heart. That's something worth shouting—"Glory to the Lord!"

When we realize that our gifts, talents, and abilities are for God's glory, the opinions of others no longer have the power to hold us back. You're not chasing after the approval of others or trying to meet the world's standards. You aren't creating to achieve worldly success; you're creating for the pleasure and delight of our heavenly Father.

So whether you sing, write, lead, or raise a family, walk in the freedom Christ died to give you. Embrace your creative expression—your God-given identity. Let His Spirit inspire you to step out in new ways, to push the boundaries of what's possible, and to reflect His glory in everything you do. Let your life be marked by a bold and uninhibited creativity.

Revel: What would it look like to step into your identity as a person who creates uninhibitedly? How would your life change if you embraced your divine calling to create alongside God in every area—in work, relationships, and your personal walk with Him?

Take time today to reflect on this and journal about the possibilities that come to mind. Ask God to reveal areas where you can co-create with Him, letting His freedom and creativity flow through you.

Day 57 Create Uninhibitedly

Align: Let's check in—how did you show up yesterday? Did you take a step (even a small one) toward the dream God has placed in your heart?

If not, don't spiral—get strategic. What slowed you down? What threw you off? Now, what can you shift today to get back in alignment and back in motion? Keep showing up and let God show off!

Dream Stack: Today, what's one new thing you can create with the Lord that will move you closer to your dream?

Think beyond the usual. Get out of the box. Step out of the boat. Paint outside the lines. Build what hasn't been built yet. Say what hasn't been said. Do what you've never dared to do. This is co-creation with heaven. You + God = something the world has never seen before.

So … what will you create today? Write about it here. Go live it out there.

DAY 58

Abundance: A Better Way to Live

[Jesus said,] 'The thief comes only to steal and kill and destroy. I came that they may have life and have it abundantly.'

—John 10:10 ESV

WHEN YOU HEAR THE WORD *abundance*, what comes to mind? More money or more stuff? Some of you might be thinking, *"Oh yeah—make money, money; make money, money!"* While others of you are ready to check out because you're thinking, *Oh please—not another prosperity message.*

I promise, this is not a prosperity message. It's a promise message. It's about *overflow*. Abundance is not about how much money is in your bank account or how much stuff you accumulate; it's about the richness of your relationship with Jesus, who, believe it or not, was on a mission for you so you would live abundantly. At the same time, there is an enemy who opposes everything God has for you, and his mission is the opposite of abundance. This is how we can clearly distinguish between the hand of God and the work of the enemy. The Scripture for today makes the contrast clear: The thief comes to steal, kill, and destroy, but Jesus came so that you would have life and have it *in abundance*.

The enemy's mission is to steal, kill, and destroy. That means, if something in your life looks, smells, or feels like death, despair, depression, or anxiety—that's the enemy at work. He's after not only your soul but also the quality of life God has made available to you. This is why it's important to recognize his schemes and not confuse the challenges in our lives as punishment or reprimand from the Lord. The Bible is clear—God's mission is not to harm or dishearten you but to give you abundant life.

The word *abundance* doesn't just refer to *quantity* but to *quality*. Abundance in God's eyes is a life filled with joy, peace, love, and purpose, regardless of what we physically have. Abundance is not something you physically possess; it's something you spiritually possess because of Jesus's sacrifice and the relationship you now have with Him. Does this mean God doesn't care if you have nice things or material wealth? Not at all. But His priority is your soul prospering in Him first. Jesus didn't come just to give you more material things; He came to offer a better way to live, a better quality of life—a life that remains unattached to external things.

So what does this mean for you today?

This means He provides everything needed for a life marked by spiritual wealth and fruitfulness in Him. It means that your life should be marked by the fruits of the Spirit—love, joy, peace, patience, kindness, goodness, faithfulness, gentleness, and self-control—expressing in how you live. It means that true abundance comes from your being one with Jesus, receiving the overflow of His Spirit, and living freely on the daily in the inheritance that is already yours. Though the world may measure abundance by possessions, God measures it by the fullness of a life lived in Him—something no one can take from you.

Practically speaking, when you live from the overflow of His Spirit, it equips you to make decisions that are led by the Spirit and aligned with His heart. A joyful soul makes joyful choices. A peaceful soul makes decisions rooted in peace. A soul filled with self-control makes disciplined decisions. Ultimately, the abundance you're seeking externally is found in the quality of life that only He can give—one that fills you internally and lasts eternally.

Today, I encourage you to stop striving for *quantity* and start receiving the *quality* of life He is freely giving you. May your life reflect the overflow of His goodness.

That is the abundant life He promises.

Revel: Have you been more focused on quantity over quality? How can you realign yourself today to receive His abundance—a soul that prospers in His presence?

Reflect on the goodness of God and the abundance of life He provides through the Spirit. Begin to ask God for a heart that is hungry for His abundance, His *quality* of life. Ask for a life filled with the fruits of the Spirit—love, joy, peace, patience, kindness, goodness, faithfulness, gentleness, and self-control.

Day 58 Abundance: A Better Way to Live

Align: Today's devotion is all about true alignment—a genuine shift within our internal world that leads to transformation in our external world. Because here's the thing: Alignment isn't just about checking off a task or making surface-level moves; it's also about the internal journey—the thoughts you think, the posture of your heart, the mindset you carry. That's what fuels real, lasting, external change.

As you reflect on yesterday, ask yourself: What needs to shift inside of me in this moment so I can move forward in full alignment today—with God, with purpose, and with who I'm becoming?

The real work happens within—and from there, everything else follows.

Dream Stack: Today, what is one thing you can do that will bring you closer to your dream? Remember, it seems impossible only to the person who has never tried. Note it here, then give it everything you've got.

DAY 59

One Encounter

Jesus replied, 'If you only knew who I am and the gift that God wants to give you, you'd ask me for a drink, and I would give you living water.'

—John 4:10 TPT

WE LIVE IN A TIME WHEN SOCIETY—and sometimes even parts of the church—has normalized sinful lifestyles by twisting phrases like "All are welcome" or focusing only on one perspective like "Black lives matter" without the broader context that in God's Kingdom, "All lives matter." And yes, all are welcome, but that doesn't mean we stay as we are when we encounter Him.

The story of the woman at the well in today's verse is indeed one of the most powerful encounters in Scripture and beautifully demonstrates a core truth about Jesus: He will always meet you exactly where you are, but He won't leave you there.

Here we find a woman with a complicated story. She's had five husbands and is now living with a man who isn't her husband. In that culture, her past would've made her the subject of whispers, judgment, and isolation. And the fact that she's drawing water in the middle of the day—when the sun is hottest and when no one else would typically be at the well because most women would have drawn water in the cool of the morning—tells us a lot. She's likely trying to avoid the crowd, avoid the shame, and avoid the pain of being seen.

But Jesus sees her anyway. And He meets her right where she is. Not by accident, not as a detour—on purpose. He doesn't avoid her mess. He walks right into it. Not to shame her but to invite her into something better—something eternal. He speaks directly to the reality of her life, not to condemn her but to offer her *living water*, a whole new way of being. Here we see how Jesus has the ability to meet us in our brokenness, see and love us completely, and call us into wholeness.

This principle applies to every encounter with Jesus—whether it's the first time we experience His presence or in our ongoing journey as believers. When we encounter Jesus, He meets us in our brokenness, shame, confusion, and deepest place of need. But His love and truth compel us to grow, transforming and empowering us to leave behind the things that hold us back. And He doesn't do that for some of us; He does it for all of us.

Let's break down some key insights from the story of the woman at the well in the book of John:

You are dependent upon whatever you call your source. *Wearied by his long journey, he sat on the edge of Jacob's well, and sent his disciples into the village to buy food, for it was already afternoon. Soon a Samaritan woman came to draw water. Jesus said to her, 'Give me a drink.' She replied, 'Why would a Jewish man ask a Samaritan woman for a drink of water?' (For Jews have no dealings with Samaritans.)* (John 4:6–9 TPT)

When Jesus first encounters this woman, she is minding her own business, coming to a literal well to get her physical need for water met. Up to this point, the well was her source. When Jesus asks the Samaritan woman for a drink, she was surprised that a Jewish man would even speak to her. But Jesus responded (in today's verse), *'If you only knew who I am and the gift God wants to give you, you'd ask me for a drink, and I would give you living water.'"* In one encounter, he shifts her focus from her need to Him. Here, the woman once dependent on a physical well meets the true source of her thirst.

Jesus didn't want to just give her a drink of water—He wanted to be her *living water*. Jesus didn't want to just meet her physical need; He wanted to satisfy the deep thirst of her soul. He didn't want her to be dependent on water; He wanted her to be dependent upon Him.

Don't downgrade God to fit the size of your need. When the woman began to realize who Jesus was, she said, *'Let me drink that water so I'll never be thirsty again and won't have to come back here to draw water'* (John 4:15 TPT). Jesus was offering more than a one-time solution. He was offering Himself as the permanent answer to her deepest desires.

Often we see our needs as the biggest thing in our lives, and we ask God to fit into those needs. But God's desire is not to just meet a temporary need; He wants to become our source. We must be careful we don't minimize who He is just to fill our need. He wants to bring us into a place of overflow—abundant life in Him, where our souls are filled beyond measure.

Jesus will meet you where you are, but He won't leave you there. *Jesus said to her, 'You don't have to wait any longer, the Anointed One is here speaking with you—I am the One you're looking for'* (John 4:26 TPT). Jesus lovingly met the woman at the well right where she was and pointed out her sin—not to shame or condemn her but to invite her into a deeper reality, Him! He wanted her to understand that her current life, shaped by temporary relationships and unmet needs, was not the life He had for her.

He acknowledged her sin, yet he called her higher, out of her sin into a better way to live, and in this one moment, her life would never be the same! She was deeply transformed by her encounter.

True transformation comes from encountering Jesus. *All at once, the woman left her water jar and ran off to her village and told everyone* (John 4:28 TPT). When the woman at the well encountered Jesus, her life was never the same. She went from a broken, shame-filled woman to an evangelist, running back to her town and telling everyone about the Messiah she had met. She was completely transformed, never to be the same, because when you see Jesus, you remember who you are.

The Samaritan woman's encounter with Jesus restored her identity. Once she saw who He was, she understood who she was. This is foundational to our

Day 59 One Encounter

transformation—knowing who Jesus is reveals who we are meant to be. Jesus didn't just meet her need; He restored her sense of worth, identity, and purpose.

Jesus didn't come to simply change your mind; He came to change your heart. He doesn't just meet you in your place of sin, He transforms you. It's not about behavior modification—it's about identity in Him. When we encounter the living Jesus, we see Him for who He really is, and that changes everything about who *we* are.

One encounter with Jesus changes everything!

Jesus didn't meet the woman at the well just to have a conversation. He exposed her past, not to condemn her but to invite her into a new life of freedom and abundance. He acknowledged her thirst, both physically and spiritually, and offered her living water—Himself. This encounter changed her identity and her future.

Every true encounter with Jesus carries this same power. He meets us in the middle of our struggles, our fears, and our sins, but His love propels us forward into healing, restoration, and new life. When we encounter Him, we are called to leave behind old patterns, dependencies, and sins, because He offers something far greater for us—transformation.

Jesus is meeting you in the same way today. In fact, every day. He does not encounter you to condemn you, nor will he let you stay where you are. May your daily encounter with Him transform you and send you into each and every day looking more like Him.

Revel: What could happen if you meet Jesus at the well of your need today? Will you allow Him to meet you where you are, no matter the weight of your burdens or the depth of your struggles, and will you allow Him to call you higher?

Ask the Lord to meet you where you're at today. Allow Him to lead you out of your brokenness and false identities into a life of abundance, joy, and transformation. One encounter with Him will completely transform who you are.

Align: Today, pause for a moment—as if you were meeting Jesus at the well. Let this be a sacred space where you pause in His presence, reflect honestly, and remember who you are because of who He is.

As you look back on yesterday, ask yourself: Did I take a step toward the dream He's placed in my heart? Did I walk in alignment with who He says I am?

If not, don't shrink back—get still. Sit with Him. Let Him reveal what held you back. Then, from that place of grace and clarity, decide how you'll realign today. Your identity is secure. Your purpose is still alive. And the sacred well is always there waiting for you to come and be filled.

Dream Stack: From a place of divine overflow, what's one bold move you can make today to move closer to your dream?

Most people wait around for inspiration—but not you. You move because you've encountered Jesus. So pause, encounter Him today, and let that encounter inspire your next step. Write it down, then go—boldly, faithfully, and full of purpose.

DAY 60

Lord, Where Are You?

[Jacob thought,] Surely the Lord is in this
place, and I was not aware of it.

—Genesis 28:16

CAN YOU RELATE? Maybe you're going through a tough season, and it seems like no one else could possibly understand what you're feeling. You've even found yourself asking, "Lord, where are you?"

God's Word assures us that He is always with us in every season—whether good or challenging. So, the question isn't whether He's with us or not, but do we have the eyes to see Him?

I can remember a memory from when I was seven years old. My mom and I had gone on vacation to Florida, and we decided to visit Disney World and Universal Studios. What was supposed to be "the happiest place on earth" felt overwhelming to me as I found myself surrounded by thousands of people. There I was in a sea of people, feeling totally lost in the crowd and somehow completely alone.

"Let the show begin!" an enthusiastic man called out as he directed the crowd's attention toward the stage. "Come one, come all!" People pressed forward. I felt crushed. My mom must've noticed, because she grabbed me and lifted me up onto her shoulders. There I could see over the heads of thousands of people and had a clear view of the stage. "Volunteers! We need five volunteers!" My heart raced. *Never in a million years,* I thought.

Then, out of nowhere, my hand shot up. I had not raised it, nor was this the divine hand of God. It was my mom. As I sat high on her shoulders, she lifted my hand for all to see. "YOU! In the glasses!" the man said. And just like that, I was chosen.

I didn't want to go. I couldn't go. No way. No how. Not on my life. But my mom insisted. Despite my protests, it was showtime, and "the show must go on." They threw feather boas around me, handed me oversize glasses, big dresses, and shoes that didn't fit. The microphone didn't work, and though they tried to make it seem like fun, it wasn't for me. I stood there on stage paralyzed with fear and embarrassment. There in a sea of thousands of people, I had never felt so alone.

The laughter, the faces, the pointing fingers—it was too much for me. After faking my way through the act, I exited the stage feeling like something inside me had died. A belief formed within me that day that said: "If you see me, you will reject me." From that moment on, I learned to hide.

But just because I learned to hide in that moment didn't mean God didn't see me. Just because I felt so alone didn't mean I was. Yet the belief I formed—that being seen meant being rejected—created a false sense that God had disappeared. Deep down, I unconsciously believed He wasn't with me anymore. Perhaps you've experienced something similar.

It took me twenty-nine years to realize how wrong I had been—and I had to relearn how to see God. To see Him in everything, in every situation, just as today's Scripture so clearly calls us to do.

Life doesn't always turn out the way we hope, and in those difficult or lonely moments, we may feel abandoned. But God is always with us. He is present in every detail of your life, so instead of questioning whether or not He's with you (He is), the real question is: *Can you see Him?*

One of the greatest breakthroughs in my healing journey came when I revisited that moment at Universal Studios and realized that the Lord was with me all along. When I viewed that memory from heaven's perspective, I could see things differently. What once felt like a painful, embarrassing memory became a moment where I was performing for an audience of one—Jesus.

If there are painful moments in your life, in the past or today, where you feel like you can't see Him, simply ask, "Lord, give me eyes to see You!" As you begin to look with fresh eyes, you'll find that He was there all along, and He is with you even now.

God is constantly speaking to you. Are you listening? He is always moving on your behalf. Can you see Him? He is always with you. Can you recognize His presence?

Today, I pray you sharpen your awareness of His nearness.

Revel: Take a moment to reflect on a memory that felt like God was nowhere to be found. Close your eyes and go back to that moment. Now ask Him, "Lord, where were *you*?"

As you quietly sit in His presence, allow yourself to see Him in that space. Recognize that He was with you then, just as He is with you now. Let His presence bring comfort and allow Him to heal the wounds of that memory. His never-ending, always-present love surrounds you—let it wash over the pain and bring peace to your heart. Develop the eyes to see that He is with you, now and even in the hardest places.

Day 60 Lord, Where Are You?

Align: Today, during your aligning time, I encourage you to ask a deeper question: Where did I see God yesterday?

It's easy to get caught up doing things for God and forget to notice where He's moving in us and around us. But alignment isn't just about tracking progress—it's also about becoming more aware of His presence. It's recognizing that He's not only with you in the work, but He's also in you as you do it.

Yes, reflect on the steps you took toward your dream—but more important ask if you saw Him in those steps? Did you notice Him walking with you, guiding you, strengthening you? Pause. Reflect. Realign. Because He's not just in the dream you're chasing—He's in you, every step of the way.

Dream Stack: Today, what is one proactive step you can take toward the dream in your heart? (PS If you spend too much time thinking about it, you'll be less likely to do it. Don't think; write it down and do it.)

DAY 61

Self-Sabotage

Through my experience of this principle, I discover that even when I want to do good, evil is ready to sabotage me. Truly, deep within my true identity, I love to do what pleases God. But I discern another power operating in my humanity, waging war against the moral principles of my conscience and bringing me into captivity as a prisoner to the 'law' of sin—this unwelcome intruder in my humanity.

—Romans 7:21–23 TPT

HAVE YOU EVER FOUND YOURSELF knowing the right thing to do then choosing not to do it? You know you shouldn't eat that cookie if you want to lose weight, but you eat it anyway. Or maybe you recognize emotional pain that needs healing, but you avoid counseling. Perhaps you see a pattern where you achieve something great—whether it's in finances, relationships, or personal growth—then ruin your own progress. This behavior has a name: *self-sabotage.*

We all know the term, and we've all experienced it in some way. It's so common that we can find ourselves tolerating it, downplaying it, or even joking about it. But self-sabotage is not something to take lightly, nor should it be minimized.

Here's the truth: Self-sabotage is a sign that we are not viewing ourselves as God views us. It reveals a disconnect between our internal beliefs and our external results. If our soul or mind believes something contrary to what's going on around us, we will act in ways that align with that false belief, even if we don't consciously want to. For example, if you believe deep down that you are unworthy of success, you may sabotage your success—even though you consciously desire it—because your internal belief system is out of alignment.

This is what today's passage is all about. Though we're reminded that, *deep within my true identity, I love to do what pleases God*, there is another force—this *unwelcome intruder*—that wars against our conscience, a disconnect that tries to bring us back into captivity. This disconnect leads to a constant internal struggle. You might go to church, pray, or read your Bible, but if you still carry false beliefs about God or yourself, you won't experience the fullness of His promises.

Self-sabotage is not just a behavior problem; it's also a belief problem. To overcome it, we must unlearn the lies we've believed about ourselves and God. We can't simply add more information or learn more Scripture; we have to *unlearn* the falsehoods that have shaped our beliefs. Only then can we walk in alignment with God's truth.

I challenge you with this idea: What if the reason you're not seeing the mighty works of God in your life, in your family, in your career, or in your community isn't because God isn't capable but because of the beliefs you've held onto? Too often, we accommodate our false beliefs instead of testing them against God's truth. We act according to what we think we know rather than stepping out in faith to trust God's promises.

The truth is: *Self-sabotage is not who you are.* You are a child of the Most High God, and His Spirit lives within you. You weren't born to be anxious, a people pleaser, a procrastinator, or a self-saboteur. These are learned behaviors, often formed to protect ourselves or avoid pain. But they don't define you.

So what do we do when we feel the pull of self-sabotage?

As today's passage continues: *What an agonizing situation I am in! So who has the power to rescue this miserable man from the unwelcome intruder of sin and death? I give all my thanks to God, for His mighty power has finally provided a way out through our Lord Jesus, the Anointed One!* (Romans 7:24–25 TPT) This passage shows us two key steps. First, we need to recognize the behavior in real time. The next time you catch yourself in a pattern of self-sabotage, stop. Notice what's happening and interrupt the behavior. Once you recognize it, you can do something about it.

Second, we need to call upon the name of Jesus. Jesus has already provided a way out. His Spirit empowers you to overcome the habits and beliefs that keep you trapped. Instead of ignoring the behavior, pretending it away, or willpowering your way through it, seek Him with all your heart and allow His grace to provide a way out. That means consciously choosing not to sabotage the blessings He has for you. Instead of believing the lie, walk in authority using God's truth.

Today, I encourage you to allow the Lord to transform you and align your internal beliefs with His truth, so you can walk in the freedom and power that are yours in Christ.

■ ■ ■ ■ ■ ■

Revel: Spend some intentional time with God today and ask Him, "What false beliefs have I been holding onto? What do I need to unlearn, so I may walk in greater levels of freedom?"

As you sit in His presence, allow His Spirit to gently reveal the lies that have been holding you back. Then let His truth and blessings wash over you, aligning your heart with His love, grace, and purpose for your life.

Day 61 Self-Sabotage

Align: Reflect on yesterday—did you take any steps toward your dream? If not, use this aligning time to identify what held you back and why. Then from the overflow of God's grace, find a way to overcome that obstacle today.

....

....

....

....

Dream Stack: What's one action you can take today that will bring you closer to your dream? Life is too short to do the things that don't matter. Write it. Do it. Let your results tell the story.

....

....

....

....

DAY 62

The Power of Faith

But without faith it is impossible to [walk with God and] please Him, for whoever comes [near] to God must [necessarily] believe that God exists and that He rewards those who [earnestly and diligently] seek Him.

—Hebrews 11:6 AMP

TRUTH BE TOLD, living a bold life requires faith. For us dream chasers, it's literally the fuel that gets us going—it's how we start the day and helps us show up all day long. Faith should also be a defining characteristic of our lives as believers. That's why it's essential to understand what Biblical faith is, what it produces within us, and the impact it brings into our lives. When we grasp this, we can confidently live it out every single day.

What is faith? Scripture gives a clear definition of faith. Hebrews 11:1 tells us that *faith is confidence in what we hope for and assurance about what we do not see*. Often we can misinterpret this verse, which is why our faith can feel strong one day and absent the next. I suggest that it's not that we lose faith, but that our faith has been misplaced in the wrong things.

The phrase *confidence in what we hope for* is less about the specific things we hope for and more about *what* or *who* we place our hope in. If our hope is solely in what God will do for us, we risk being disappointed when He doesn't act the way we expect. True Biblical faith rests not in the results of God but the character of God. It is literally anchored in the character of who He is, not in the outcomes we desire. If our faith is in God's character—His goodness, love, and faithfulness—then it remains steady, even when life doesn't go as planned.

What does faith produce? When our faith is grounded in God's character, it produces something powerful in us: *action*. Hebrews 11 outlines what faith looks like:

- By faith, Abel offered a better sacrifice.
- By faith, Noah built an ark.
- By faith, Abraham obeyed, not knowing where he was going.
- By faith, Sarah conceived, even when it seemed impossible.

Faith moves us. It compels us to take steps in obedience, even when we can't see the outcome. These heroes of faith acted because they had faith in who God is, not just what He said. Like them, we may not always see the answers to our prayers in the way we expect, but God is still working, and His purposes are eternal. When our faith rests in God's character, not just in the results we desire, we find strength to trust Him in every situation—whether we're in the waiting, walking through hardship, or witnessing His promises fulfilled. Faith in His character will produce the boldness, the willingness, to take the next step.

So ask yourself: Is your faith moving you? Are you taking steps of obedience, even when the future is unclear? If your faith is rooted in God's unchanging character, it will produce action in your life, and you will see the fruits of that faith. Faith that produces action is living, vibrant, and effective.

What is the result of faith? The ultimate result of faith is twofold: It gives us peace of mind in God, and it pleases Him. First, faith isn't just answered prayers or fulfilled dreams. The true outcome of faith is *confident rest* in God. Hebrews 4:3 (TPT) says, *For those of us who believe, faith activates the promise and we experience the realm of confident rest!* When your faith is in God's character and you are taking steps of faith, you experience His peace, even in the midst of uncertainty.

This is what the heroes of the faith in Hebrews 11 are commended for. These men and women are not celebrated because they received every promise in their lifetime, but because their faith was in *God Himself.* Hebrews 11:13 tells us: *All these people were still living by faith when they died. They did not receive the things promised; they only saw them and welcomed them from a distance.* Their faith was not in just the promises of God but also in God's eternal plan that extends beyond this life; therefore, they rested in Him.

This confident rest allowed them to operate from a place of peace rather than fear or worry. The same is true for you. Instead of being driven by anxiety, comparison, deliverables, and deadlines, you are grounded in the love and purpose of God, and you are set free from the pressure of outcomes.

The second result and a powerful truth from today's Scripture: Your faith pleases God. The Kingdom measures faith, not results. It is not about getting it right or even doing everything perfectly; it's your faith that pleases God. Your faith is your offering; it is your sacrifice to Him that blesses Him the most. Bottom line, your taking a risk on God pleases Him, and this is where He rewards you—not when you cross the finish line of completion but when you cross the starting line of faith.

As you walk in faith today, know that you *are* pleasing God. He doesn't need you to do anything for Him; He just wants you to walk with Him.

Day 62 The Power of Faith

Revel: Has your faith been in the results of God or the character of God? Today, realign your attention to focus more on who God is and what He says, instead of what He can do for you.

Is your faith mobilized? Are you taking a risk on God? Today in your dream stacking time, be sure your choices reflect your faith.

Are you experiencing a rest-in-faith life? If not, how can you lean into Hebrews 11 and be encouraged by your levels of *faith*fulness and not just your results? Remember, the Kingdom measures faith, not results.

....

....

....

....

Align: Take a moment to reflect on yesterday—did you take any steps of faith toward your dream? If so, celebrate that! Even if you haven't seen the full results (yet), know this—God is pleased. He delights in your obedience, your courage, and every bold step you take in faith.

Today, align your heart with His. Fan the flame of your faith by remembering all the ways you're choosing to live by faith, not by sight. Let that remembrance fuel your next step. He sees you, and He's in it with you.

....

....

....

....

BOLD

Dream Stack: Choose one faith-filled action today that will bring you closer to your dream. Write it down. Make sure your choices reflect your faith—and let your steps give your dreams wings!

DAY 63

Beyond Balance: Embracing God's Perfect Alignment

[Jesus said,] 'But seek first the kingdom of God and his righteousness, and all these things will be added to you.'

—Matthew 6:33 ESV

BALANCE. WE ALL STRIVE FOR IT. We buy coffee mugs and T-shirts that celebrate it. We sign up for courses and read countless books to learn how to achieve it. Yet the more we pursue it, the more frustrated we become.

Personally, I've never liked the word *balance*. For many, it's their life mission! Yet for us as believers, this cannot be our goal in life. But if balance isn't the goal, why do we feel so compelled to chase it? And why do we fail so miserably in the process?

Balance, as it's commonly understood, means making everything even, giving equal weight and attention to every part of life. It's like seeing your life as a pie chart where each slice—work, family, faith, rest, health—gets the same amount of time, attention, and energy. Sounds practical, right? Work hard; play hard.

But here's the thing—it doesn't work.

This kind of balance often leads us straight into misplaced priorities and false responsibility. We start believing it's our job to keep everyone together and everything running smoothly, to hold all the pieces together, and to never let any of the balls drop.

Before we know it, we've made ourselves the center of it all—as if life is supposed to revolve around us. And because we're trying to give everyone and everything equal attention, we end up drained, distracted, and disconnected. That's why we feel pulled when we're at work, like we should be at home. And when we're home, we feel like we should be doing more.

It splits our focus, drains our energy, and—maybe worst of all—it keeps us stuck managing everything instead of moving forward in what actually matters. And that kind of constant juggling? It doesn't just cost us time—it costs us our peace, our potential, and ultimately, our greatness. In fact, you won't find the word *balance* (at least how we are defining it) anywhere in Scripture. Trust me—I've looked.

When we stretch ourselves too thin in the name of balance, we end up diluting the very thing God is trying to do through us. Ask any new parent if they feel balanced. They'll laugh. Ask an athlete in training or a missionary on assignment. Ask Paul, Moses, or Noah. None of them lived balanced lives. You cannot be both balanced and great, nor can you be balanced and fully on mission for God. That doesn't mean you pile more on your plate. It means you get clear on what really matters, and you learn to prioritize what God is calling you to and releasing what He's not.

This is called *alignment*.

Alignment comes from doing the right things, in the right order, in the right season, with God at the center. Today's Scripture speaks directly to this and shows us that true Kingdom alignment takes the emphasis off ourselves, other people, and our circumstances and puts it where it needs to be: on *the kingdom of God and His righteousness*. It shifts the focus off you and back onto Him. It's not about managing the parts of your life equally—it's about stewarding your whole life intentionally.

In the *Oxford English Dictionary*, alignment means "a position of agreement or alliance." Alignment means positioning yourself in alliance with God and seeking Him above all else. It means being in agreement with what He says and His order for your life. This kind of alignment means focusing on what matters most—your relationship with God, your relationships with the people He's brought into your life, His calling on your life, and His purpose for you. It's about aligning yourself with His dreams and visions for your life rather than chasing after the world's version of success or significance. Focus on His will over your will, His timing over your timing.

In my own life, this truth changed everything after the birth of my fifth child. I was learning to parent five kids, manage a team, write, be a wife, and homeschool, plus attempting to get a workout in, and, oh yeah, sleep. I was pushing myself to the limits, trying to keep everything balanced. My attempt at balance fell apart, not because I couldn't handle it all, but because my eyes had drifted away from Jesus. I was losing heavenly perspective. In that season, I realized that balance wasn't the answer—alignment was.

When you align with God's heart, your heart becomes like His. Your desires and dreams reflect His desires for you. As you do this, you begin to trust that He will add everything you need in the right order and according to His perfect timing because He is a good and faithful Father. Ultimately, this posture allows you to surrender your need to balance the things around you and instead, align the things within you. Alignment is divine order.

All progress happens when we prioritize God's Kingdom first. Therefore, don't seek balance, which keeps you focused on what's going on around you. Instead, seek alignment, which keeps you focused on Him, then *all these things will be added to you*.

This is the better way.

Day 63 Beyond Balance: Embracing God's Perfect Alignment

Revel: What would it look like for you to let go of the idea of balance and instead seek alignment with the Lord? How can you prioritize your relationship with Him and trust Him with every detail of your life?

Spend some time reflecting on this, then begin to reorder your life according to His priorities, knowing that your life depends on it (because it does). Then use your dream stacking time to reflect the next best aligned steps to take!

....

....

....

....

Align: All right, I know I say this every day, but it's that time again: alignment check! Look back on yesterday—did you take any intentional steps toward your dream? Were you doing the right things, in the right order, in the right season, with God at the center of it all?

Today, take a moment to sit with this deeper revelation of alignment. Let God shift you further into His grace, deeper into His plan, and fully into His will and His way. Because alignment isn't just about action—it's also about posture. And He's always ready to lead when we're ready to follow.

....

....

....

....

BOLD

Dream Stack: What's one aligned step you can take that moves you closer to your dreams? Write it down and go have some fun, would ya?!

....

....

....

....

DAY 64

Awkward Until Awesome

[David said,] 'I will become even more undignified than this, and I will be humiliated in my own eyes.'

—2 Samuel 6:22

THE OTHER DAY, MY SON looked at me and said, "Mom, you're so awkward."

Ouch. Let's be real—no one enjoys being called awkward, especially not by their own child. We all want to seem like we've got it together. We want people to affirm us, to look at us and think, "Wow, they've really got this!" But if we're being honest, that desire to appear confident and competent often stems from insecurity and a longing for approval. It's not really about what we think of ourselves; it's about what others think of us.

Sure, that's a normal human tendency. But as believers, we're called to live a *new* way—a way that values God's opinion above all else.

So my response to my son was, "Yep, I'm awkward ... but I'm on my way to awesome!" Truth be told, he wasn't wrong. I was a bit awkward when I was learning something new. Second truth to be told, awkward is temporary. It is not the destination—awesome is!

Here's another truth: On the road to fulfilling God's promises for your life, you're going to do a lot of things awkwardly at first. That's just part of the process. No one started out great. No one extraordinary started out that way. This isn't even a spiritual matter, it's for real in any area of our lives as we try something new or strive for greatness.

Far too often, we don't chase after our dreams or take a risk of being awkward because we care so much about what other people think. You don't chase your dreams to look cool in someone's eyes; you chase your dreams because you are being obedient to the Lord! Think about Peter walking on water, or Noah building the ark. Neither of them were experts when they started. And if we're being honest, they probably looked downright crazy at times. Or how about my favorite example—David dancing before the Lord

As we see in the book of 2 Samuel, chapter 6, something powerful unfolds as we see David embracing this awkward until awesome journey. After a long and complicated journey—one marked by both tragedy and reverence—David finally brings the Ark of the Covenant to Jerusalem, the very symbol of God's presence among His people. This moment wasn't just political or ceremonial—it was deeply personal and profoundly spiritual.

Overcome with joy and awe, David danced before the Lord with all his might. He didn't hold back. He wasn't concerned with appearances. He was completely unashamed and undignified, expressing wholehearted worship in response to God's faithfulness. When Michal, daughter of Saul, criticized him for looking foolish, I love the purity of how David responds in today's Scripture:: *I will become even more undignified than this.*

David didn't care about looking dignified or keeping up appearances. Why? Because it wasn't about him. It wasn't about what other people thought. It was about fulfilling

God's purpose for Him. David was willing to sacrifice his ego, his reputation, and his need for approval to do what God called him to do.

That's the key for you too. You have to surrender your need for validation from others, your desire to look good, and your fear of looking foolish. You have to be willing to embrace the awkwardness, so God can do something awesome in and through you.

Will people think you're awkward? Yep.

Will people call you undignified? Probably.

Don't do it for them; do it for the Lord!

When you start something new, it's not going to be perfect. You won't have all the answers, and it will probably be messy. But when you're connected to something bigger—when you're aligned with God's purpose for your life—those things don't matter anymore. Embrace your awkward beginnings, don't shame the messy middle, and don't let insecurity keep you from stepping into the awesome things God has planned for you.

Make sure your heart is in the right place, put your eyes on Jesus, and dance—undignified and unashamed—before the Lord.

It's OK to be messy on your way to the miracle.

It's OK to be awkward on your way to awesome.

Revel: Is there something God is calling you to do, but fear of feeling unqualified or uncomfortable is holding you back?

Today, I encourage you to release the need for approval and embrace the awkward, uncomfortable beginnings, trusting that God will produce amazing results in His perfect timing. Remember, no one starts off great—God shapes us and grows us through the journey.

Day 64 Awkward Until Awesome

Align: Let's rewind—how did you show up yesterday? Did your actions move you even a little closer to the dream God's placed in your heart?

If not, there's no shame—just clarity. What got in the way? What slowed you down or pulled you off course?

Now ask yourself: What needs to shift today so you can move forward with focus, intention, and alignment? Because every day is another chance to course-correct and chase what matters most.

Dream Stack: Today, be like David—unapologetic, unashamed, and even undignified—as you go after your dreams. They might look crazy to everyone else, but they are beautiful to God.

Identify one step you can take today that pulls you out of your comfort zone and into your dream zone. Write it down. Make it happen. (And remember, comfort is boring—and it's the enemy of all progress.)

DAY 65

Less Is More

And he sent them out to proclaim the kingdom of God and to heal the sick. He told them: 'Take nothing for the journey—no staff, no bag, no bread, no money, no extra shirt.'

—Luke 9:2–3

WE LIVE IN A CULTURE that constantly tells us, that more is better. More stuff, more success, more followers, more recognition—this is what the world says will make us happy, valued, and fulfilled. But if you ask anyone who has achieved more, they'll tell you that it's often a mirage, a chase with no end. This constant craving for more creates a never-ending cycle—want more, do more, spend more, need more, and on and on. There's got to be a better way.

There is! In His wisdom, Jesus always offers a different way—and we see it clearly in today's passage from the book of Luke. Jesus sent His disciples out with a mission, just as He's sent you. Only He didn't tell them to gather more resources or to prepare with endless supplies. Instead, He gave them purpose then told them the opposite of the cultural norm. He told them *to proclaim the kingdom of God and to heal the sick*. And immediately after, He said something radical: *"Take nothing for the journey."*

This was Jesus's way of teaching us, His disciples, one of the most profound lessons in life—less is more. God isn't opposed to your having nice things or wanting more things. But He is deeply concerned when *those* things start having you.

If we look at this lesson, we see that He wasn't asking the disciples to have less for the sake of having less; He was asking them to have less for the sake of *depending on Him more*. He was inviting them into deeper trust and intimacy, stripping away their reliance on worldly things, so they could discover that everything they needed was already found in Him.

If we look closely, the five items Jesus specified they not bring—staff, bag, bread, money, and extra shirt—all represent things we often turn to for our own safety, security, stability, provision, sustenance, and self-sufficiency. But in each of these areas, Jesus wants to be our source. He isn't teaching us to go without; He is teaching us that He, Himself, will provide everything we need.

Jesus's invitation for us to journey with Him and be on mission for Him means walking even more in our God-given purpose. Though this is the greatest ride we could ever go on, it often requires us to let go of excess attachments we have on the things around us, our baggage, if you will—both physically and emotionally. It's about learning that less really is more when we're connected to the true source of life. Jesus isn't unaware of the needs you have, but He doesn't want those things to have you.

As an example, imagine you're a climber with the ultimate goal of summiting Mount Everest. No matter how eager you are, you can't scale the mountain in a single day. You must acclimate at several base camps along the way, allowing your body to adjust to the changing elevation. This process is essential—not only do you need to adapt to the lower oxygen levels, but each stop is also an opportunity to rest and release unnecessary gear. The higher you climb, the lighter your load becomes. It's not that the gear wasn't helpful up to that point; it's that what worked at the lower elevations isn't needed for the final ascent.

In much the same way, the tools, strategies, attachments, and mindsets that brought you to where you are now may not be what you need to take you to where God is leading you next. As you grow and follow His call, you may need to let go of things that once served you but are no longer necessary for the higher places He's taking you. The higher you go, the more you must rely on Him, and the less you can hold onto things of this world. This is why Jesus tells us not to store up treasures on earth but to store up treasures in heaven (Matthew 6:19–20). The treasures of this world—whether material possessions, accomplishments, or our old ways of thinking—can weigh us down if we're not willing to release them when it's time to climb higher.

Today, Jesus is calling you to let go of anything that competes for the place only He should hold in your heart. When you loosen your grip on worldly attachments and reconnect to the source—God Himself—you realize that less truly is more, because in Him, and you find everything you need.

Climb higher with confidence—carry less; trust more!

■ ■ ■ ■ ■ ■

Revel: Take some time to reflect on your heart. Are there things holding space that only the Lord should occupy? Identify anything that might be taking His place. Then repent, release what's no longer needed, and reconnect with your true source—Jesus.

Day 65 Less Is More

Align: Time for a little soul-searching and goal-checking! Did you take a step toward your dream yesterday—or did you hit that snooze button all day long? If something tripped you up, name it, claim it, and course-correct.

Here's the deal: Whether you crushed it yesterday or not, don't let yesterday distract you from today. Get back in alignment, shake off any dust, and step it up—one faith-filled foot in front of the other. Your dream's not on pause ... unless you are.

....

....

....

....

Dream Stack: Today, what's one action that will allow you to climb higher, bringing you closer to your dream? Take a deep breath, write it down, then make it happen.

....

....

....

....

DAY 66

Authority

When the seventy missionaries returned to Jesus, they were ecstatic with joy, telling him, 'Lord, even the demons obeyed us when we commanded them in your name!' Jesus replied, 'While you were ministering, I watched Satan topple until he fell suddenly from heaven like lightning to the ground. Now you understand that I have imparted to you my authority to trample over his kingdom. You will trample upon every demon before you and overcome every power Satan possesses. Absolutely nothing will harm you as you walk in this authority.'

—Luke 10:17–19 TPT

TODAY MARKS AN INCREDIBLE milestone—Day 66 of your daily journey of dreaming with God! In my course *Arise & Align: Master Your Morning Routine*, I talk about research that proves habits are often solidified in sixty-six-day cycles. Good job—you did that!

For the past sixty-five days, you have been doing hard things—creating new habits, beating the odds, staying committed to dreaming with God, and taking consistent action toward those dreams. This is a moment to acknowledge your perseverance and growth. You are not just thinking about dreaming; you are also doing something about your dreams! You're now walking in new levels of authority.

Authority! That's a bold word.

But did you know that you have been given the authority of heaven? This divine authority empowers us as believers to act in Jesus's name doing what He's called us to do. We see this in today's Scripture.

Talk about authority! But what exactly does authority look like in our daily lives?

Authority is defined in *The Concise Oxford English Dictionary* as "the power or right to give orders, make decisions, and enforce obedience." Based on this definition and Jesus's own words, we must recognize that He has imparted His authority to us. He has given us the power and the right not only to make decisions but also to enforce Biblical obedience. This is an enormous mission for us as His church, yet it's one He gave to us. If we fail to fully understand this, we risk shrinking back and surrendering unnecessarily to the enemy's schemes.

With that in mind, it's important to understand that the authority we've been given enables us to play proactively. We are not here to react to the schemes of the enemy. He doesn't happen to us; we happen to him. Just like in a game of basketball, there's a difference between offense and defense. Offense moves forward, takes ground, and scores; defense reacts to prevent the opposing team from advancing. As believers, Jesus has already played our defensive game by defeating death and sin on the cross. He now passes the ball to us and tells us to go—to advance with confidence in the authority He's given us.

Too many believers today live defensively, reacting to the enemy's schemes rather than actively taking the ground God has promised us. Jesus said clearly: *'I have imparted to you my authority.'* It's time for us to live on offense in the authority we've been given.

Additionally, the authority of Jesus empowers us to say no to the forces of hell and yes to the promises of heaven. This means we have the power to trample over demonic forces. Jesus said, *'You will trample upon every demon before you and overcome every power*

Satan possesses.' As we go into all nations with His authority, we don't just proclaim the good news—we break strongholds, demolish arguments that oppose the name of Jesus, and destroy the enemy's works. I am here to remind you that we are not a weak church; we walk in the authority God has given us.

It's time to step into that authority, to live like we mean it! If you wax and wane in this, or when the enemy tries to defeat you with destructive words and phrases around your identity, simply remember *who you are because of whose you are*. You are a child of God, and your Father has empowered you to trample over the enemy's plans. Don't stand still in moments of struggle—pray with authority, take action with authority, and watch as God moves through you. Authority is active; it's a movement, and as "a body in motion stays in motion," so too does a church in motion stay in motion.

Today, walk in the fullness of your authority, continue saying no to hell and yes to heaven.

Now let's play ball!

Revel: How can you stop playing defense and start living more on offense in the spiritual authority God has given you? What areas of your life need you to say no to the enemy's lies and yes to God's promises?

Start today by reflecting upon the authority you've been given, then in your dream stacking time, step out in your God-given authority and watch God move.

Day 66 Authority

Align: Let's take a minute to reflect on yesterday and consider where you said no to the enemy and yes to the things of the Lord.

Did you take a step toward your dream—your yes to God's calling? I have a feeling you did.

Now ask yourself: What helped me stay in that yes mindset? How can you keep operating from that same space today—faith-filled, focused, and fully aligned?

Once you've tasted the power of a God-aligned yes ... you will never want it any other way!

....

....

....

....

Dream Stack: How can you create even more momentum today by walking in even greater authority?

Decide on one action that will bring you closer to your God-given dream. It doesn't have to be massive—it just has to be meaningful. That one step can create a ripple effect. That one decision can be the spark that ignites a movement—not just around you but within you. Write it down, then go make it happen!

....

....

....

....

DAY 67

Presence

Every evening I will explain my need to him. Every morning I will move my soul toward him. Every waking hour I will worship only him, and he will hear and respond to my cry.

—Psalms 55:17 TPT

HAVE YOU EVER STARTED YOUR DAY off right feeling filled up, peaceful, and in the presence of God only to find yourself drained by the time the day ends? Or have you ever been in worship feeling energized by the Spirit only to feel empty again once you step outside the four walls of the church?

If we're not careful, we may think that the filling of the Holy Spirit is a one-time event. We may assume that we're filled up only during our quiet time, worship sets, or in our designated time with God. But the truth is, God promises to be with us every moment of every day. So why do we feel so filled up in one moment and so drained the next? Why do we sometimes struggle throughout the day to keep the peace we felt in the morning? It's because we need to learn how to bridge the gap—and we need to expect God to do what He promises He will do.

David's life offers us a raw, real framework for this. He was no stranger to emotional highs and lows. I love him, because I can relate to him—one moment he was rejoicing in God's goodness; the next he was crying out in despair. But despite these ups and downs, David kept pursuing God with an unwavering heart. His life was not defined by his circumstances but by his commitment to seek God's presence.

In today's Scripture, David shows us the power of what I call bridging the gap. Every evening, he comes before God, pouring out his heart and expressing his need. By morning, something shifts—his soul moves toward God, drawing fresh strength from Him. And it gets even better. We see David, every waking hour, worshiping the Lord with full confidence, knowing that God hears him and responds.

What a picture. David models what it looks like to live in constant communion with the Lord—from morning to evening and every moment in between. A life that doesn't visit God occasionally but stays aligned with Him hour by hour. Consider this divine framework to bridge the gap:

Every evening I will explain my need to him. What would it look like to explain your need to God and not just at nighttime but anytime? To unapologetically and honestly pour out your heart to Him? Too often we either ignore our emotions or give them too much power. But David exemplifies how to do this without allowing his emotions to define him. He expresses his feelings but doesn't let them take control. David shows us how to give our needs to God trusting that He hears and holds us close.

Every morning I will move my soul toward him. Allow God to see all of you. Every part of you—your thoughts, emotions, desires, and even your overwhelm. Picture yourself sitting with Him, laying it all out honestly—no filter, no fixing. Just you and Him, connecting.

And don't stop there— pause in the middle of your day as well. Don't let it be a brief encounter—think of it as a constant partnership throughout the day. It's not about coming to Him for a quick fill-up then rushing off to the next task. He wants to walk with you through every moment. He wants you to connect with Him, to be one with Him.

Every waking hour I will worship only him, and he will hear and respond to my cry. Instead of compartmentalizing our time with God—experiencing Him only in our quiet moments or in worship—David teaches us to live in a constant awareness of God, *every waking hour* as we worship Him and only Him. This is the way to bridge the gap. When you invite Him into every part of your day, you experience His presence continuously, not as an isolated moment but as a constant companion.

Picture standing beneath the rush of a waterfall. The water envelops you, touching every part of you, and you cannot escape its flow. In the same way, when you invite God into every detail of your day, you allow His grace, peace, and love to saturate your every action, conversation, and decision. Instead of standing on the outside of that waterfall holding a bucket and filling up only when you run dry, step into the waterfall's flow of His presence that's already there. Immerse yourself in it. Immerse yourself in Him, allowing Him to cascade over every aspect of your life.

In the good moments, He is there celebrating with you. In the hard moments, He is there comforting you. This is what David meant when he said, *he will hear and respond to my cry.* As long as you stay conscious of His presence, you can sit back, relax, and trust that He is God. This continuous connection with Him, day in and day out, bridges the gap, allowing His presence to guide, strengthen, and sustain you through every part of your day.

So when you find yourself stressed or overwhelmed during the day, remind yourself to realign and reconnect with this partnership with God. Allow Him to envelop you, touching every part of you. Just as a waterfall never ceases to pour out water, God's presence unceasingly cascades over every aspect of your life; it is not confined to one specific moment of prayer or worship. It's not just a trickle that appears when you make time for Him—it's a continuous outpouring that drenches your heart, mind, and soul.

See your relationship with the Lord as an all-day, every-day journey. Experience His presence 24/7 flowing over every aspect of your life.

Day 67 Presence

Revel: Picture yourself under the cascading waterfall of God's presence. Like David, pour out your heart to Him right now—your needs, fears, and dreams. Move your soul toward Him as you invite Him into every part of your day. Then commit to worshiping Him throughout your day. If it's challenging, set reminders to pause and praise Him. Watch how He fills you with His peace as you continually invite Him into your routine.

Align: As you reflect on yesterday, pause and sit under His waterfall of grace. Don't just think about what you did—reflect on who He is.

Let His grace wash over you, then rise up and ask: What can I shift today to move forward in alignment with Him? Because His presence doesn't just reveal the gaps—it empowers you to bridge them.

Dream Stack: What's one thing you can do today to move closer to the dream God has placed on your heart? Write it down. As you stand under His waterfall of grace, let it wash away striving, doubt, and fear. Let His presence refresh your perspective. Then from that place of overflow, do the thing.

....

....

....

....

DAY 68

Faithful Friendship

Faithful are the wounds of a friend, but deceitful are the kisses of an enemy.

—Proverbs 27:6 NKJV

I RECENTLY HEARD A STATEMENT that hit me hard: "Most friendships are built out of convenience."

It's sad yet undeniably true. Think about your circle of friends. We all have friends who live near us, attend the same church, have kids in the same schools, or work in the same place. It's easy to be friends with them, at least when schedules line up. Though there's nothing wrong with these connections, we need to be cautious not to settle for surface-level friendships built out of convenience that lack depth and maturity.

Let's be real—true friendship isn't always easy to find, and it can be even harder to keep. That's because it's not just built in the good times—it's also tested and strengthened in the hard ones. Real friendship requires consistent commitment, vulnerability, and intentionality.

Too often we see friendships fall apart after one disagreement, a tough season, or even something as simple as switching churches, changing jobs, or relocating.

Yet friendship is a gift designed by God to enrich our lives, not just in the fun moments but also in the difficult ones. The Bible is full of examples of deep friendships—David and Jonathan, Ruth and Naomi—relationships where loyalty, encouragement, and faithfulness were at the core. Today's Scripture speaks to this profound truth. It reveals that true friendship goes beyond shared interests and laughter, convenience, or surface-level conversations; it's about supporting each other, lifting one another up, walking through life's highs and lows together, and being faithful to one another. The word *faithful* means to remain loyal, steadfast, and true—to the facts, to the original, and to what is right—holding to God's truth, even when it's hard.

Today's Scripture reminds us that a godly friend doesn't simply tell us what we want to hear—they also tell us what we need to hear, words that are inspired by the Lord. Their words may sometimes sting in the moment, but they are meant to heal, protect, and sharpen us.

True friendship in Christ is rooted in truth, not flattery. It's the kind of love that risks discomfort for the sake of calling us higher, closer to the heart of God. And though the easy route might be silence or sweet-sounding words, a faithful friend chooses honesty—even when it costs them—because they love you enough to care about your soul more than your comfort.

This truth challenges us and causes us to consider: Are we surrounding ourselves with people who love us enough to speak the truth, even when it's hard? Are we going to always get it right? Of course not. Do not confuse faithful friend with perfection. Yet it is a higher call for both parties involved to walk in loyalty, steadfastness, and honesty.

Godly friends simply reflect the glory of God to one another and express the voice of God to one another.

Unfortunately, many of us weren't taught how to do this, nor did we have many friends who actively practiced this. But as I've grown in my relationship with God, I've realized how important this is, and I've become way more intentional with my friendships. I now have friends who not only speak encouragement into my life but also speak God's truth. They know my weaknesses, they pray for me through the good and the hard, and they hold me accountable to who God says I am. They've seen my failures but remain steady and faithful. I've learned to do the same. That is the kind of friendship that helps us grow and walk in the calling God has for us. This may be new for you, but it doesn't mean you can't learn how to do it.

Friendship matters, because God didn't design us to walk through life alone. We were created for connection, to love and be loved, to encourage and be encouraged. In a world that often prioritizes independence, friendship reminds us that we are stronger, braver, and better together. And I propose that friendship is also given to us by God to treat with the utmost respect and to speak the honest truth of God over one another's lives.

Today, I encourage you to embrace faithful friendships. Though it takes some work and effort, you'll be glad you did. The path won't seem as lonely, the jokes will be funnier, the ups and downs won't be as scary, and the moments of celebration will be much more fulfilling.

Revel: Take a moment to reflect on your friendships. Are these relationships encouraging you to grow and aligning you with the purpose of God for your life? Do they call you higher and speak truth to you?

Now turn the reflection inward—what kind of friend are you? Are you faithful, speaking truth in love to those around you? Ask God to reveal areas where you can grow in being a Christ-like friend, embodying His heart for the people He's entrusted to you.

Today, take a step—whether through a simple text, call, or act of kindness—to connect with the faithful friends He's placed around you.

Day 68 Faithful Friendship

....

....

Align: Reflect on yesterday—did you take any steps toward your dream? If not, identify what held you back and find a way to realign and overcome today.

....

....

....

....

Dream Stack: What's one thing you can do today to move your dream forward? Write it down. Then reach out to a faithful friend and take that step together!

....

....

....

....

DAY 69

Choose Wisely

Be very careful, then, how you live—not as unwise but as wise, making the most of every opportunity, because the days are evil.

—Ephesians 5:15–16

LIFE IS INTERESTING IN THAT circumstances are not biased. The weather, the wind, the trees aren't swayed by preference. But we, as humans, are *super* biased.

Think about the last time you woke up to a cold, dreary, snowy morning seven days in a row. Maybe it's just me, but by the seventh day, it causes me to think, *Ugh, this is a terrible day!* Or how about a day where the sun is shining, the birds are chirping, and you just know today is *your day?*

It reminds me of a trip I took with my director of operations to Phoenix, Arizona. While she went to serve, I wanted to get some sun. I had spent months in cold, snowy weather, and my soul was longing for warmth. But the weather didn't cooperate—we had three days of rain and below average temperatures. My team member, who's from Tillamook, Oregon, is used to rain, so she was thrilled with the occasional small patch of sun and said, "Wow, what an incredible day!" Meanwhile, I was disappointed and grouchy. The difference between us was how we *chose* to interpret that day based upon the weather.

This is the reality: Every experience in life is just that—an experience. It carries no inherent meaning until we assign it one. The meaning we attach to each experience comes from our interpretation, which then influences our decisions, often without us realizing it.

For example, if I decide that cloudy weather is bad and choose to feel grumpy, my day will likely follow suit. The grumpiness doesn't stem from the weather itself but from my interpretation of it. On the other hand, if I choose joy despite the gloomy skies, my day may feel lighter and more fulfilling. The weather remains unchanged, but how I interpret and respond to it determines the quality of my day. In the same way, the quality of your day is determined by the choice you make.

The instructions in today's verse, though clear and concise, are easy to overlook. But Paul is helping us understand how to live our lives to get the most out of it. So if you are a junkie for living your best life and you believe in making it better every day, this is for you.

When Paul says, *Be very careful,* he means to see or discern. But this isn't just about vision or perception; it's also suggesting an action, representing something we do. He's encouraging us to actively watch and discern how we are living. Then he goes on to say, *not as unwise*—meaning don't live in a way that's foolish, reckless, or without considering the consequences. He's also implying that we don't disregard God's guidance and wisdom or essentially make poor decisions based on a lack of understanding or good judgment from the Lord. This may be as reckless as doing the wrong thing even when you know it's wrong or not considering God's will as you decide which steps to take.

Then Paul says to live *as wise,* defining wisdom in this context as *making the most of every opportunity. Every* means all. Not some, not only the perfect moments, nor the ones where all the stars align, but *every* single moment. And *seizing* it, grabbing it with all you've got. Wisdom is seeing the opportunity to do God's will no matter who you are, where you are, what you're doing, or what challenges or obstacles life may throw at you. Making the most of an opportunity doesn't mean choosing the easiest path; it means choosing the path that aligns with God's will.

The beauty—and challenge—of life is that every moment, we have the opportunity to make the most of it! Paul is not saying that to frustrate us or to pretend hard, gloomy days don't happen. He gives us truth wrapped in hope. He's not downplaying whatever you might be going through; he's showing you the power of your choice despite the hardest of times.

God, in His love for us, has given us the opportunity to make choices, just as He did in the Garden of Eden. Adam and Eve had everything they needed, yet God gave them the opportunity to choose to follow His voice or not. God didn't desire a relationship based on control but one grounded in love, and love always offers the freedom to choose. God doesn't force our hand—He lays out the path of life and death before us, urging us to choose wisely, but ultimately, the choice is ours. Just as any true relationship is built on mutual trust and freedom, so is our relationship with Him. He desires that we choose Him out of love, not obligation, reminding us that wise decisions lead to life, and unwise ones lead to destruction.

This means life is not happening *to* you; it's happening *for* you, and God is working for your good (Romans 8:28) *if* you choose to see it that way. Life is a collection of circumstances, and God gives you the opportunity in each to make wise choices—or not. The real question is not, "Why is this happening to me?" but "How will I choose to respond?" Will you choose to respond as Jesus would?

Not as unwise but as wise, making the most of every opportunity, because that's who you are.

The hard news is that gloomy days will happen; the great news is, how you interpret them and respond to them is within your control. You can't always control what happens, but you do have the opportunity to choose your response. This creates endless opportunities for growth and alignment with God's will, no matter what happens.

God doesn't promise things will happen the way we want, but He gives us the opportunity to choose wisely. This is your day; what will you choose?

Day 69 Choose Wisely

Revel: How are you really doing most days—are you living wisely and making the most of each situation?

Take a moment to ask God to reveal any areas where you may not be making wise choices or where you're relying on your own understanding. Surrender those areas to Him and allow Him to renew your mindset. Today, choose to walk in wisdom and let His guidance shape your decisions.

....

....

....

....

Align: Today's passage reminds us to make the most of every opportunity—to choose wisely. Now take a moment and reflect on yesterday—did you take a step, even a small one, toward the dream God's placed in your heart? If so, what was the choice? Write it down and take note.

If not, pause and ask yourself: What held me back? Was it fear, distraction, doubt, or simply a missed moment? Then today, choose to align your actions with your purpose. Choose to be proactive, not reactive. Because each day is a fresh chance to move forward—and what you choose today shapes tomorrow.

....

....

....

....

Dream Stack: What's one wise step you can take that will bring you closer to your dream? Make note of it. Then make the decision to choose it—and live it out—in your actions today!

....

....

....

....

DAY 70

Worry

Do not be anxious about anything, but in every situation, by prayer and petition, with thanksgiving, present your requests to God.

—Philippians 4:6

IT'S NORMAL TO FEEL WORRIED AT TIMES. But many people have learned to cope with worry as though it is part of their life. I'm here to tell you that Jesus didn't die on the cross for us to merely cope with life's struggles or walk on the path of worry. He died so that we could have abundant life, a life that overcomes every tactic the enemy uses to distract us—including worry.

For us as believers, worry is ultimately a matter of perspective. Think about the last thing that weighed heavily on your mind. How often did you find yourself revisiting that thought? Worry has a way of cycling through our minds until it becomes overwhelming, stealing our peace throughout the day or keeping us awake at night. The more we focus on it, the bigger it seems to grow.

The key to overcoming worry is in shifting your focus. Whatever you think about, you focus on. Whatever you focus on expands. And whatever expands becomes the most dominant force in your life. This is why our problems often seem bigger than God. Not because they are, but because we give so much attention to what could go wrong or what has gone wrong, that the things we're thinking about become bigger than the thoughts we have about God. Our thoughts empower our worry, and suddenly, those worries overshadow the Lord's presence and promises.

So today, what are you focused on? Are you focused on the problem or on God's power? Are you focused on what's gone wrong or on His promises? Are you focused on the statistics or on His miracle-working potential? Are you focused on the darkness or on the light? Here's the truth: Your focus matters, and you can't allow your misaligned focus to reduce the power of God to fit the size of your worry.

The Bible doesn't promise us a life free from challenges or things to worry about, but it does give us the tools to overcome them. The moment worry comes knocking—and it will—today's Scripture shows us exactly what to do. Instead of focusing on everything we have to worry about, we're invited to turn to prayer.

In every situation, by prayer and petition, with thanksgiving, we are to *present [our] requests to God.* This is the authority we carry as children of God—not to be overwhelmed but to overcome using prayer.

This process is ultimately teaching you how to meditate on the Lord, not your worry.

If you've ever said, "I can't meditate," but you have worried, guess what?—you've already been meditating. Meditation is the practice of thinking deeply and focusing one's mind for a period of time. Therefore, worry is a form of meditation; you've just chosen the wrong subject matter.

Good news is, you're a fabulous meditator; the only thing you need to change is the subject of your meditation. Instead of worrying, focus on prayer—over and over again. Why? Because as you do, you shift your mind toward the power of the cross. You redirect your thoughts to align with God's truth and His promises. Then something amazing happens—your heart begins to fill with gratitude. Your spirit remembers what it has known all along: God is good. He is the alpha and the omega, the beginning and the end. He holds everything in His hands, including your life. As you pray and give thanks, God's Word promises this: *And the peace of God, which transcends all understanding, will guard your hearts and your minds in Christ Jesus* (Philippians 4:7).

This kind of peace, the kind we all crave, the kind that transcends our understanding means we must give up our right to understand. Peace in the Lord does not mean you will understand it all; it means you're choosing to focus on the One who does. Your focus on the Lord, not on an answer, will allow you to breathe deep and trust God even more. By exchanging your worry for prayer, you are ultimately changing what you're focused on, which changes what expands in your life. Focus on worry and you're going to get a life of worry. Focus on prayer and you're going to get a life filled with peace.

I don't know about you, but that's the woman of faith I want to be! Despite the wind, the waves, and the worry, I want to be the one who overcomes through persistent prayer, thanksgiving, and gratitude—leading me back to the stillness and peace found in the Lord.

Today, don't worry … pray!

Revel: What is one worry that's been weighing on your mind? How can you shift your focus from the problem to God's promises today, from worry to prayer?

Take time to pray about your concerns, thanking God in advance for His peace. Don't pray just for an answer; pray also for His presence. Then trust that, as you continually present your requests to Him, His peace will guard your heart and mind.

Day 70 Worry

Align: Take a moment to reflect on yesterday—did you take a step toward the dream God has placed in your heart, or did worry take the lead?

If you found yourself stuck in worry, it's time to realign. Shift your posture through prayer. Focus your mind, center your heart, and give it all to Him.

Today, choose prayer over pressure. Lay it all at His feet and move forward in faith, not striving. You weren't meant to carry it all. You were meant to bring it all to Him.

....

....

....

....

Dream Stack: What's one thing you can do today, even in the face of worry, that will move you closer to your dream? Write it down. Take the step, praying as you go, and get it done. Progress and prayer go hand in hand. You've got this.

....

....

....

....

DAY 71

Connection over Confidence

[The Lord said,] 'But blessed is the one who trusts in the Lord, whose confidence is in Him.'

—Jeremiah 17:7

IF I HAD A DOLLAR FOR EVERY TIME I've heard someone say, "I wish I had more confidence," I'd be rich. We live in a world that pushes us to believe that confidence comes from doing better, having more, or looking the part. So we chase after it: We work harder, buy new clothes, read more self-help books, and hire life coaches. Though these things can help temporarily, they don't provide sustainable confidence. So the more we have and the more we do, the less confident we actually feel. Why is that?

Because we're putting our confidence in the wrong things. We're relying on our own strength and our own resources, expecting a divine result from human effort. Your input determines your output, and if your confidence is built on things of this world, your foundation will always be shaky.

If you're placing your confidence in what you can acquire or possess—whether it's money, success, or approval—you'll always find yourself needing more. More shoes? You'll want more closet space. More money? You'll find more ways to spend it then only need more of it. More achievements? They'll give you a temporary boost, but they won't truly satisfy. The issue with relying on external things such as these is that you'll feel secure when you have them but insecure when you don't.

If you're placing your confidence in others—whether it's your spouse, the government, or even church leaders—remember that though they can support your life, they're not meant to be its foundation. You can't rely solely on them, because they're human too, and at some point, they will make mistakes or let you down. If your trust is entirely in them, your world will crumble when they fall short. They can't provide lasting security or stability, because they are resources, not the ultimate source.

Similarly, when you place your confidence in yourself—your skills, abilities, or appearance—there's always the chance of failure. No matter how skilled you are, you're still human, and there will be times when you fall short. Plus, there will always be someone who outshines you, which can leave you feeling inadequate. This happens because we're relying on ourselves rather than the One who holds us.

The confidence we seek can only come from trusting in God—the One who never changes, never fails, and who offers us security that is unshaken by circumstances. True confidence is found in knowing that no matter what we have or don't have, do or don't do, achieve or don't achieve, our security comes from Him. The Lord is the foundation of our life and today's passage reminds us of this.

When Scripture says, *Blessed is the one who trusts in the Lord*, that word *blessed* signifies a state of joy and well-being that comes only from fully relying on God. Though we may look to the things of this world to satisfy us or make us feel better about ourselves, true blessing comes when we trust in the Lord. *Trusts in the Lord* means relying on God's power, faithfulness, and promises. It's about prioritizing our faith in Him over our self-reliance. Yes, developing yourself and pushing your limits are great, but we can't let our own personal development take the place of faith in God. The truth is, we don't need more self-confident people—we need more God-confident people.

God-confident people are those *whose confidence is in Him*. Lasting confidence doesn't come from what we can do but trusting in what *He* can do. When your confidence is rooted in your trust in God, it doesn't matter how much you have or how successful you are. Your confidence isn't based on your performance or even a feeling; it's based on your connection to Christ. It isn't about having it all together or doing everything perfectly. It's about trusting in the One who does.

If you want more confidence today, draw closer to God. The strength of your connection with Him is what fuels the strength of your confidence. The closer you are to Him, the more unshakable your confidence will be. He's your firm foundation (Isaiah 33:6), your anchor in every storm (Hebrews 6:19), your safe place when life feels uncertain (Psalm 91:2). He's the One who made the heavens and the whole earth (Genesis 1:1–3), the alpha and omega, the beginning and the end (Revelation 22:13), and he knows every hair on your head (Matthew 10:30). He holds your pain, your dreams, your needs, and even your destiny. I don't know about you, but that is someone to be confident in.

Your goal isn't confidence in yourself—it's connection with the Lord.

Revel: Have you been struggling with self-confidence? Maybe your focus has been on the wrong things. Today, put your confidence in the Lord and choose connection with Him over self-confidence.

Take time today to prioritize your faith in God over your own skills and abilities. Intentionally connect with God—through prayer, reading His Word, or simply sitting in His presence. Ask Him to realign your heart as you place your confidence in Him.

Day 71 Connection over Confidence

Align: Look back on yesterday—did you take ground toward your dream? If something tripped you up, name it. Then guard your alignment today as if it matters—because it does. Spend a few minutes today closing your eyes, envisioning the dream He's placed inside you, and sensing His presence drawing near. Stay in that place—linger there—until you feel your heart come back into alignment with Him. Protect the path God has you on and move forward with bold intentionality. Then, from that place of alignment, dream stack it.

Dream Stack: Today, what is one step you can take that reflects the level of confidence you have in the Lord? Focus on His power, write it down, and get it done.

DAY 72

Kingdom Impact

The Lord is my shepherd, I lack nothing. He makes me lie down in green pastures, he leads me beside quiet waters, he refreshes my soul. He guides me along the right paths for his name's sake.

—Psalm 23:1–3

CAN YOU IMAGINE A WORLD full of men and women making an impact for the Kingdom of God? A world where we live out our God-given purpose in such a way that heaven touches earth. Where our influence as believers leaves a lasting, eternal mark—not just on people but also on culture, communities, and generations.

It's leadership that reflects Jesus. It's business that builds people. It's churches that go beyond the four walls of the building itself. It's parenting that makes disciples for generations. It's decisions driven by faith, not fear. Where bold dreams, big faith, and daily obedience create ripple effects for eternity. That's not only a world we should imagine; it's the kind of world we're called to build.

I believe our desire for Kingdom impact is vital in the years to come! *Vital!* Our heartfelt, real, authentic craving to see heaven on earth must increase. Our appetite for the impossible must grow. Our faith must expand. Our heart for people, God's purposes, His will must be bolder than ever before!

However, though the desire for Kingdom impact is vital in these times, we must be cautious not to confuse impact with success measured by numbers, achievements, or recognition. We must understand that if we want to make an impact for the Kingdom, we need to recognize that it has less to do with what we're doing out there and more to do with what God wants to do in here, within our heart.

Our real focus must not be solely on doing more for the Lord but also on deepening our intimacy with the Lord. Because true Kingdom impact doesn't come from striving; it flows from intimacy. The truth is, your greatest impact will not come from your abilities or efforts but from your connection to God. Your level of dreaming is tied to your level of freedom, and your level of freedom depends on your level of dependence on the Lord. This means that *your greatest impact is found in your quiet time with Him*—in your relationship with Him, not in your performance for Him.

The most transformative impact happens when we get still before God. We don't make an impact by pushing our agenda; we make an impact by being pulled by His graces. Instead of striving to do more for the Kingdom, we need to be with the king more.

Of all the characters in the Bible, King David stands out as a powerful example of someone who made a huge Kingdom impact, and if you notice in His life, He lived in constant pursuit of God's presence. He deeply longed for God's heart and was even called *a man after God's own heart* (1 Samuel 13:14). His influence wasn't just in his public victories; they also were in the quiet, intimate moments with the Lord. It was in those still places that he encountered God time and time again. In today's Scripture, we see a powerful example of this—and a clear invitation to live from that same beautiful framework.

The Lord is my shepherd. David begins by acknowledging that the Lord is his shepherd. This signifies a life of total surrender and trust in God's leading. David didn't rely on his own strength, abilities, or wisdom; he knew that his success and victory came from following the Lord's guidance. To make an impact for the Kingdom, we first must understand that God is our shepherd leading us through every season of life. Our plans, ideas, and strategies are secondary to being aligned with His will and purpose.

I lack nothing. David expresses that with God as his shepherd, he lacks nothing. Often we feel held back in making a Kingdom impact because we think we're lacking the resources, skills, or support. But David reminds us that in God, we have all that we need. If He calls you to something, He will provide for it. God is the source of every resource we need, and His provision is abundant. When we see Him as our source, we can confidently move forward, knowing that we lack nothing essential to fulfill His calling.

He makes me lie down in green pastures. Green pastures symbolize God's presence, a place of rest and sustenance. David understood that his greatest desire wasn't to make an impact but to be in the presence of God. True Kingdom impact flows from intimacy with God. Before we set out to do great things for Him, we must learn to be with Him, to rest in His presence, and to draw strength from His nearness as a lifestyle.

He leads me beside quiet waters, he refreshes my soul. The quiet waters David speaks of are peaceful and restful places where our souls can be refreshed and renewed. Impact in the Kingdom isn't about striving—it's about trusting in the shepherd who leads us to places of peace. As we follow Him, we are refreshed, and our strength is renewed. Kingdom impact flows out of a place of rest, not stress. In these quiet waters, our focus shifts from what we can do to what God can do through us.

He guides me along the right paths for his name's sake. David knew that God would guide him along paths of righteousness, leading him higher step by step. The phrase *circular paths* refers to the way shepherds lead their sheep up the hillside in spirals, slowly and steadily ascending. Likewise, God guides us along a path that may seem slow or repetitive at times, but it is purposeful. Each step is taking us closer to His heart and to the greater heights He has prepared for us. Even when the journey feels like we're going in circles, He is leading us upward, transforming us from glory to glory for the sake of His name.

David's impact for the Kingdom didn't come from his own strength but from his deep relationship with the Lord. He learned to trust God, rest in His presence, and follow His guidance. Like David, your greatest Kingdom impact doesn't begin with doing more out there. It begins with a heart fully surrendered to God in here. When your heart is aligned with His, the fruits of your life will naturally flow out into the world.

Make your ultimate goal to be a man or woman after God's own heart. Let this be your greatest place of impact!

Revel: Ask God to develop within you not just a heart for Kingdom impact but a heart that longs for Him above all else. If you've been so focused on making an impact that you've neglected getting quiet with the Lord, ask Him to realign your heart today. Seek intimacy with Him that surpasses anything you can do for Him.

....

....

....

....

Align: Take a moment to reflect on yesterday—not through the lens of what you didn't get done but through what you did. There were a hundred things pulling for your attention, but you still made choices that aligned with who God says you are and the dream He's called you to pursue. Honor that. Celebrate the progress, no matter how small.

Write it down. Let it remind you of who you're becoming. Then choose it again—with even more intention today. Alignment is built in the repetition.

....

....

....

....

Dream Stack: After spending time in the presence of God, ask Him, "What kind of impact do you want to make today, Lord?" Allow Him to guide you and then take one or maybe even two bold steps with Him. Write them down and make them happen.

DAY 73

Spiritual Gifts

He "ascended" means that he returned to heaven, after he had first descended from the heights of heaven, even to the lower regions, namely, the earth. The same one who descended is also the one who ascended above the heights of heaven, in order to begin the restoration and fulfillment of all things. And he has appointed some with grace to be apostles, and some with grace to be prophets, and some with grace to be evangelists, and some with grace to be pastors, and some with grace to be teachers. And their calling is to nurture and prepare all the holy believers to do their own works of ministry, and as they do this they will enlarge and build up the body of Christ. These grace ministries will function until we all attain oneness into the faith, until we all experience the fullness of what it means to know the Son of God, and finally we become one into a perfect man with the full dimensions of spiritual maturity and fully developed into the abundance of Christ.

—Ephesians 4:9-13 TPT

HAVE YOU EVER FOUND YOURSELF asking God, "What's your plan? When will you show up and fix all of this?" It's easy to assume that God will one day step in and make everything perfect. And yes, Scripture tells us that one day, He will return, as Revelation 19:11–16 describes so powerfully. But until that day comes, God's plan involves us. As we sit near Him, in an ever-abiding relationship with our shepherd, as we learned yesterday, our impact with the Lord and what He can do through our lives is infinite. Though He doesn't have to work through us, He chooses to. Therefore, it is an honor, a privilege, and a responsibility to respond to His call.

Today's passage in Ephesians reminds us that Jesus has done His part—He came, descended to earth, lived, died, resurrected, and ascended back into heaven. His ascension marked the beginning of the restoration of all things. But that restoration involves His church—you and me. Jesus did his part, so now what? Well, it means it's your turn. You are part of His plan, and these Scriptures tell us how—empowered by His grace gifts.

Scripture goes on to say that Jesus has appointed some to be apostles, prophets, evangelists, pastors, and teachers, each with a specific calling to nurture believers, helping them to grow spiritually and step into their own ministry. But their role isn't to do all the work—it's to empower the entire Church to participate in building up the body of Christ (Ephesians 4:15 TPT).

Many believe that these spiritual gifts were only for the early church, but Scripture is very clear. Every believer, not just those with titles, is called to action. We are all tasked with the job of maturing spiritually, growing into the fullness of Christ, and contributing to God's plan on earth by using these grace ministries, grace gifts, that are given to us by God.

A grace gift is a gift from God that is undeserved and given through faith in Jesus. You don't earn it; you receive it. Once received, then you have to use it. I theorize that we all have the gifts, yet few are using them.

Imagine having a beautifully wrapped gift in your hands—valuable, full of potential—yet you leave it unopened or, worse, open it but never use it. Your spiritual gifts are much like that. They matter, and so does your understanding of them. Just knowing about them isn't enough, nor is having them without using them. You must recognize what they are, develop them, and actively use them for the Lord's purposes. Your gifts play a vital role in God's plan, and without embracing and using them, you miss out on the impact you were created to make.

You are part of heaven's grand plan, called to actively participate in restoring everything back to God's design. This isn't just your purpose—it's your destiny. So when you encounter problems, don't wish or pray them away. And don't pass them off to your pastor or church. Instead, ask God how He's equipped you to be part of the solution. Perhaps He has given you the passion, the skills, and *the spiritual gifts* to create change. If you see obstacles, remember that God has empowered you to overcome them through His grace and by using the gifts He's given you.

As today's passage continues, we not only see the importance of the global church and the role of our spiritual leaders, but more important, we see that every one of us is called to be an active part of God's mission. We're not waiting for Jesus to come back and make everything perfect—He's waiting for us to rise up, mature, and build up His Kingdom on earth, one body of believers, unified. It's time for us individually and collectively to step up and step in.

God's plan for the restoration of all things involves you. Don't wait on the sidelines. Step into your calling. Grow in spiritual maturity and the awareness of the gifts He's given you. And together, let's build the Church and expand God's Kingdom on this side of eternity.

The plan is in motion, and you are a vital part of it.

■ ■ ■ ■ ■ ■

Revel: Take time to dive into the spiritual gifts outlined in Ephesians 4, where Paul describes the unique gifts Christ gives to strengthen and build up His body. Explore this chapter or perhaps 1 Corinthians 12, Romans 12, or 1 Peter 4 to deepen your understanding of the spiritual gifts and unlock new levels of insight.

As you reflect on your own life, consider the unique gifts God has placed within you. How can you use these to strengthen the people around you—whether at home, in your church, among your family, or within your community?

Day 73 Spiritual Gifts

Align: Let's celebrate your progress—did you take a step toward your dream yesterday? Even the smallest step matters!

And if you didn't—there's no stress, just growth. Today, don't focus on what you didn't do, pause and ask, What *did* I do? Reflect on it. Celebrate it. Stay committed to the journey. Because small wins, stacked daily, go a long way. Keep going—you're building something that lasts.

Dream Stack: Consider how your grace gift could support you in taking divine action today. What's one thing you can do today to move your dream forward by using a spiritual gift God has given you? Write it down and make it a priority. You will feel inspired and fulfilled!

DAY 74

Boundaries

For our struggle is not against flesh and blood, but against the rulers, against the authorities, against the powers of this dark world and against the spiritual forces of evil in the heavenly realms.

—Ephesians 6:12

I'VE NEVER BEEN FOND of the word *boundaries*. In fact, I think it reflects a concept that often sets us up to fail.

How many times have you read books, listened to podcasts, or searched for advice about setting boundaries? And how many of those strategies have actually worked long-term? Exactly.

The problem isn't with the concept itself but in how we approach it. A boundary is a line that marks where something ends and something else begins—a clear dividing line between the two. While well-intentioned, this mindset can lead us to operate from a place of fear. It becomes *you versus me,* creating unnecessary division, not just between people but also within ourselves. This is why boundaries often fail to foster the deep connection we crave in our relationships.

Boundaries often come from a reactive place: *You aren't treating me the way I want.* Fair enough. But this focuses on the other person's shortcomings rather than God's divine will. It's a protective mechanism that puts *us* in control but doesn't necessarily bring us more freedom, because it's rooted in fear. When we set boundaries out of fear or frustration, we don't build connection—we build walls. And fear, by nature, separates us from others and from God's plan for true connection.

Here's the thing—connection is the true goal of any relationship. So what if, instead of focusing on setting better boundaries, we shifted our focus to aligning with God's truth and living the way He's called us to live? A better word than boundaries might actually be *standards*. When we raise our standards to reflect heaven's standards, we begin to mirror God's heart in our relationships.

It's important to understand the difference: boundaries often emphasize what others *aren't* doing, while standards keep our focus on who God is—and who He's calling us to be. Boundaries can draw hard lines in the sand. But standards? They reflect a certain level of quality or expectation, often used as a measure or model for how something (or someone) should operate or be represented.

As believers, we're called to live in a way that sets a clear example—both to those in the faith and those outside of it. We're called to reflect the quality and character of Jesus in how we love, lead, and live. That's our purpose: to embody His standard in every area of our lives so that everything we do points back to Him.

Unlike boundaries, which are often reactive and designed to protect, standards are proactive and rooted in heaven's reality. Though boundaries are designed to defend, leaving most feeling more divided or defensive, standards ground us in God's truth, allowing us to call people higher from a place of love and conviction. Looking at the life of Jesus, we see how He remained perfectly aligned with the Father's will, while continually inviting others to do the same. For instance, in Matthew 16, the Pharisees frequently tested Jesus regarding the law (boundaries), but Jesus responded in a way that demonstrated His purpose wasn't to keep or break the law but to fulfill the law (standards). In Luke 5, when Jesus withdrew from the pressing crowds to pray, it wasn't about keeping people out (boundaries) but about maintaining closeness with God and nurturing His intimacy with the Father (standards).

So how do we live this out when we face difficult people or situations, especially when others repeatedly take advantage of us? It's natural to feel the need to draw a boundary and keep people at a distance. Though this instinct seems reasonable on the surface, we must remember that every challenge we face is spiritual at its core. Today's passage reminds us of that and helps us recognize the spiritual dimension behind our struggles, which allows us to approach people with a mindset aligned with God's truth.

This is where discernment and wisdom from God are essential. When we can see the spirit behind the conflict, we can respond in both love and authority as we set a heavenly standard. Setting a heavenly standard is about aligning with God's will, not reacting to someone else's behavior; therefore, our standards should reflect heaven's reality and draw us closer to the Father, transforming our behavior, while encouraging others to do the same. Fear keeps people out and perpetuates the behavior; love draws people in and transforms us. Therefore, a good standard calls everyone higher.

God never said it would be easy, but when we live by His standards, we find stability, because we are grounded in Him, standing on His truth. We are free because of His grace, not because of the control we try to maintain over others. When we align with heaven, we tap into a deeper, richer understanding of God's heart and are able to invite others into it. If they won't participate, then keep your heart pure, steadfast in the truth of the Father. Forgive relentlessly and remain focused on the path He's set before you. Follow Jesus's example: Point others to the truth, model a better way, and if they're unwilling to follow, continue to walk in grace and purpose. Stay rooted in love and conviction, trusting that your faithfulness to God's call will make an impact, whether others choose to join or not. Keep moving forward with a heart fully surrendered to Him. Jesus didn't come to make the world a better place by setting boundaries—He came to bring heaven to earth by aligning our reality with his. Let's partner with Him by living in that truth.

Today, I encourage you to look higher. Don't set boundaries—set standards that mirror heaven's truth. Don't wait for others to change—be the change who brings heaven's standard into your relationships and circumstances.

Day 74 Boundaries

■ ■ ■ ■ ■ ■ ■

Revel: Take time to pray and ask God to reveal where you've been setting boundaries out of fear rather than raising your standards in faith. As you begin to assess the best standards to set for your life, ask yourself, "Does this align with God's heart?" and adjust accordingly.

Ask Him to show you His heart for the relationships in your life and begin to align your will with His as you walk in new levels of forgiveness, love, truth, and freedom.

....

....

....

....

Align: Here we are, Day 74. That means you're seeing the progress, feeling the momentum, and doing the hard things!

Now let's shift gears. From here on out, it's no longer a question of if you're moving—because you are. It's time to track what you're doing. Because documenting your progress? That's how you build real trust and confidence. Tracking progress brings clarity, and clarity is what makes things move.

Take a moment and reflect on yesterday—what steps did you actually take toward your dream? I'm not asking if you did something... I'm asking what you did!

....

....

....

....

BOLD

Dream Stack: Today, what is one proactive step you can take to pull heaven down and bridge the gap between heaven's reality and yours? Get clear, write it down, and do it (because tomorrow, you will take accountability for it)!

....

....

....

....

DAY 75

What's Love God to Do with It?!

So now I live with the confidence that there is nothing in the universe with the power to separate us from God's love. I'm convinced that his love will triumph over death, life's troubles, fallen angels, or dark rulers in the heavens. There is nothing in our present or future circumstances that can weaken his love.

—Romans 8:38 TPT

WE'VE ALL HEARD COUNTLESS sermons on love—God's unconditional love, the power of love, and how we should walk in love. But I suggest that though we think we know a lot about love, our lives show we have a lot more to learn—or at least, we need to bring what we understand from a head level to a heart level.

I also suggest that our ability to dream and create without limits is directly tied to our level of freedom. And our level of freedom is directly related to how deeply we grasp God's love. The more you know and truly believe that you are loved, the freer you will be. Notice I didn't say "the more you feel loved," because you already are loved, fully and completely. You could do nothing more to earn it, nothing to lose it. It's not about how good you are, how much you do, or how proud you make God. It's about recognizing that you already are completely loved because of who He is. This love is based on His character, not how you perform. Knowing this truth is the key to freedom.

Romans 8 speaks to this truth—a powerful reminder of God's never-ending, all-consuming love. Verse 1 says, *So now the case is closed*. Imagine that—*the case is closed*. Once a legal case is closed, it's done. Yet many of us live as though we're constantly trying to reopen the case against ourselves, gathering evidence of why we're not good enough, why we need to do more or be more. But God is clear: The case is closed. When you gave your life to Christ, your mistakes, your past, your failures—He paid for them all.

The verse continues: *There remains no accusing voice of condemnation against those who are joined in life-union with Jesus, the Anointed One. For the 'law' of the Spirit of life flowing through the anointing of Jesus has liberated us from the 'law' of sin and death* (Romans 8:1–2 TPT). So when you feel overwhelmed by your past or get caught up in self-criticism, simply say, "The case is closed. Thank you, God." Respond with gratitude and stop revisiting what God has already forgiven.

That means you are free to live—not by the flesh—but by the *dynamic power of the Holy Spirit* (Romans 8:4 TPT). Yes, Jesus has given you freedom, but living in that freedom is a daily choice. Every day, you must proactively choose to walk by the Spirit, not by the flesh.

We do this by living in step with the *impulses of the Holy Spirit … motivated to pursue spiritual realities* (Romans 8:5 TPT). The more you set your mind on what's above—on heaven, on Jesus, on His love—the more you'll live from a place of freedom and peace. And that's exactly what you're training yourself in, day after day, here in this *BOLD*, daily dreaming devotional.

As today's Scripture so beautifully depicts, when you live from love and the truth that God's love has set you free, everything changes. You stop striving for approval, for success, or for validation. Instead, you begin to dream, live, and create from a place of freedom and confidence, knowing you are fully loved and accepted, no matter what.

This is more than a nice idea; it's the reality God wants you to walk in every day. Not only for your sake but also for this lost and dying world that needs an encounter with a loving God. Our world needs to see a love that is bold, radical, and unapologetic—a love that doesn't conform to the world's standards but is rooted in the unshakable truth that we are God's beloved children. How else will they see it but in and through your life? What a testimony!

Let His love be the foundation of your life and watch how it unlocks your ability to dream without fear, create without limits, and lead, live, and give wholeheartedly.

※ ※ ※ ※ ※ ※

Revel: Begin your reflection time with this statement: "Lord, show me your love for me."

Ask God to deepen your understanding of His love today. Let go of any old narratives of striving or proving yourself and live in the truth that the case is closed. You are free, you are loved, and you are called to live in that freedom. Pray for a greater revelation of God's love that moves from your head to your heart. And as you walk in this freedom, let it fuel your dreams, your creativity, and your calling.

Day 75 What's Love God to Do with It?!

Align: Reflect on yesterday—what steps did you take toward your dream? Count them. Stack them. Celebrate them. Then lift your eyes and dream on.

....

....

....

....

Dream Stack: With love as your foundation—unshakable, unwavering, and rooted in God's truth—what's one bold step you would take today, wholeheartedly and unapologetically, to pursue your dream? Identify one clear, courageous move that aligns with who you're becoming.

Clarify it. Write it down. Schedule it as if it matters—because it does. Stack the dream. One faithful step at a time.

....

....

....

....

DAY 76

Patience: There's Power in the Pause

[Job said,] 'The Lord gave and the Lord has taken away; may the name of the Lord be praised.'

—Job 1:21

ARE YOU PATIENT?

Actually, let me ask it a different way: If I asked the people who know you best, would they say you're patient?

And just so you know—"sometimes" or "on occasion" aren't real answers. And that's exactly where the problem shows up. Patience isn't something you have when everything is going according to plan. It's not tested when timing feels perfect or answers come easily. Patience shows up when you don't get your way. When things are delayed. When the answer is "not yet" or "wait."

Biblically, patience means enduring delays, difficulties, and even difficult people with grace, without giving in to anger, frustration, or hopelessness. It's about staying steady in hope, trusting that God's timing is perfect even when ours isn't.

Patience isn't just the ability to wait—it's also about how we wait.

So, I'll ask you again: Are you patient?

The Bible tells us that *whoever is patient has great understanding* (Proverbs 14:29). Great understanding comes from the ability to perceive the bigger picture, recognizing that acting in haste or anger often leads to poor decisions and consequences. When we are patient, we allow time for reflection, discernment, and listening to God's guidance. This kind of patience shows a depth of understanding about life, relationships, and spiritual truths that transcend immediate emotions or frustrations.

Let's consider the life of Job, a man whose story teaches us about the power of patience. Job was a wealthy man, deeply faithful to God, and blessed with a large family and many possessions. But in an instant, his entire life unraveled. In the book of Job, we see Satan challenge God, claiming that Job loved Him only because of the blessings he received. That's probably the first place we should stop and pause.

Could it be that this tactic of the enemy isn't something reserved for Job but a strategy used against anyone who, like Job, walks in deep faithfulness to God? Anyone who is pursuing their God-given dreams and making an impact for the Kingdom? The enemy wants to test the genuineness of our faith, to see if our love for God is conditional upon our blessings, success, or comfort.

Satan's challenge wasn't just about Job's circumstances—it was also about his heart posture. And it's a challenge that many of us, especially those who are committed to following God, may face in different forms. When everything is going well, it's easy to praise God, but what happens when life falls apart? What happens when our dreams seem delayed, our plans are interrupted, or we face unimaginable loss? The enemy's tactic is to convince us that our relationship with God is fragile and dependent on external blessings. He whispers, "If God really loved you, He wouldn't let this happen."

Then we see God allow Satan to test Job's faith. One thing after another, Job loses everything: his livestock, his wealth, his servants, his wife, and his children. To make matters worse, Job's health failed, and he was covered in painful sores. I know this is a challenging part to digest. It raises deep questions about suffering, temptation, and God's sovereignty. When we ask why God allowed Satan to tempt Job, we are diving into the mystery of how God's goodness and power coexist with human suffering and the existence of evil.

One reason God allows Satan to test Job is to demonstrate the purity and strength of Job's faith. Satan had implied that Job worshiped God only because of the blessings and protection he received. God allows the test to prove that Job's faith is genuine and not based on his material blessings or favorable circumstances. This teaches us that true faith is not transactional—it doesn't depend on what we receive from God but rests on trust in who God is, even when life turns upside down. Though it can be hard to intellectually understand, Job's story should stir up our faith, as it shows us that real faith in God can endure even the most extreme hardships.

We see in today's Scripture, despite all this tragedy, Job chose to worship God instead of giving in to despair. Job's ability to pause in the midst of unimaginable loss shows us the true meaning of patience—trusting God even when we don't understand.

In our fast-paced world, it's easy to become impatient when things don't go our way. Whether it's a difficult relationship, a tough season in your career, or waiting for a breakthrough in your personal life, we can be tempted to rush ahead, get frustrated, or even give up hope. But patience is your *place of power*. It's the ability to pause—not as a passive act but as an intentional moment to trust God's timing and wisdom over our own.

The next time you feel frustrated or anxious about a situation, practice the power of the pause. Take a deep breath and count down from 10. Reflect on Job's story and remember that God's timing is perfect, even when we can't see the full picture.

- 10, 9, 8 ... Breathe. Trust.
- 7, 6, 5 ... Remind yourself that God is in control.
- 4, 3, 2 ... Let go of the need to rush.
- 1 ... Surrender to His plan.

Day 76 Patience: There's Power in the Pause

Patience is not just waiting; it's trusting. It's trusting that God is always at work, even in the waiting. So the next time life feels overwhelming, remember the power in the pause and trust that God is moving, even when you can't see it.

Pause.

Revel: How can you find power in the pause?

Take time to reflect on the Biblical principle of patience. Begin training your heart and mind to pause before the Lord—not just in the morning but throughout your day, especially when you need it most. Let each pause become a moment of renewal and alignment in His presence.

Align: Look back on yesterday—where did you move the needle toward your dream? Name the steps you took with the right mindset, heart posture, and actions. Honor them. Let them fuel your momentum for today.

Then lift your gaze—take a deep breath, because there's more to dream and more to do. Arise, aligned!

BOLD

Dream Stack: Count 'em—up to this point you've taken seventy-five steps. That's seventy-five intentional steps you've taken to stack your dream! That's no small thing. Now ask yourself: What's one more bold move I can make toward this God-given dream? Write it down. Own it. Then give it everything you've got—heart, soul, and grit. Today, let's make it 76!

DAY 77

Unexpected Gifts

[Jesus said,] 'Blessed is anyone who does not stumble on account of me.'

—Matthew 11:6

THE NUMBER ONE REASON people stop daring to dream with God is the pain of disappointment. We have expectations that things will work out, but then they don't. We hope for good news and receive bad news instead. We pray to hear from God and sometimes it feels like He's silent. We believe in prophetic words, but they don't come to pass—or at least, not when we want them to or in the way we think they should. Or, worst of all, we work toward a dream for years only to face failure. Huge blow. Massive disappointment.

The pain of disappointment can often feel more unbearable than the pain of never hoping or trying at all. Disappointment is the result of unmet expectations, trapping us in the pain of the past. For example, we pray for healing, expecting God to move in a specific way, but when He doesn't, our expectations go unmet, leaving us overwhelmed with disappointment and feeling stuck in the past of all the things He didn't do.

In everyday life, I might have an expectation (even unconscious in nature) to return from a work trip to a clean house, dinner ready, with the kids behaving perfectly and their schoolwork done. Yet I come home to a messy house, the kids are running around screaming, and I'm met with, "What's for dinner?" Unmet expectations leave my heart heavy with disappointment, and my mind tells me, *Well, I won't do that again*, because the pain is now rooted in my past experience. This cycle is why so many people carry the weight of disappointment and stop dreaming altogether. Yet Jesus's life shows us how God works through unmet expectations to reveal unexpected gifts.

Everything about Jesus defied expectations. People expected a king, but they received a baby born to a poor, unwed couple in a barn. Instead of a royal announcement, shepherds were the first to hear of His birth. Many expected him to be a leader from a young age, yet his ministry didn't start until He was thirty, and instead of ruling with political power, He broke every expectation by challenging traditional laws and revealing Himself as the fulfillment of the law.

Jesus didn't fit people's expectations, and many stumbled because of it. Yet today's Scripture reveals to us God's ultimate heart. When Jesus says, *'Blessed is anyone who does not stumble on account of me,'* He means blessed is the one who does not lose faith or doubt Him. *On account of me* refers to not being deterred by Jesus's teachings, persona, or circumstances based upon what you can conceive or intellectually understand. Jesus was saying, "Don't be offended by me because I don't meet *your* expectations!" If that's not a wake-up call, I don't know what is!

Instead, Jesus invites us into something greater than our own expectations—an unexpected gift, a blessing for anyone who believes! *Blessed* in this context implies a state of happiness and spiritual fulfillment that comes from unwavering faith in Jesus. This gift was a lifetime of unwavering joy for those who didn't stumble when expectations weren't met, who trusted Him beyond their disappointment. The unexpected gift that was available then and available to you now is an encounter with the living God, something more powerful than any of us could ever imagine.

So my question to you today is this: Will your unmet expectations cause you to stumble? Though your pain and disappointment may be valid, holding onto them will only keep you from embracing the true gift of God's ultimate plan.

Will there be disappointment in this life? Yes. Will God always meet our expectations? No. Is He still good and still God? Yes. Can He give us unexpected gifts in the midst of unmet expectations? Absolutely.

When we trust God and believe, despite disappointment and unmet expectations, we open ourselves to receive the unexpected gifts He wants to give. But if we cling to our unmet expectations, we stay trapped in the pain of loss and defeat. In times of disappointment, you will be forced to choose whether to believe that God is good, that His ways are higher, and His thoughts are better—or not. The choice will be yours.

God's promises are always *yes* and *amen,* and He is faithful—even when His timing or His ways are beyond our understanding. True faith holds onto His character and trusts in His eternal promises, which surpass our immediate desires.

Today, I pray that you see the blessing of laying down disappointment before the Lord. Bring your pain, questions, and unmet expectations of the past to the cross. Let Him meet you in the process. May you discover the greatest gift—the presence of Jesus Himself—and find spiritual fulfillment, even when your expectations aren't met. The greatest gift of all is already yours.

■ ■ ■ ■ ■ ■

Revel: Where in your life do you need to bring the pain of disappointment to Him and exchange it for the most unexpected gift of all—Jesus Himself?

Take time to reflect on the blessing of knowing that Jesus came not just to meet but to exceed your wildest expectations. He is the fulfillment of every promise of God. Let Him meet you in the space of your disappointment and trust that He is more than enough.

Day 77 Unexpected Gifts

Align: Look back on yesterday—where did your footsteps line up with the call of heaven on your life? Where did your choices reveal the truth of God's Word and the identity He's written over you? Take a moment. Notice the alignment. These are the signs that you're walking in step with Him—and that what you're doing is making a difference.

Dream Stack: What is one thing you can do today to move forward in achieving your dream? Write it down, schedule it, then give it everything you've got!

DAY 78

"But God"

I have planted, Apollos watered; but God gave the increase.

—1 Corinthians 3:6 KJV

DELAY. HAS ANYONE EVER BEEN delayed and hated every minute? Let's be real; no one likes delay. I have a plan, I want to stick with it, and no, I don't want traffic, missed flights, or other delays to keep me from where I want to be, when I want to be there.

OK, I'm done.

Yesterday we spoke about one of the greatest obstacles to dreaming with God, disappointment. Well, here's another one for you: *delay*.

Whenever we face an obstacle, resistance, or a dead end, it's so easy to focus on that delay, not the promise. "Lord, I did what you told me to do—now what?" Or "Lord, I've prayed for healing, but it hasn't come. Now what?" Or "My dream is not coming to fruition. This seems impossible ... now what?" Ever been there before?

Life's delays can seem overwhelming when we aren't seeing the results we want, when we want, especially after putting in the hard work. It's one thing to grumble and complain when you've done nothing to support the cause, but when you feel like you've done everything you can, it's easy to grow hopeless.

When we focus only on the results we aren't getting, we begin to focus on everything that's not working. We begin to shame ourselves, blame others, and wonder if God is really doing His part. The more we fixate on it, the more hopelessness sets in. The more we allow it to set in, the more the quiet desperation grows, and the more it grows, the smaller God can appear in our minds. Fear then takes the driver's seat, and we've given it authority over our lives. The Word of God tells us we will face trials, and that includes seasons of disappointment and delays, but it also gives us two powerful words that change everything when we face such seasons: *but God*.

How big is your *but God*?

The disappointments, delays, and struggles we face may be bigger than we are, but are they bigger than God? No. Nothing is bigger than God. Scripture is full of testimonies where people faced walls of delay, *but God* was greater.

- *No temptation has overtaken you except what is common to mankind. And God is faithful; He will not let you tempted beyond what you can bear.* —1 Corinthians 10:13
- *Then they took Him down from the cross and laid Him in a tomb. But God raised Him from the dead.!* —Acts 13:29–30 TPT
- *Jesus looked at them and said, 'With man this is impossible, but with God all things are possible.'* —Matthew 19:26

- *My flesh and my heart may fail, but God is the strength of my heart and my portion forever.* —Psalm 73:26
- *You intended to harm me, but God intended it for good to accomplish what is now being done, the saving of many lives.* —Genesis 50:20

Do you see the pattern? The circumstances did not end at the comma; they were followed by *but God*. Every extraordinary act begins with someone's willingness to push through "the commas," the delays in life, the improbabilities, the moments you feel like you've done everything you can do, and boldly declare: "but God!"

When we say, "but God," we shift our focus from hopelessness to faith, from our own limitations to His unchanging, everlasting power. In today's Scripture, we see Paul living out this transformative truth. First, he acknowledges the value of his own effort: *I have planted*. He did what he was capable of doing. Too often, we expect God to handle everything, but though He can move mountains, He requires our faith and action. God needs your step of faith—your planting—to bring the increase.

Second, Paul didn't work alone. He understood the importance of partnership. Dreaming and acting in faith can feel daunting, lonely, and overwhelming, but Paul, seeing the value in shared responsibility, invited Apollos to join him. Apollos took on his role, watering what had been planted.

Finally, we see Paul highlighting something that is important for us today: Though we must plant the seed and water it, there are things only God can do. I wish I could say that God will do things exactly how you want Him to, when you want, but He doesn't work that way. Scripture reminds us, as we saw in yesterday's writing, that He *will* surpass our expectations and wildest dreams—but that doesn't mean it will happen without delay. You must remember that the day you plant the seed and the day you harvest that seed are two totally different days. The real question is: Can you keep your faith during the waiting?

It is God who brings the increase. He's the One who adds more after your "I'm done" and His strength to your exhaustion. He brings life where there seems to be only death. But you have to move beyond the delay, past the comma—you must believe in the *but God* moment! Keep planting seeds of faith. Be diligent in watering them. Then trust and believe.

Today, declare "but God" over your life and every delay you are facing. Don't stop until you see the miracle-working power of our victorious God.

Day 78 "But God"

Revel: Are you feeling discouraged by delays, wondering when or if things will change? Do you feel like you're stuck before the comma of *but God*?

Take time to reflect on the areas of delay in your life, and instead of focusing on what's not happening, press into Scripture and align your heart with the promises and power of God. Recognize that delays are not the end of the story. Begin to build up your faith by boldly declaring, "but God," knowing that He can shift any situation in His perfect timing and turn it for His glory. Let your faith rise in the waiting.

Align: What choices yesterday came from a place rooted in God's truth? Where did you move with clarity, courage, and conviction in who He's called you to be? Pause. Reflect. Let those moments anchor your momentum and strengthen your conviction.

BOLD

Dream Stack: Even as you diligently wait on the Lord for His wonder-working power, what is one thing *you* can do today to move closer to your dreams? Write it down, then do it!

....

....

....

....

DAY 79

To Forgive or Not to Forgive?

Then Peter came to Him and said, 'Lord, how often shall my brother sin against me, and I forgive him? Up to seven times?' Jesus said to him, 'I do not say to you, up to seven times, but up to seventy times seven.'

—Matthew 18:21–22 NKJV

LET'S BE HONEST—we can all think of one or more people we need to forgive, even if that person is ourselves. Forgiveness, though easy to understand as a concept, isn't always the easiest to implement in our day-to-day lives. Yet as believers, our lives should be marked by forgiveness.

Now let me be clear with you, forgiveness doesn't release the other person from what they've done—it sets you free to do what God has called you to do. Without it, you remain tied to the pain of the past—emotionally, mentally, and spiritually bound until that pain consumes you. It's been said that refusing to forgive is like drinking poison and expecting someone else to die. Unforgiveness, like delay and disappointment, can keep us from experiencing the fullness of God's promises.

Though unforgiveness feels rational, because it validates our hurt, allowing us to compartmentalize the pain we've experienced, the Word of God points to a better way. Your pain is valid, the hurt is real, and there is someone who can acknowledge everything you've ever experienced even better than unforgiveness could—God! He is your vindicator (Psalm 37:6) and your healer (Psalm 30:2). But in order to fully experience His healing, you must give Him all your pain—including the unforgiveness you harbor.

But how do you even begin to forgive when the pain is real?

When we think about forgiveness, most of us see it as a one-time act—either extending it to someone or receiving it for something we've done. But if you look a little deeper, it's actually described as a process of forgiving or being forgiven. And that's the key word—process. Forgiveness doesn't always happen overnight. Though we may say it with our mouth, "I forgive you," there is a process in our hearts that has to take place. It *is* a process and it's one we must choose—have the willingness to step into the process. There's another key word—*willingness*.

Do you remember how we talked about how boldness is defined as the willingness to say yes to what God is asking, even when we want to say no? Forgiveness is the same. Like boldness, forgiveness is not something you always feel like doing. But it's something you choose to do, because it's what God asks of you. Therefore, forgiveness requires the *willingness* to let go and let God.

But they've hurt me too many times, you might think. Or maybe you think, *I've made the same mistake over and over again, why should I choose to forgive myself again?* Peter probably thought he was being generous when he asked Jesus if he should forgive seven times. But in His response, Jesus reveals the very heart of the Father—one of mercy, grace, and boundless forgiveness—as He declares we are to forgive *seventy times seven*. In doing so, He not only answers the question, but He also sets the standard for us to follow.

Jesus doesn't ask for details about how Peter was wronged. He doesn't inquire about the severity of the offense. Instead, He gives Peter a clear and profound answer—*forgive without limit*. The phrase *seventy times seven* (490) isn't meant to be a literal count. It symbolizes boundless forgiveness, a grace without end. It's a call to extend compassion and mercy as many times as necessary—as Jesus does for us.

This doesn't mean you must ignore your standards or allow others to continue to hurt you. It's about aligning your heart with Jesus. When you look at Him and remember His sacrifice—the love and grace He extended to you—it transforms your perspective on forgiveness because He first loved *and* forgave you over and over again. His forgiveness should inspire and transform us, not as an excuse to continue sinning but as a motivation to live differently. Then it should encourage us to do the same.

You will never be done sinning, which means you will never be done receiving God's grace. And because you are constantly receiving His grace, you are also called to give it. Forgiving others does not mean you have to trust them again or let them keep hurting you, but it does mean that you release them from the grip of your heart and extend the same grace you receive from God.

Let the process begin. Start by forgiving yourself—profoundly, often, and daily. Allow the blood of Jesus to transform you, not shame you; to change you, not condemn you. His love invites you closer and encourages you to *go and sin no more* (John 8:11 KJV). As you experience this transformation, the next step is to extend the same grace you are given to those around you.

Forgive them first in your heart. Then, when you're ready, offer that forgiveness outwardly, knowing that trust does not have to be immediately restored. Trust is something that must be earned over time. However, forgiveness is an act of grace. When you offer it, you begin to invite others—those who have hurt you—into that same process of forgiveness you have been in. In doing so, you point them to Jesus. Your goal is not only to restore your relationship with them but also to help restore them unto Him. Let His love and grace flow through you, not only to reconcile with others but also to direct them toward the One who can truly heal and redeem them. Forgiveness becomes a channel for God's transformative love to work in their hearts—as it has in yours.

You won't always feel ready to forgive, but do it anyway. Be willing to forgive, even when it's hard, because forgiveness is a pathway to freedom. Don't forgive just for them; forgive also for Jesus. Forgive because that's what He asks you to do. Forgive because it's a reflection of who you are in Him.

Day 79 To Forgive or Not to Forgive?

Unchain yourself from the pain of unforgiveness and bitterness and step into the fullness of His grace. Receive His eternal forgiveness for you—completely, undeservedly—then give it away, not once, not seven times, but seventy times seven. Let the freedom that comes with forgiveness transform your heart and your life.

* * *

Revel: Who do you need to forgive? How can you begin the process of forgiving—for yourself and for others—so your life reflects the love of Jesus?

Spend time with the Lord relearning what true forgiveness looks like. Open your heart to His unconditional love and allow Him to show you how to forgive well so that you can stay free.

Align: Take a moment to reflect on yesterday; it holds clues. Where did you live as if you believe what God says about you? Where did your actions line up with His calling? Take a few moments to notice and name them. That's how divine alignment becomes your new norm.

BOLD

Dream Stack: What is one bold step you can take today to bring you closer to your dream? Write it down, put it at the top of your to-do list, and make it happen! Can't stop; won't stop.

....

....

....

....

DAY 80

Stop Doing; Start Becoming

Even in times of trouble we have a joyful confidence, knowing that our pressures will develop in us patient endurance. And patient endurance will refine our character, and proven character leads us back to hope.

—Romans 5:3–4 TPT

MOST OF US LOVE the *idea* of having a dream—the excitement of imagining a future where we've accomplished something great, done the impossible with God. Whether it's losing weight, starting a business or ministry, or achieving financial success, the dream does offer a level of blissfulness that's undeniable. It makes us feel good. The feeling of accomplishment, the admiration we receive from others, the aesthetic of the after pictures—we can't get enough of it. But when it comes to actually doing the work? Well, that's another story.

That's where we hit a wall.

We all have dreams, though few live through the hard times in between to make those dreams a reality. We've discussed a few of the pitfalls along the way—disappointment, delay, unforgiveness—now we face another harsh reality: The process of your dream isn't going to make you *feel* good. It's designed to make you *be* good. This is why most people don't try and many more fail.

Statistically speaking, anyone who's ever set a goal, like a New Year's resolution, knows exactly what I mean. Have you ever set a goal and not hit it? You had every good intention to see it through to completion, but somewhere along the line, you lost motivation? You're not alone. Research shows that only 9 percent of Americans who make resolutions actually complete them, with 23 percent of people dropping their resolutions by the end of the first week and 43 percent by the end of the first month. These statistics reflect a deeper issue beyond just goal-setting—they point to a lack of sustained commitment, and more important, a lack of a deeper understanding of the point of a God-size dream.

The truth is this: We all want the dream; we just don't want the struggle, the discipline, or the discomfort it takes to get there. We want the goal, but we don't want the journey. We want the result without the process, the good without the hard, the dream without the pressure. But as P.T. Barnum, the famous nineteenth-century showman, so eloquently said, "Comfort is the enemy of progress."

We see other people's success on social media—the perfect Instagram posts, the before and after photos, the stories of triumph—and we get fixated on the outcome. It's easy to forget that behind every ta-da moment is a long process of unseen effort, setbacks, and perseverance. But here's the reality: True success doesn't come from obsessing over the outcome but from learning to love the process. The journey of growth, of becoming more disciplined, more patient, and more resilient, is where the real transformation happens. The goal is not just to achieve something but to *become* someone in the process.

The problem isn't in having dreams or setting goals. The problem is in thinking it should be easy or comfortable. The path to your dreams is not easy, and it is anything but comfortable. I'm here to tell you, in the kindest way possible, God isn't interested in your comfort. He's interested in you—your character, your growth, and your journey of becoming more like Him. We learn this in today's verse from the book of Romans.

Here we see that God uses pressure and hardship to develop *patient endurance* in us, which refines our character and makes us more like Him. This isn't about quick success in the world around us but the long-term transformation that happens within us. It's not about doing but becoming.

When we have dreams and set goals without understanding that the real value lies in who we become along the way, we set ourselves up for failure. God's goal isn't just for us to achieve something; His ultimate goal is for us to *become* someone—a reflection of Him and His character.

So how do we shift our mindset?

Understand that pressure is part of the process. Life, and particularly the pursuit of goals, inevitably creates moments of pressure. But pressure has a purpose: It builds endurance and refines character. Instead of tapping out when things get hard, see the struggle as an opportunity for growth.

Focus on who you're becoming, not just what you're doing. God is more concerned with your transformation than with your achievements. Ask yourself this very powerful question: Who do I have to become so that my dreams are just a by-product of who I became? Maybe it's becoming more disciplined, more trusting, or more patient. Start your process of becoming by first laying out all your hopes, dreams, goals, and ideas before the Lord, then become.

Trust in God's timing. As we learned yesterday, God's timing is perfect (even if it's not yours). God isn't in a rush, even if you are. He's not looking to build something fast; He's wanting to build people who last. He doesn't just want you to get there, to achieve more; He also wants you to become more so when you get there, you have the character required to hold the weight of the blessing. Your growth in character is His priority, and it's what will enable you to carry the blessings He has in store.

Today, I pray you begin to see your character development in the Lord as the most important goal you could ever have. I pray you see that God is not just trying to build something through you; He wants to build *you*.

Don't just dare to dream; dare to be everything God created you to be.

Day 80 Stop Doing; Start Becoming

Revel: As you reflect on today's devotional and the previous days, consider how the challenges of disappointment, delays, forgiveness, and even pressures are shaping you. What areas of your character are being exposed that may need refinement? Rather than focusing on what you need to do, take time today to seek who God is calling you to become in this season as you pursue your God-given dreams. Ask God: "Who do I need to become, so I can do what you've called me to do?" Wait patiently, fervently, for His response.

Align: Reflect on yesterday—where did your steps show that you're not just doing but also becoming? When you're rooted in Christ, your actions flow from identity, not striving. So pause and consider: Where did your movement reflect the overflow of who you are in Him?

And if you found yourself on the struggle bus yesterday—hey, that's OK. There's grace for that. Grace upon grace. But don't stay there. Let His grace wash over you today—lifting you, realigning you, calling you higher.

Come back into full alignment. You'll be so glad you did.

Dream Stack: From this place of becoming, what is one action you can take today to move closer to your dream? Write it, become it, do it.

....

....

....

....

DAY 81

Your Forever Home

Surely your goodness and love will follow me all the days of my life, and I will dwell in the house of the Lord forever.

—Psalm 23:6

I CONSIDER MYSELF A BIT unconventional in that I've lived in twenty-five different homes over thirty-eight years, and that's not even counting all the temporary places we stayed while living in an RV. What about you? How many places have you called home? Maybe you're on the other end of the spectrum and have lived in the same house in the same town for forty-plus years. Even though our roof count may differ, the idea of home is universal.

When we think about what makes a house a home, it's not walls and a roof but a place of safety, security, and stability. It's where we can be ourselves, where consistency reassures us, and where we feel sheltered from the unpredictability of life. Even if you didn't experience this type of home growing up, it's something you can foster for yourself as you grow. Home is where you retreat after a long day, where you find safety when life feels uncertain and comfort when people let you down. But imagine if the love and security we find in our physical homes don't even begin to compare to the love of the Father and the true home we're meant to find in Him.

Where do you live? Where do you call home?

Truth be told, God has already given you an eternal home in Him. That's the message of today's Scripture. God's love is chasing after you, not just on your good days but on the tough ones too. He doesn't want you to live in Him when you've got it all figured out; He wants you to establish yourself in Him on the daily. He doesn't just want you to have a physical house; He wants to be your house—your abiding home.

Maybe you grew up in a home that didn't feel safe or secure, or maybe your current home doesn't bring you the peace you need. If that's the case, this topic can make you feel a little vulnerable and cause apprehension about making a home in the Lord. But if we're not careful, we can spend our whole lives hiding our pain, running from the love of the Father, and trying to find the home we didn't have. It's time to return.

The story of the prodigal son in the book of Luke beautifully illustrates the power of returning to the unconditional love of our heavenly Father. In the parable, the son made a choice to leave his father's house, chasing after the allure of freedom and independence. He squandered his inheritance, and when everything fell apart, he found himself in a pit of despair, realizing he had nothing left. In his lowest moment, he remembered his father's house—a place of safety, provision, and love.

With a heart full of humility and shame, he decided to return, not knowing how his father would respond. But to his amazement, as he made his way home, his father saw him from afar and ran toward him with open arms. His father didn't scold him or condemn him for his mistakes. Instead, he embraced him, clothed him in fine robes, and celebrated his return with a feast.

This is the picture of God's love for us. No matter how far we may stray, or how much we think we've messed up, God is always waiting with open arms, eager to welcome us back into His presence. He doesn't want us to stay lost or distant; He longs for us to run back to Him and dwell in Him, our home, where we find rest, healing, and unconditional love.

Here's the truth: God sent Jesus so you wouldn't have to seek your safety, security, stability—your home—in anyone or anything but Him. Jesus wasn't sent for those who have it all together; He came for the broken, the messy, and those in need of healing. He came for people like us. Jesus didn't come for the perfect; He came to be the answer for the imperfect. And even if you run, His love will never stop pursuing you with relentless grace.

I can tell you firsthand that when I finally stopped running from the pain of my broken home and chose to dwell in God's love, I realized just how powerful and healing it really is. God wasn't unsafe—He was the definition of safe. He wasn't conditional in His love, He was unconditional, and He had been pursuing me all along. His love, though extravagant and sometimes hard to grasp at times, met me where I was and transformed me. When I let Him love me fully, I found my true home in Him.

No matter what your past or present homelife looks like, I encourage you to let Jesus meet you right where you are. Give Him access to your heart and let Him wrap you in His unconditional love. Even if you feel messy, broken, or unsure, His love is big enough to heal and transform you. Don't run from Him—run toward Him. Run home.

Our response to this relentless love should be to turn and about-face. It's the conscious choice to stop running and to dwell in His love, to make Him our home. God's love for you is unshakable and relentless, constantly pursuing you.

Take a moment to stop running and consciously decide to dwell in His love. Let His goodness and mercy wash over you, heal your heart, and renew your spirit. His love is pursuing you, calling you home—how will you respond?

Day 81 Your Forever Home

Revel: How will you respond to God's love today? It's not a question of whether He loves you—His love for you is certain. But will you continue to run—or will you turn and dwell in His house forever?

Take a moment today to about-face and run toward the Lord, allowing His transforming love to heal and lead you. Let His embrace guide every step as you make your home in Him.

Align: As you reflect on yesterday, ask yourself: Did I walk in step with God's truth? Did my choices reflect His promises and the identity He's spoken over me? Let those moments rise—notice them, celebrate them, let them remind you of the growth already happening.

And for anything that felt out of sync—thoughts, emotions, or actions that missed the mark—bring them to Jesus. Lay them at His feet. Give Him what you've got ... so He can give you what He's got. Because His grace is always enough, and His exchange is always better.

Dream Stack: What's one thing you can do to manifest the dream God's given you? Keep it simple, make it bold, write it down, and live to tell about it tomorrow.

....

....

....

....

DAY 82

Count the Cost

[Jesus said,] 'So don't follow me without considering what it will cost you.'

—Luke 14:28 TPT

AS MY KIDS HAVE GROWN, it's been fun to watch them reach new levels of maturity. And having five kids means I get the opportunity to experience each stage more than most people. I have spent fifty months (over four years!) being pregnant, have changed diapers for over a decade, and have answered "Mom, where are my shoes?" more times than I can count.

We're now at the stage where they're learning about money—how to make it, tithe it, save it, and, of course, how to spend it (a skill they've always had). It's funny though, because when it's not their money, they say they want everything "so bad!" It doesn't matter what it is or how much it costs, when it's my money, they *want* it so, so badly. If you have kids, you know what I mean. They have no sense of the value of money; they just want things. But as soon as they're holding their own twenty or fifty dollars, it's a different story.

For example, the other day my daughter Aslan said, "Mom, I really want those jeans" (even though she has eleven pairs). I said, "You don't need jeans, honey." She saw it from a different perspective and said, "No, Mom, I do. I don't have that exact color. I want them SO bad!" I get it—jeans vary in color; that's valid. So I said, "Totally go for it—with your own money!" Suddenly, the desire shifted. "No, I don't want them *that* bad."

The truth is, she wanted the jeans—but not once she counted the cost.

In life, everything has a cost. It's easy to grasp when it comes to money. If I want milk, it costs $3.33. If I want to see a movie, it's twenty dollars. Investing in my future may cost me hundreds or thousands of dollars. There's always a cost, and that often determines how much I truly want something.

The same applies to our time. We all have twenty-four hours in a day, and how we choose to spend that time determines the price we're willing to pay for each activity. When people say, "I don't have enough time," it's not really about time—it's about priorities. We all have the same amount; the difference is about priorities. Ultimately, it comes down to counting the cost and deciding what matters most and how we want to spend the time we have.

Consider this: If you were going to build a house, what would you do first? You wouldn't just pick a lot and start buying materials without architects, blueprints, or financing. You'd sit down first and figure out how much time and money it was going to take to complete the project or dream. Counting the cost is something you would want to determine at the start, not halfway through. Once you determine the overall cost, you can figure out how badly you want it. If it costs too much in time or money, you might realize it's not worth it to you.

As believers, our walk with Jesus is no different. In today's verse, we see this so clearly. Jesus speaks with truth but always wrapped in love. He doesn't water it down, and He doesn't avoid the hard stuff either. Instead, He looks His disciples in the eye and tells them, *Don't follow me without considering what it will cost you.'* Not to discourage them but to prepare them.

As followers of Christ, our goal isn't to avoid hardship, run from pain, or chase after comfort. It's not about looking good or feeling good. It's about being good—being more like Jesus, *no matter what it costs*. We're called to embrace the mission He's given us, trusting that every battle is worth it, because in Him, we have the victory. A life lived with Jesus, fully on mission for Him—though it's the best and most fulfilling way to live—will often require sacrifices that others may never be asked to make or be willing to make, for that matter. And yes, it will cost you.

- It may cost you your ego.
- It will cost you your fear.
- It will cost you convenience.
- It may cost you friendships.
- It will cost you resources.
- It will cost you your will, your way, and your time.

Yet here's the beautiful truth: God never asks us to give up something without offering something even greater in return. When our hands are open to Him—after we've counted the cost and surrendered everything we have, even if it's a simple "Yes, Lord"—He pours back into our open hands more than we could ever contain.

Look at the examples in the Bible.

Abraham: It cost him his son! Or so he thought. Abraham thought he would lose Isaac, the son of promise, yet in his obedience, God made him the father of many nations and fulfilled His covenant beyond what Abraham could have imagined. (Genesis 22)

Noah: It cost him his reputation! Or so he thought. Though his reputation was on the line as he built the ark in obedience to God's command, by trusting God's plan, Noah ultimately saved the world and became an example of faithfulness for generations to come. (Genesis 7)

Esther: It cost her her life! Or so she thought. Esther risked her life by approaching the king uninvited, but in doing so, she saved not only her own life but also the lives of the entire Jewish people, becoming a key figure in God's plan of deliverance for the Jews. (Esther 5–7)

Day 82 Count the Cost

Joseph: It cost him his dream! Or so he thought. As Joseph gave up his own dreams of family and freedom when he was sold into slavery and thrown into prison, God used his trials to elevate him to a place of power, allowing him to save his family and countless others from famine, fulfilling God's greater plan. (Genesis 37)

In each case, they counted the cost. They were willing to lose everything they had and yet found something even greater—God's faithfulness. What they gained on the other side of sacrifice far exceeded their expectations. No matter how we look at it, everything costs us. It will cost you to follow Jesus. It will cost you to not follow Jesus. It will cost you to live your dreams. It will cost you to not live your dreams. How bad do you want it and what cost are you willing to pay?

Today, I pray this doesn't cause you to hesitate in your journey with the Lord but to remind you that counting the cost for Jesus isn't designed to scare you but to prepare you. Following Jesus isn't always easy, but it's definitely worth it.

Count the cost.

❈ ❈ ❈ ❈ ❈ ❈

Revel: What is the cost of your following Jesus? What will it cost you to follow the dreams He's given you?

Reflect on this today. Count the cost, then give Him everything you've got. Trust that He will fill your hands with even more than you could ever imagine.

Align: Reflect on yesterday—what choices came from a place rooted in God's truth? Where did you move with clarity, courage, and conviction in who He's called you to be and what He's called you to do? Pause. Reflect. Let those moments anchor your momentum for today.

....

....

....

....

Dream Stack: What is one bold thing you can do today to move your dreams forward? Count the cost. How badly do you want it? Write it down, map it out, and take account for it tomorrow.

....

....

....

....

DAY 83

Meditation

[The Lord said,] 'Keep this Book of the Law always on your lips; meditate on it day and night, so that you may be careful to do everything written in it. Then you will be prosperous and successful.'

—Joshua 1:8

WHEN YOU HEAR THE WORD *meditate*, what comes to mind? For many, it creates this image of sitting quietly, all alone, far from distractions or interruptions, emptying one's thoughts and reaching some state of tranquility. It feels like being in a bubble, not reality. Or at least, that's how I viewed it for a long time—and it's also why I avoided it. I thought it was all about doing it right or being good at it, and because of that, I just didn't do it at all. The more I tried, the louder the chatter became. The more time I gave it, the worse I got. But truth be told, that mindset caused me to miss the true purpose of meditation.

What if I told you true meditation could positively impact your success in life? Would you be more apt to do it? Of course you would! We all want to be more successful in this life; yet, I wonder, are we willing to do what we need to do? Lasting success in life has more to do with meditation than one may think. I propose that aligning your mind with God's wisdom is what will give you the clarity, peace, and focus you need and will directly influence your daily actions and long-term goals.

It can be easy to look to the world's quick fixes or easy solutions for what we don't understand, but true wisdom begins with the Word of God, not a successful technique or quick app with step-by-step directions. Yet we google, we download, we buy books on the subject in order to empty the mind, and though there's nothing wrong with this approach, according to Scripture, meditation is not about emptying the mind but filling it with God's truth.

True meditation isn't about finding extended moments of peace while sitting on a mountaintop or in a yoga class or feeling good in just the present moment; it's about the deeper transformation happening inside of you. It's what shapes your thoughts, aligns your heart with God's truth, and produces the richness and fulfillment we often seek in external things. Through meditating on God's Word, we're cultivating a life that thrives not because of temporary feelings but because of an enduring foundation rooted in His promises. It's an inside-out process and leads to true prosperity and success, far beyond anything this world can offer. As believers, we understand meditation is not a one-time event or a specific moment in our day; *it is a way of life*.

Today's Scripture tells us to *keep this Book of the Law always on your lips*, and it shows us how to do so—by meditating on it. That word *meditate* means to reflect, contemplate, or ruminate. To ruminate is to think deeply, or as the phrase goes, "chew the cud." We don't use that phrase every day, but it describes how animals like cows, sheep, and goats, classified as ruminants, regurgitate and rechew their food. This process helps them break down the food and absorb the nutrients, especially when they're difficult to digest. In a similar way, we often need to chew on God's Word repeatedly, breaking it down, reflecting on it, and absorbing its truth over time. Like ruminating animals, we need to process God's principles over and over as we move them from our head to our heart. This is how we turn intellectual knowledge into wisdom through real encounters with His Word.

Notice that the passage says to meditate *day and night*. This tells us that meditating on the Lord and His Word isn't just something we do occasionally—it's meant to be a constant practice, an ongoing rhythm in our daily lives. Biblical meditation isn't about emptying the mind; rather, it involves continuously filling our minds with God's truth, promises, and wisdom—every moment of every day. It's not a one-time event or a weekly routine; it's a lifestyle. It's the intentional training of our minds to focus on God, allowing His Word to shape our thoughts and guide our decisions.

The Lord also instructs us to keep the Word *always on your lips*. This means that meditation is not just an internal reflection; it's meant to be spoken. The words we speak have power, and we are called to proclaim God's Word aloud. As we meditate on His truth, our mouths should echo what's in our minds, spreading wisdom and light to those around us. Meditation, then, isn't just a private experience—it also impacts what we say and how we influence others. The truth we meditate on in our hearts must also be declared with our lips. As a verbal processor, I've found that one of the most valuable parts of my meditation practice is sharing what I'm learning as I learn it. I talk about it online, with my kids and husband—with anyone who will listen. I'm not sharing it to position myself as an expert but to solidify my own understanding and, hopefully, encourage those around me with what I'm discovering.

Finally, the verse tells us that living a life of meditation on God's Word is the key to true prosperity and success. Can't beat that! But the prosperity and success mentioned here go beyond material wealth and external achievements. True prosperity in this context means to thrive spiritually and flourish in God's will. Success in the Kingdom is marked by wisdom, discernment, and the ability to make sound judgments—all of which come from being rooted in God's truth. Could it be that the real blessings we're looking for are on the other side of the meditation we're avoiding? Absolutely! When we make the choice to meditate on God's Word, to think it, speak it, and live it, we position ourselves for the kind of success and prosperity that God desires for us.

If you want to experience true prosperity and success, meditation isn't just a good idea—it's essential. Meditating on God's Word isn't optional; it's the foundation for the life He's called you to live.

Day 83 Meditation

Revel: What thoughts are you meditating on each day or, better yet, chewing on? Are they aligned with God's Word?

Today, start meditating on God's wisdom as a lifestyle. And don't just keep it in your mind—speak it out and let it transform the world around you. Then be sure that your *daily action* reflects the truth of God's Word.

Align: What an incredible opportunity—especially in light of today's reading—to pause and truly reflect on your journey. This is your invitation to come into full alignment: mind, body, spirit ... mindset, heartset, dreamset.

Take a few extra moments today to do a deeper inventory. Maybe that looks like journaling your growth. Or maybe it means carving out time to talk it through with someone who's walking this journey too. However you do it—don't rush it. Look at how far you've come—what you've learned, who you're becoming, and what you're actively doing to walk out the dream God's placed in you.

Keep surrendering to the process, yes—but do it with intention. Release what no longer serves you. Double down on what does. Alignment looks good on you.

BOLD

Dream Stack: What's the next bold step you can take to manifest your dreams today? Dream it, define it, write it down, and do it!

....

....

....

....

DAY 84

Flip the Script

If then you have been raised with Christ, seek the things that are above, where Christ is, seated at the right hand of God. Set your minds on things that are above, not on things that are on earth.

—Colossians 3:1–2 ESV

YESTERDAY WE LEARNED ABOUT Biblical meditation. Today, I am going to show you how to do that in real time—the JG way. For me, meditation isn't a quiet walk in the forest or long periods of meditative states without interruptions. I've got five kids y'all! For me, meditation is a proactive, all day long, rewiring of my thoughts to match God's thoughts, drop-kicking the things I think for the ones He's thinking.

For far too long I settled for a life lived well beneath heaven's design. I got stuck within the barriers of my own mind, hiding behind my limiting beliefs and self-deprecating talk tracks. Until I learned how to *flip the script*. Today, it's your turn!

We've all heard terms like *limiting beliefs* or *narrative* in personal development circles. They refer to the subconscious *scripts* that shape our daily thoughts, emotions, and actions. Have you ever left a conversation feeling like you and the other person were speaking two different languages? That's because we all have these narratives, talk tracks, or *scripts* going on in our minds, and why two people in the same conversation can be talking about two totally different things.

The scripts in your mind have been developed over time. Research shows that every thought creates a pathway in the brain. The more you think a thought, the wider that path gets; the wider the pathway gets, the easier it is to think the thought. Those pathways become talk tracks and, ultimately, your scripts. These scripts start to feel real. You begin to act as if they are real. And when life starts reflecting them back to you, you call them truth—even if they're not. It's a vicious cycle.

Science also supports this in cognitive behavioral therapy, a kind of psychotherapy based on the idea that our thoughts shape our emotions, our emotions shape our actions, and consistent action determines our results. Simply put: The thoughts you have impact the way you think, and the way you think impacts the scripts you use.

So, what scripts are you using?

You know you have a script when it feels nearly impossible to break free from certain habits or thought patterns. If your scripts are patterned to focus on survival: safety, security, and stability, you will never feel like you have enough. Your thoughts will be stuck in patterns like, "There is not enough. I don't have enough. I am not enough." Truth be told, you can't expect to thrive if your thoughts are scripted to focus on simply surviving.

Or maybe your script is focused on people-pleasing, trying to feel loved, affirmed, or accepted by others; therefore, you constantly worry about what other people think, keeping the peace, or wanting everyone to be happy. Though those are natural needs, when we focus on them above everything else, we are left constantly chasing approval—approval that never truly satisfies and feels impossible to change. It's not impossible; it's a script. A script that has been learned over time, which means, with enough intention, it can be retrained and given new patterns to follow.

Here's the good news: These are just scripts. And though they feel hardwired, they're learned behaviors and thought patterns, which can be unlearned. With enough intentionality, you can rewrite your mental scripts with new patterns of thinking using God's Word.

God has the most profound way of calling us into something greater, allowing us to flip the script of our lives by aligning our thoughts with His. Today's Scripture from the book of Colossians gives us the key: *Seek the things that are above*. Here we see God inviting us to refocus our thoughts on heavenly things, on His truths, on His Word, and on His promises, not on the things of this world.

Here's how to flip the script with SCRIPTure:

Align with God's truth. Ask yourself: Do the scripts you're running in your head (i.e., the thoughts you're thinking) align with God's Word? If it uplifts, convicts, or speaks life and hope, it's from God. If it condemns, shames, or brings guilt, it's not from Him.

Be purposeful. Scripture says to set your mind on *things that are above*, not on earthly things. If a thought lines up with the truth of God's Word, meditate on it as you learned yesterday. Chew on it, repeat it, and let it shape your emotions, actions, and ultimately, your life.

Drop-kick the lies. If a thought doesn't align with Scripture, drop-kick it immediately. Replace it with God's truth and stand firm in that truth until it becomes your new narrative.

Persevere in rewriting your script. Some days, flipping the script will be tough. That's because you're breaking long-held beliefs that don't serve you anymore. But just because the truth feels unfamiliar doesn't make it less true. Keep meditating on Scripture, even when it's hard, and watch as God's truth rewrites the narrative in your mind.

Remember, mastering your thoughts isn't an option—it's essential to living a life that honors God and is filled with His joy, peace, and purpose. The more you align your script with SCRIPTure, the more you'll experience the fullness of life that God has promised. The key to living abundantly is to think abundantly—set your mind on things above and let God's Word guide you.

Day 84 Flip the Script

Revel: What current scripts (thought patterns) are playing out in your mind right now? Are they aligned with God's truth or are they driven by old patterns of fear, insecurity, or a need for control?

Take time to reflect on some specific scripts that are not in agreement with God's Word. Then dive into the Scriptures and seek God's truth to rewrite those scripts. Allow His Word to renew your mind, transform your thinking, and shape your heart in a way that brings honor and glory to Him. Then, as we talked about yesterday, meditate on it day and night.

Align: Mindset, heartset, dreamset—you're getting the hang of this! So how did yesterday go? Were all parts of you firing on all cylinders? Were you moving and grooving with the Lord?

Take a moment to reflect—yes, even on the mundane stuff (you know you secretly love it). Because inspecting what we're expecting? That's the number one discipline of a conquering dreamer.

BOLD

Dream Stack: Today, what is one action that will bring you closer to your dream? Make that a priority. Write it down, put it at the top of your to-do list, and don't leave home without it.

....

....

....

....

DAY 85

Live to Tell About It

They triumphed over him by the blood of the
Lamb and by the word of their testimony.

—Revelation 12:11

LIFE CAN HIT HARD. The enemy's attacks often feel relentless—sometimes coming not in single blows but in waves. It's as though when one storm clears, another rolls in, making it feel like tough times come in threes or, worse, last for decades. How do we stand firm when the pressure seems never-ending, when it feels like the enemy is throwing everything at us?

Well, it's simple. Or shall I say, simple, stupid, hard? But don't stop. The only way out is through. No matter what, keep going. Then live to tell about it.

In a world overwhelmed with problems—personal and global—the last thing it needs is one more person complaining or highlighting what's wrong. What the world desperately needs is a group of people shining the light of Jesus, proclaiming the power of His testimony despite all odds. And they need you doing it in style!

If not now, when? If not you, who?

The testimony of Jesus is the most powerful tool we have. Jesus is the fulfillment of all of God's promises. His life, death, and resurrection ushered in a new era, one where God's heavenly Kingdom is both present and coming. As followers of Christ, we are not bystanders—we are called to bear witness and testify to the reality of His Kingdom.

Today's Scripture from Revelation confirms that we are in a spiritual battle, but it also reveals how we overcome—*by the blood of the Lamb and by the word of* [our] *testimony*. We already know the end of the story—God wins. But there are still souls on the line, lives hanging in the balance.

It's easy to get caught up in the grind of daily life, focused on paying bills, building careers, or just surviving. But let's be real—the true battle is not about earthly success. After our seventy to eighty years, there is an eternity ahead. And with billions of souls still unreached, the stakes are high. We have a job to do but not by playing the role of savior—that's Jesus's job. Our job is to declare the blood of the Lamb and share our testimony about who He is and what He's done in our lives.

Jesus has already shed His blood for us, securing our victory over sin, death, sickness, and fear. The blood of Jesus delivers, heals, cleanses, and restores. It's not about what we can do—it's about what He has already done. This is the greatest testimony we have, yet it becomes transformational when his blood becomes personal in our own lives.

What does Jesus's shed blood do for you, today, thousands of years later? Look back for a moment and think about how far you've come, the times God stepped in, lifted you up, dusted you off, and restored you. Remember the healings, the prayers answered, and the miracles you've witnessed. These are not just memories—they are moments where the blood of Jesus redeemed you, forgave you, justified and cleansed you, reconciled you, gave you access to God, healed you, and helped you overcome! These miracles are part of not just your story; they're also part of your testimony—God's bigger story!

Your testimony, the story of what He's done in your life, brings victory into the here and now. Even as you consider all He's done, it encourages you, edifies you, and even anchors you into the present moment. It reminds you of his goodness and his faithfulness and builds your faith. Equally so, it is the very *word of* [your] *testimony* that brings the victory into someone else's life too.

Here's the thing: If God has done it before, He will do it again. The testimony of Jesus is the spirit of prophecy. That means your story has the power to encourage others and remind them that God is real, alive, and working in their lives too. You don't need to be perfect in sharing your testimony. This isn't a polished TED Talk—it's your story. It's real, raw, and personal. And it not only blesses others, but it also strengthens them and reminds them to keep going.

Don't let the current battle make you forget all the victories you've already seen. Keep pushing forward and *live to tell about it*. This is how you overcome in style!

Revel: Today, take some time to write about the goodness of God in your life. What battles has God brought you through? What obstacles has He helped you overcome? As you reflect upon His goodness, consider that what He's already done for you can sustain what He will do for you.

Then live to tell about it! Share your testimony with someone—whether it's a friend or family member or in a small group setting. Let your testimony be a light that points others to Jesus.

Day 85 Live to Tell About It

Align: Today's Word is a perfect reflection of what you've been doing for the past eighty-four days—living the testimony.

In case you need the reminder—you're bridging the gap. You're part of God's bigger story. Yes, you're letting Him be God—but you're also rising up, taking bold, courageous steps day after day. And guess what? Your results are becoming the testimony of Jesus in motion.

Do you see what just happened there?! Every moment of this journey has been on purpose leading to this day. The day you start recognizing God's hand woven through every part of your story. The day your obedience turns into a living, breathing testimony. This is a moment worth pausing for. Worth celebrating. And definitely worth sharing.

OK. But also don't forget to align. Too often people quit because it starts to work, but that's all the more reason to stick with it and keep at it! Arise, align, and be mobilized.

....

....

....

....

Dream Stack: You're smack-dab in the middle of your miracle. So let's keep the momentum going. What's one thing you can do today to keep those dreams moving forward? Write it down and throw caution to the wind.

....

....

....

....

DAY 86

The Power of Prayer

I will pray until I become prayer itself.

—Psalm 109:4 TPT

OVER THE PAST WEEK, we've spent a lot of time reflecting on what it means to *become*. Becoming who God created us to be despite the pressures, distractions, disappointments, delays, and the weight of unforgiveness. Becoming as we learn who we really are in Christ, counting the cost, and sharing our testimony boldly and unapologetically.

With that in mind, I want to highlight one more crucial aspect of becoming: *prayer*. What an incredible privilege we have as believers to communicate with the creator of the universe! Yet it's so easy to underestimate or overlook the immense power prayer holds in shaping our lives.

Many admit they pray, just not when anyone else is around, as though there is a right or wrong way to do it. Others admit they pray "when all else fails." This implies that prayer is a last resort, something we turn to when we have run out of options. Or for some, prayer is one of those simple, profound practices that works so well that too often we just don't do it as much as we should. As a recovering doer, I struggled with prayer, simply because I had the wrong perspective. While others were praying, I was busy trying to make things happen—go, go, go; do, do, do was my mantra. Sure, that works for a while, but it eventually leads to burnout, exhaustion, and frustration.

But what if there isn't a right or wrong way to pray? What if it isn't our last resort for emergencies or crises, or just the first thing we do before we go about the rest of our day but is a consistent part of our day to day? What if prayer isn't just something we do but is a part of who we are? I propose that prayer is not just communication with God; it's also *communion* with God. It's a connection to Him. Sure, prayer can absolutely be a dedicated time set apart to be with the Lord, as Jesus frequently did by retreating to spend time with the Father. But prayer is more than a scheduled moment with the Lord. *It's also a place where we become like Him.*

This is the power of prayer!

We see David stepping into the fullness of prayer in the book of Psalms. In the midst of his greatest trials—trials so intense they put him face-to-face with death—David doesn't just pray; he *becomes* his prayer. We see this in today's Scripture when he says, *I will pray until I become prayer itself.*

David's life shows us something truly powerful. Here we see his life and his prayers are completely intertwined. His prayers weren't separate moments reserved for his prayer closet; they were woven into every part of his life. His relationship with God was so profound that prayer became a lifeline, not a mere item on a spiritual checklist. David didn't turn to God just to ask for things or seek relief—he also prayed to be transformed, to become the person God intended him to be. His prayers were an ongoing surrender to God's presence, allowing his heart to be molded daily. It wasn't a routine; it was a lifestyle of intimacy and trust.

Ask yourself: In your day-to-day moments of life (including hardship), where do you turn? Do you run to prayer as your first response, or is it an afterthought? Do you pray with the same intensity and focus that David had, or is your heart divided? Most of us don't reach the point where we *become prayer itself*, because we often don't pray with the depth that fully surrenders everything to God—praying not just for answers but becoming the very prayers that we pray.

But imagine how transformative it would be if we did. If we saw prayer not just as a means to an end but as the essence of our transformation in the Lord. If we prayed until we became *one* with the prayer, fully aligned with His will. It's not just about the words we speak; it's about letting our whole lives become an offering, a prayer in and of itself. This perspective could radically change not only how we pray but how we live—living each moment in communion with God, with hearts fully surrendered, trusting Him even when life feels overwhelming. It's a challenge, but it's also an invitation to experience the fullness of God in a deeper, more intimate way.

When prayer becomes our way of life, we experience the fullness of God where we learn from God, commune with Him, and petition for His will to be done on earth as it is in heaven. It's in this place of prayer with God, that we wage spiritual battles, surrender ourselves, and seek heavenly transformation. It's through prayer that we are shaped by God, molded into His likeness, and empowered to live in alignment with Him, so we can live like heaven on earth.

Let your life become a prayer. Begin in your prayer closet, yes, but don't leave prayer behind when you step out into your day. Let your whole life be an ongoing conversation with God. Don't just pray for change; be the change. Let your actions, your attitude, your heart, and your words be infused with prayerful connection to God that causes you to become what you pray for. If you're praying for peace, I pray you become peace. If you're praying for joy, I pray you become joy. If you're praying for your family, community, church, or nation to be on fire for God, I pray you become the fire.

May your life *become* your prayer.

Day 86 The Power of Prayer

Revel: How can your prayer time become the place where your life becomes a prayer?

Spend time talking with, communing with, and partnering with God daily. Then take what you've prayed for and live it out. Don't leave your prayers behind in your prayer closet—become them.

Align: As you reflect on yesterday and the steps you took toward your dream, remember, how you moved matters more than what you accomplished. Were your steps prayerful? Were you walking in communion with the Lord, aware of His presence in every breath, every move, every brick you laid toward the dream He's entrusted to you?

Today, as you align, be intentional. Stay in step with Him. Walk with Him. Talk with Him. Build with Him—every moment, every step of the way.

Dream Stack: Today, what is one action step you can take to make your dreams a reality? Write it down. Then don't just walk it out; pray it out!

....

....

....

....

DAY 87

Do Better: A Call to Excellence

Then this Daniel became distinguished above all the other high officials and satraps, because an excellent spirit was in him. And the king planned to set him over the whole kingdom.

—Daniel 6:3 ESV

WE LIVE IN AN INFORMATION AGE, which means anything we want to know, we can know with the click of a button. Yet why is it that the more we google, the more we know, but the more we know, the less we do.

As believers, our lives should be marked by the revelation of God's Word. The more we understand His truth, the more it should be reflected in how we live. This isn't about striving for perfection or living performance-driven lives. It's about allowing the revelation of God to produce something extraordinary in us. The more we receive His wisdom, the more our actions should align with that wisdom. His Word isn't meant to just fill our minds but to transform our lives—leading us to high levels of *excellence* in all we do.

Excellence is defined as the *quality* of being outstanding or extremely good. Synonyms for *excellence* include *brilliance*, *greatness*, and *transcendence*. As the body of Christ, we should live in a way that reflects the goodness of God. We are not God, but we are mirrors of His character and power. That means our lives should showcase what's possible when a person aligns their heart with God's truth and heavenly realms.

Daniel is an incredible example of this. The phrase *an excellent spirit was in him* from today's Scripture speaks volumes about Daniel's character and how he carried himself. This wasn't only about his outward abilities or success; it was also about an inner quality—a spirit of excellence that was rooted in his relationship with God.

Are you reflecting the brilliance and greatness of God in all you do?

Are you living in holy excellence?

Chances are, you're not always hitting that mark. But that's OK. It doesn't mean you're failing—it means you're human, and you may have forgotten what's available to you. Today, I'm here to remind you that excellence lives in you! It's who you are. It's who you were created to be.

You are created in the image of God. His Spirit dwells in you, and because of that, you have the capacity to reflect His excellence in everything you put your hand to. You don't need to strive for it; it's woven into your very identity.

This kind of excellence isn't about perfectionism that stresses you out. It brings life and peace. It doesn't drive you to constantly strive but invites you to rest and trust that His grace is sufficient for you, even in your imperfection. It won't leave you feeling drained; instead, it will fill you with purpose and energy as God works through you. Whether you're changing diapers, cooking dinner, building a business, or leading a team, God's love will inspire you to operate in excellence, not out of obligation but as a natural overflow of His grace in your life.

This kind of excellence isn't about seeking approval from others or validation through accolades, stats, or followers. It's not about people-pleasing or achieving worldly success. Instead, it's about doing everything for Jesus—with your whole heart—out of a genuine desire to honor Him, which is rooted in love.

So how can we live this out practically? It starts by drawing near to God and staying connected to His presence daily. When we dwell in His presence, we are constantly reminded of who we are and who He is. From that place of intimacy, His Spirit begins to flow through our actions, thoughts, and words. Excellence becomes less about performance and more about partnership with God.

The closer we are to the Father, the more His excellence flows through us. Our connection to His love becomes the source of everything we do. It is this love that empowers us to rise above mediocrity and reflect His character to the world around us. When you operate from this place of divine love, your work isn't just good—it's extraordinary, because God is behind it.

Today, as you go about your day, ask yourself: Am I reflecting God's brilliance and greatness in this moment? Am I doing this for His glory? Allow His Spirit to guide you, and let His love draw out a new level of excellence in your life that points back to Him. In doing so, you'll be walking in the fullness of who you were created to be—an extraordinary reflection of the God who loves you.

Don't just know more; do more with what you know.

Revel: What would Biblical excellence look like for you today? How can you rise up and walk in the greatness and brilliance of God's Kingdom in your everyday life?

Now ask yourself: Are there areas where you've been holding back, cutting corners, or lacking excellence? How can you realign yourself today, ensuring that everything you do is done with an excellent Spirit? Let this realignment set the tone for walking in His power and presence in every aspect of life.

Day 87 Do Better: A Call to Excellence

Align: Let today's principle guide your aligning time. As you reflect on yesterday, ask yourself: Did your steps reflect who you are, whose you are, and what you know you're called to do?

If not, there's no shame—just clarity. Pinpoint what held you back. Name it. Then decide how you'll rise above it today, so your actions start lining up with the truth you already know. Let your results testify to what you know to be true!

....

....

....

....

Dream Stack: What's one thing you can do today to move closer to your dreams—and how can you do it with a spirit of excellence?

Write it down clearly:

- Action step: (What exactly will you do?)
- How you'll do it with excellence: (What attitude, focus, or standard will you bring to it?)

Be specific. Excellence isn't about doing it perfectly; it's about doing it with full heart, full focus, and a commitment to honor God in the process.

....

....

....

....

DAY 88

What You Got?

Get wisdom, get understanding; do not forget my words or turn away from them.

—Proverbs 4:5

HAVE YOU FOUND YOURSELF READING any of these daily devotionals, or perhaps any book of the Bible, and admitting to yourself that it's hard to apply what you're learning? It makes sense as you read it, but you seem to fail at the application? Or as you read my motivational speech from yesterday about the call to excellence and knowing more so you can do better—you get it; you're just not doing better? What gives?

Good news, Proverbs gives us insight into why this is happening. It has a simple yet profound purpose: to connect us with divine wisdom and offer the guidance we need for our everyday lives. As I've read through it chapter by chapter I have noticed that Solomon, the author of this unforgettable book of the Bible, doesn't make things overly complicated. His words are clear and direct, and the application of its principles is a can't-fail, sure-proof plan to succeed. Yet despite its simplicity, applying this wisdom can sometimes feel like the hardest thing to do. #simplestupidhard

In today's passage, we see two words that may sound similar but carry distinctly different weight in how we live: *wisdom* and *understanding*. Though they're often paired together, their separate use here is intentional—and worth paying attention to. The distinction reminds us that each holds unique value and plays a different role in our day-to-day walk with the Lord.

Gaining *understanding* means acquiring knowledge, learning how things work, and grasping deeper insight into God's will, ways, and promises. Understanding is essential because it helps us intellectually comprehend God's Word and its relevance to our lives.

Wisdom, different from understanding, is the ability to take what you have learned and apply it in real-life situations. Wisdom forces you to move beyond knowledge and information and transform what you know into action and ultimately into who you become.

This confirms that understanding alone isn't enough. You can learn a lot and still lack the ability to apply it. One of my favorite quotes is from the philosopher Søren Kierkegaard: "If a person does not become what he understands, then he does not understand it either."

Think of it like this: Learning Scripture and applying Scripture are two different things, true or true? Knowing God's commands is one thing, but living them out is what sets us apart. Scripture tells us that even the demons know the Word of God, but that doesn't mean they're applying it. Our lives should be marked by understanding *and* wisdom.

Too often we learn about the love of God or His forgiveness, and we learn about His ways and His commandments, and then we wait to *feel* our way into living out God's principles. We wait until we *feel* loved before we live as if we're loved. We wait until we *feel* forgiven before we live as if we're forgiven. But God's Word teaches us to learn His principles then *apply* them, not feel them out. As believers, we aren't supposed to wait to feel a certain way about Scripture before we act accordingly. We have feelings; we're not our feelings. We are who God says we are; we do what He says we can do. When we take God's principles from head to heart by learning them, meditating on them, imagining them, *and* then living them out, we begin to align our lives with His wisdom. It's a process that requires repetition, guidance from spiritual mentors, *and* real-life application. Over time, applying what we've learned causes us to act our way into a new way of thinking and feeling. This is key!

Then when it works, because it will, don't stop living in wisdom's path. Proverbs reminds us in this same verse to *not forget* the wisdom God gives us. It's easy to fall back into old habits or let the pressures of life cause us to forget what we've learned by no longer applying it. But Solomon encourages us to stay alert, to hold tightly to the revelation God gives, and to keep applying heavenly wisdom to our lives.

So *what you got?* I encourage you today and every day above everything—above money, success, approval, or fame—to seek understanding *and* get wisdom. Let it be the thing you hunger for, the thing you can't live without. And as you do, remember, success in God's eyes isn't about perfection or worldly measures of achievement. It's about consistently pursuing His ways and living out His truth. When you do this, success—true success—is inevitable.

Get it? Got it. Good!

Revel: In what areas of your life do you need to seek deeper understanding from the Lord? Identify where you feel uncertain or unclear and use your time with God to grow in your knowledge of Him, His ways, and His truth.

Next consider the areas of your life where you already know the principles of His Word but haven't fully applied them yet. How can you begin to put that wisdom into action in real, tangible ways? Incorporate that into your dream stacking today.

Day 88 What You Got?

Align: As you reflect on yesterday, where did you see yourself move toward your dream? Notice the steps you took, because they're proof you're not just learning, you're also growing in the Lord. You're not just talking about His Word—you're also living it, walking it out one faithful step at a time. Celebrate that today!

And if you find any places where you hesitated or pulled back, don't beat yourself up. Instead, step under the waterfall of His grace. Let His love wash over you, reminding you of who He is, and let Him hand you the keys you need to live like Him—with hands ready to serve and feet willing to go.

Dream Stack: *What you got?* What's one thing you can do to chase after your dreams today? Don't just intellectually know what you need to do; write it down and do it. Apply that wisdom today.

DAY 89

Stewardship

[Jesus said,] 'For it will be like a man going on a journey, who called his servants and entrusted to them his property. To one he gave five talents, to another two, to another one, to each according to his ability.'

—Matthew 25:14–15 ESV

OFTEN THE FIRST QUESTION we ask someone when we first meet is: "What do you do for a living?" Walk into any networking event, social gathering, or small group setting, and you'll be asked within the first thirty seconds, "What do you do?"

Though society cares deeply about what you do for a living, the Lord cares more about how you do what you do. He cares that you use what He's entrusted to you, in a mindful and thoughtful way. This is called stewardship.

Biblical stewardship is recognizing, utilizing, and managing all resources God provides for His glory and the betterment of His creation. The essence of Biblical stewardship is managing everything God brings into our lives in a way that honors Him. It's the recognition that *all* of this is God's—that He has placed it in our care to borrow, nurture, and multiply for His glory.

It's like when my kids argue over whose room it is. Malachi says, "It's my room!" and Zion insists, "No, it's mine!" I quickly remind them, "Actually, it's neither of yours—I bought the house, and I'm letting you both use the room. I'm entrusting it to you to take care of, use wisely, and yes, share it." Reminding them that what they have is a gift they're responsible for stewarding usually ends the argument. When we see ourselves as stewards, partakers and beneficiaries of divine borrowing from the Lord, it shifts not only *what* we do but *how* we do it—or at least, it should.

Jesus teaches this principle in the parable of the talents, a unit of gold or silver used as money. In it, we see a master entrust his servants with talents. In those days, a single talent was worth about twenty years' wages, so this was no small gift!

Later in today's parable, we are told the two servants who were given the most invested what they were given and multiplied it. But the one who received only one talent, out of fear, buried it—and was met with disappointment. All were entrusted with something valuable, but how they chose to steward it made all the difference.

I propose that the parable of the talents isn't just about raw skill or ability—it's about actualizing ability, meaning what we choose to do with the gifts and potential we've been given. *According to his ability* isn't a fixed measure; it's a call to recognize and activate our gifts, doing what we can to the best of our potential.

Too often we claim we don't know what God is asking of us, or we hide behind a lack of clarity while habitually following the patterns of the world—going to college, getting a degree, finding a job, and pretending to be fine. We buy more to fill the emptiness, post photos of momentary excitement, and wonder why we still feel unfulfilled. If we're asked what we do for a living, we answer immediately. But if we're asked, "Are you stewarding the abilities God's given you?" we have no idea what to say.

But if we don't know how to steward the abilities He's given us, how can He multiply them? The parable of the talents shows us that the recognition of our gifts is important, even crucial. Often we walk through life without fully realizing what God has placed within us, wondering why we don't know our purpose or why we're not receiving the blessing that comes from stewardship. Yet the discovery and recognition of our abilities is equally as important as the utilization and management of them. You can't manage what you don't recognize.

Discovering your abilities and gifts requires intentional seeking, praying, and sometimes stepping out in faith to explore unfamiliar areas. It requires risk, trial and error, then utilization (i.e., stewardship). It's not about immediate perfection but about stewarding the discovery process. Stewarding the process of discovery is just as important as stewarding the gift! So no matter where you're at in the process, you can practice stewardship.

The parable of the talents also shows that God entrusts us according to the use of our ability, but that use isn't static. It can grow, expand, and deepen as we seek to understand our purpose, invest our gifts, and align ourselves with God's will. And the more we do this, committing to stewardship as a lifestyle, the more we step into His blessing.

Luke 12:48 (ESV) tells us *to whom much was given, of him much will be required*; this doesn't necessarily mean one person is born with more talent or potential than another—it means that the one who invests time and effort into recognizing, utilizing, and managing their God-given purpose is the one who becomes more and, ultimately, is given more. It's not about being better or doing more; it's about becoming more by nurturing what God has already placed within you. The more we steward, the more He can bless. Not because of merit, but because we've made room for more by faithfully developing what He's given us.

Your abilities are God-given—that's true. But the development and activation of those abilities? That's on you. That's the part that determines what God can trust you with next. It's about being a faithful steward of what you've already been given and preparing for what's to come by becoming more in Christ. God isn't concerned with your earthly job descriptions or titles; He's concerned about you recognizing the gifts He's given you, utilizing them, and managing them well. Not only is this stewardship, but it's also activated purpose.

True fulfillment comes from discovering your gifts, stewarding them well, and giving them away on behalf of the Lord. When we align our lives with God's plan and generously pour out what He's entrusted to us, we experience a deeper sense of joy and fulfillment that transcends worldly success. Living in that kind of purpose-centered stewardship is where true meaning is found.

Day 89 Stewardship

Revel: To walk in the fullness of stewardship, spend some time reflecting on these questions:

- What are my God-given gifts and abilities?
- How am I utilizing the gifts I've been given?
- How can I develop and manage them even better?
- What's the next step in actualizing my purpose even more?

Today, I encourage you to do some self-reflection and consider these big questions. Though they may not be easy or convenient to consider, they're worth asking. Every season, the answer to these questions may look different, but the recognition, utilization, and management of them are the most important things you could steward in a lifetime. Take some time to recognize, utilize, *and* manage the gifts you've been given. Then multiply them!

....

....

....

....

Align: Quick check-in—where did you make even the smallest move toward your dream yesterday? Big or small, it all counts. Take a moment to notate it, reflect on it, and recognize it as part of the bigger story God is writing through you.

And if yesterday felt a little stuck or heavy, that's OK too. Grace is already here. Use today to realign, to reset, and to step forward with fresh focus. Keep showing up—you're building something that matters.

BOLD

Dream Stack: What is one step you can take to make your dream a reality? Write it down. Make it real. Then get ready, get set, and go!

DAY 90

The More

[Jesus said,] 'All authority in heaven and on earth has been given to me. Therefore go and make disciples of all nations, baptizing them in the name of the Father and of the Son and of the Holy Spirit, and teaching them to obey everything I have commanded you. And surely I am with you always, to the very end of the age.'

—Matthew 28:18–20

YESTERDAY, WE TOOK TIME to reflect on what it means to steward the gifts God has given you. You learned that stewardship isn't about investing better or accumulating material things—it's about using what the Lord has entrusted to you for His purposes. It's not about having more but recognizing, utilizing, *and* managing the gifts, abilities, time, and resources you've been given to impact the Kingdom. God isn't focused on you having more for the sake of more; He's focused on you *becoming* more—and then multiplying!

To multiply means to increase or cause something to grow significantly. Biblical multiplication isn't about prosperity for selfish gain; it's a divine calling. We shouldn't seek the more of this world but the more of what God is doing.

We know that Jesus came to save us (Luke 19:10), to set an example (John 13:15), and to remind us that we too would do even greater works than He did (John 14:12). Then He did something remarkable: He commissioned us! His commissioning in today's Scripture wasn't just for the disciples of His time but also for all of us today. He didn't give it as an option but as a command with clear instructions.

This commissioning moment wasn't vague or up for debate. It was clear and specific. He gave specific authority (His own), specific instructions (*go and make disciples*), specific locations (*all nations*), under one name (*the name of the Father and of the Son and of the Holy Spirit*), and details on what to do (teach His commandments), then he affirmed His role (*I am with you always, to the very end of the age*). This commission was not for just the disciples at the time; it is also for every believer and follower of Christ—it is for you. Regardless of your role in life—whether you're a stay-at-home parent, an entrepreneur or business professional, a student, or retired, God is inviting you into His *more*.

The more God is inviting you into isn't about worldly gain; it's about increasing and multiplying what He's placed in your hands for His Kingdom. Multiplication happens when what we have meets God's power exceedingly, abundantly, more than we could ever think or imagine. He never intended for your personal relationship with Him to be just about you. He designed it to ignite a fire that does something within you then spreads to those around you. The gifts you've been given were meant to be used to serve and bless those around you.

With over three billion people in the world who haven't heard the name of Jesus and only 17 percent of the active church knowing what the Great Commission even is, we are not short on need. Though these facts are shocking, they should not discourage us—rather, they should fuel our passion and purpose. God has given us a mission, and it's time to step into the *more* He has for us. God isn't asking us to add with Him; He wants us to multiply with Him. Our God is not a God of sort of more or adding a little bit at a time; He is about exponential growth.

What does multiplication look like in our day-to-day life? I do believe every Christian should experience a mission trip one time in their lifetime, because it's important to get outside your norm and experience a global world, to see the extreme needs of people while experiencing the extreme heart of God in new ways. But even more important, I believe *on mission for Jesus* is the *more* we are all called to live—no matter who we are or where we are. Our mission is to know Jesus and make Him known, whether on a mission trip, through local outreach, at home, or at work. This is the more we were created for.

You were created for more. You were created to reach people, to make His name known, and to spread the Gospel. Though the need for Jesus is universal, God's call for you will be personal and unique in the way you live it out.

The *more* with God is creative, uninhibited, and filled with opportunities to work with an unrestricted God who can do anything through people willing to say yes. My prayer for you today is that you stir the gifts God has given you and ask His heart for the more. Go bold, live bigger, and step into the more that God has for you. You've been commissioned. It's time to multiply.

The harvest is ready. Are you? Of course you are. Now go!

Revel: How can you step into the *more* today? What are the creative, uninhibited ways in which God can use you to multiply His Kingdom?

Spend time commissioning yourself in the presence of God. Ask Him to open your eyes and give you a heart to know who He is and what He is doing in the world around you. Then ask Him what role He wants you to play in His plan today and how He wants you to respond. Step into the boldness of your calling, ready to be used by Him in greater ways!

Day 90 The More

Align: You're almost there—91 days of aligning with the Lord. It's simple, yet some days felt hard, and still, you showed up—calming your heart, mind, and spirit, training your mindset, heartset, and dreamset to match Heaven's blueprint. Today, pause and notice the progress—not just around you, but within you. Look back at what you're doing now that you wouldn't have dared 90 days ago. Take some time to reflect and journal on how far you've come.

Dream Stack: What's one step you can take today to move closer to your dream? Then think bolder—Go for the more! You're not just building an ordinary life—you're living out His exceedingly abundant more.

Write it down. Commit to doing it. Don't quit. Heaven's not finished writing your story yet.

DAY 91

Abide

[Jesus said,] 'If you abide in me, and my words abide in you, ask whatever you wish, and it will be done for you.'

—John 15:7 ESV

MANY PEOPLE INTERPRET VERSES like this one or Matthew 7:7 (*Ask and it will be given to you*) as if God were a cosmic genie waiting to fulfill our every request. But having traveled the world and engaged with the church in many places, I've seen the need to address this misconception—no matter how mature someone's faith may seem.

Our God is not a genie, nor is He like Santa Claus, whose purpose is to deliver all our wishes. He is the creator of the universe, Yahweh, the great I AM—our Father, healer, hope, and redeemer. Though He cares deeply about the desires of our hearts, His ultimate desire is for relationship, not transaction. He doesn't want us to merely come to Him for what He can give us. He wants us to know Him, to trust Him, and to abide in Him.

When we treat God as a means to our desires, we set ourselves up for disappointment. When our prayers are specifically to see our dreams come true, when they aren't answered as we expect, it can lead to resentment and shape our view of God in unhealthy ways. But when we shift our focus to truly abiding in Him, everything changes.

We often think we understand what it means to abide, but as we see in today's Scripture, it goes much deeper than we realize. To abide means to remain, stay, or dwell in a particular place over time. Jesus is calling us to make our home in God—to live, breathe, and be sustained by His presence. In Hebrew, words like *shakan* and *yashab* translate to *dwell* or *settle*, often describing God's presence as dwelling with His people. The beauty of abiding is that it's not about getting results; it's about deep, ongoing communion with the Lord.

Abiding in God means staying connected to Him, even when life is tough, prayers go unanswered, and circumstances don't align with our expectations. It's about having His Word not just in our minds but also deep in our hearts, shaping how we live, think, and act.

Many believers fall into the trap of focusing solely on asking God for things. But abiding in Christ has a purpose. Only in His presence are our hearts transformed to reflect His heart. The more time we spend with God, the more we become like Him. Think about it: The people you spend the most time with are the ones you start to resemble in both actions and attitudes. The same is true with God. As we dwell in His presence, we begin to develop His characteristics, and our desires start to align with His.

That's why verses like John 15:7 promise that we can ask for anything, and it will be given to us. It's not because God is handing out everything we ask for, but because when we abide in Him, our hearts and desires are transformed to align with His. We no longer seek what's in His hand; we seek what's in His heart. It's not about the ask—it's about the heart. It's about the invitation then the promise.

Abiding teaches us to stay close to God, no matter the trials or challenges we face. The words *endure* and *bear* are often synonymous with *abide*. It's this enduring relationship that produces fruit and enables us to ask from a place of deep connection with God's will. Our desires, then, are no longer self-centered but are grounded in a desire to see God's purpose fulfilled.

If you feel distant from God or if your relationship with Him has become more about asking and less about becoming, now is the time to realign. Return to abiding in Him. Settle into His presence and ask Him to reshape your heart. Give Him your desires but also ask Him for His heart.

If you're feeling like you've been asking and seeking, asking and seeking but are disappointed in how God seems to be showing up, consider not doubting Him but drawing closer to Him. Maybe you've mastered the asking but need to focus more on His heart. Trust Him with the outcomes, lean in, and get to know Him more deeply. Give Him the chance to show you what's in His heart, not just His hands. And perhaps in that place of abiding, you'll find that He gently redirects your ask.

When you learn to abide, you're no longer consumed by what God can give but by who He is. That is where transformation happens. That is where we begin to live out the truth of John 15:7, not just as a request for things but also as an invitation into deeper intimacy with the Father.

Revel: Has your time with God been more focused on asking for things than being with Him, abiding in Him?

Today, relearn what it means to abide in Him. Seek Him not for the answers to prayers or for what He can do for you but simply for who He is. Allow your heart to rest in His presence, knowing that you'll find more than answers—you'll find Him.

Day 91 Abide

Align: As you look back on yesterday, ask: Did I live aligned with God's truth? Did my choices honor the promises He's spoken over my life? Pause and notice the moments where you walked in step with Him—let those be your reminders that growth is happening, even if you don't always see it.

And for the moments that feel out of rhythm, don't hide them. Bring every thought, emotion, and misstep to Jesus. Lay it all down, so He can trade it for something better. His grace covers it all.

....

....

....

....

Dream Stack: What's one intentional step you can take today to move your dream forward? Write it down. Then put your feet to the street allowing His presence to guide your pace, your posture, and your purpose.

....

....

....

....

DAY 92

Let's Go on an Adventure

By faith Abraham, when called to go to a place he would later receive as his inheritance, obeyed and went, even though he did not know where he was going.

—Hebrews 11:8

ONE OF OUR FAMILY STANDARDS is *adventure*. And man, oh man, our lives are defined by this word. We've sold everything and traveled the country in an RV. We've stayed in rentals, not just for vacations but as a lifestyle, spending extended time in areas we hadn't lived in, all with kids in tow. We've had a farm and lived on ten acres and in a loft. Who knows where we'll be in another few years? All that to say, we take adventuring seriously.

Life with God is not static; it's dynamic and full of growth, and it's an unfolding journey as He leads you into the fullness of His plans. I say He's leading you on an adventure too!

The word *adventure* suggests physical action, taking risks, being courageous, trying new things, and seeking excitement. In the spiritual sense, an adventure with God is more than just an adrenaline rush or the thrill of new experiences—it's the bold decision to step into the unknown with faith, trusting God to leads.

Take Abraham in today's passage, for example. Abraham was called by God to leave his home (his comfort zone) and journey to an unknown land that God would show him. He had no map, no guarantees, and no idea how everything would turn out, yet he obeyed. Imagine how Abraham must have felt—perhaps a little fearful but also excited by the adventure of following God's plan.

Abraham's journey took him through deserts and mountains, and he faced countless challenges. But through it all, he trusted God to guide and protect him. His story shows us that stepping into an adventure with God might not always be easy, but it is always worth it. It requires faith, courage, and a willingness to embrace uncertainty, trusting that God will provide everything needed along the way.

Because of Abraham's obedience, his faith, and his willingness to go on an adventure with God, he was richly blessed. Not only did God bless Abraham, but He also blessed his descendants for generations to come. His life became a testimony of what God can do when we step out in faith and allow Him to lead the way just as today's Scripture so beautifully describes.

Going on an adventure with God means doing life *with* Him—following where He leads, even when the destination is unclear. Too often we find ourselves doing things *for* God, yet the truth is, He doesn't need us to do anything for Him. He wants to do life *with* us, hand in hand.

Dreaming with God is an adventure! Like Abraham, you might feel uncertain at times, but God promises to be with you every step of the way. Take courageous steps of faith, try things you've never tried, and embrace the unknown with trust, giving God the opportunity to show up in extraordinary ways. Hand in hand with God, trust that you are on the right path. Now have some fun, would ya?!

※ ※ ※ ※ ※ ※

Revel: What new adventures, perhaps disguised as risks, is God calling you to step into today? How can you deepen your trust in Him and embrace life as an adventure alongside the Lord?

Take time today to reflect on His faithfulness and the depth of your friendship with Him. Remember, adventuring with God is not just about doing things for Him but also about experiencing the joy and fun that come with walking hand in hand with Him!

Align: Reflect on yesterday—are you having fun yet? I don't know about you, but sometimes I can get way too serious about doing God's work. But what if this journey with Him—twists, turns, and all—is meant to be full of joy? Full of peace?

Maybe today, as you reflect, you let yourself lean back a little. Smile. Enjoy the ride. Receive all the goodness God is pouring into your life through this beautiful, wild journey called living with Him.

Day 92 Let's Go on an Adventure

Dream Stack: Today, what's one thing that pushes you out of your comfort zone and into your dream zone? Write it down, have some fun, and go for it, all in, all out!

....

....

....

....

DAY 93

Thank God It's Friday

This is the day the Lord has made. We will rejoice and be glad in it.
—Psalm 118:24 NKJV

I WAS SITTING AT A COFFEE SHOP the other day, and overhearing a conversation, I couldn't help but roll my eyes when someone said, "Thank God it's Friday!"

How often do we hear this saying? Or maybe we've said it ourselves. It implies relief that the workweek is over—a week likely spent in a job we don't enjoy, with people we don't connect with, and for a cause we're not passionate about. We finally get to rest, unwind, and live for the weekend, free from the Monday-to-Friday grind. But when Sunday afternoon arrives, that sinking feeling sets in, because we know we have to do it all over again.

I don't know about you, but that's not the kind of life I want to live, and it's certainly not the life God intended. Notice that today's Scripture doesn't mention yesterday or tomorrow, Friday or Saturday. It doesn't say, "Rejoice on your best day" or "when things go your way." It says, *This is the day*—today, the one right in front of you. It's not about waiting until everything falls into place or when your dream is fulfilled. I suggest this verse is inviting us not to do something different but to see each day differently.

We've all experienced the ups and downs of life, and it's easy to get caught up in the grind and take each day for granted. Perhaps you can relate. Maybe you are going through a hard season, and you've lost the light at the end of the tunnel. Or you're raising babies, and you're so overrun by all the things that you can no longer determine what day it is let alone celebrate *this day*. But here's a reminder: Life is fleeting, and none of us is guaranteed tomorrow.

The life expectancy for women living in the United States is 80.2 years; for men, it's 74.8 years. This means we have a limited number of years to make the most of each day. Scripture doesn't tell us to grind it out, pretend it away, wish for something different, or even do something different; it invites us to see each day differently—as a gift from God!

When you start to see each day as a gift from God, your perspective shifts. You begin to feel gratitude for what you have and find the courage to change what needs changing. Instead of grumbling or settling for how things are or thinking, *"I've been in this career for thirty years, so I might as well stick with it until I retire,"* you gain fresh eyes to see today for what it truly is—a gift. And with that clarity, you realize that if God has brought you to it, He's also equipped you to get through it or, even better, to make a change.

Once you choose to see each day differently, you open the door to making different choices. Though this sounds simple, I know it's not always easy. No matter how old you are, doing something different—whether it's starting a new job or career, moving cities or countries, finding a new friend group—won't happen with the snap of your fingers, and it can bring up insecurities and fears. But it's worth facing them. The stats say you'll spend around 90,000 hours of your life working. That's a lot of time. If you're not passionate about what you do, don't feel called to it, or haven't had the courage to pursue what truly matters to you, you're signing up for a significant chunk of your life doing something you don't love. If that's you, it's time to change it. If you live in a place you don't love, but you're there because you've been there for thirty-plus years, remind yourself that no one says you have to stay there. You can make a change. If you're in relationships that are not supporting you to fulfill the dreams God's given you nor to become everything God's called you to be, you can make a change.

Today is the day!

When we choose to see today as a gift, the world around us seems to change: Birds sing louder, the sun shines brighter, the things we once grumbled about don't seem to bother us in the same way, and making the appropriate changes we need to make doesn't feel so impossible. In reality, what's changed is our perspective. A changed perspective changes everything.

So, if you're waiting for Friday to find joy, make a change. Yes, you can! That's why you're here reading this devotional, pursuing a life built on your dreams. Today is your day. And every day thereafter. It's *the* day God gives you, full of choices and possibilities. Rejoice in that. If you're in the midst of challenges, today is still your day. Rejoice, no matter what day of the week it is, for this is the day God has given you. You will never get it back. It is precious. It is a gift, and you can find joy in that.

Today, if you're alive and breathing, God has given you another day—maybe it's not perfect, but it's yours. In eternity, there will be no pain or struggle—praise will flow naturally. But today, in the midst of life's challenges, you have the unique opportunity to praise Him through it all. There's something special about that.

So today—rejoice. It's the day God has made.

Day 93 Thank God It's Friday

Revel: Are there changes you need to make to break out of the "Is it Friday yet?" mindset? If so, make them today.

Spend time reflecting on the fact that today is the day the Lord has made. Ask Him to give you a heart that rejoices in each day, no matter what. If today is a day you need to make changes, find the boldness to do that. Spend time in your dream stacking time to identify and write the necessary changes you know you need to make. Then rejoice!

....

....

....

....

Align: Reflect on yesterday: Where did you see yourself move closer to the person God has called you to be? Where did your actions line up with the truth of who you are in Him? Celebrate those places—they're proof that transformation is happening step by faithful step.

If you find places where you slipped or struggled, that's not failure—it's an invitation. Hand it over to Jesus. Trust His grace to fill the gaps and keep leading you forward. His exchange is always more than enough.

....

....

....

....

BOLD

Dream Stack: What's one thing you get to do today to move closer to your dreams? You don't have to—you get to. (It's something I always remind my children.)

What an honor it is to partner with heaven and build the dreams God has placed inside you. Make a conscious choice today: Write it down, take action, then celebrate as you do it. Now that's something worth rejoicing over!

....

....

....

....

DAY 94

Worship: More Than a Song

[Jesus said,] 'But the hour is coming, and is now here, when the true worshipers will worship the Father in spirit and truth, for the Father is seeking such people to worship him. God is spirit, and those who worship him must worship in spirit and truth.'

—John 4:23–24 ESV

WORSHIP. WHEN WE HEAR THAT WORD, we often picture singing songs in church or raising our hands in praise among a group of people. But what if worship is more than just a moment we create through music or ritual? What if worship is a posture of the heart, a deep surrender that goes beyond the actual act in and of itself?

In John 4, Jesus speaks to the Samaritan woman at the well about the kind of worship the Father is seeking. If you remember from a few devotions back, Jesus didn't come to the well to just offer us water—He came to be our Living Water. He came not to abolish the law but to fulfill it. It was at this place He also redefined what it means to be *true worshipers*, no longer binding us to a specific place or tradition but becoming an expression of love and adoration for the One we live for.

Did you notice in today's passage Jesus says two times, *in spirit and truth*. He means what He's saying, and He doesn't want us to just intellectually understand it but also for us to become it.

He says *those who worship him must worship in spirit and truth*. When Jesus tells us to worship in *spirit*, He's pointing to the inner transformation that takes place when we are born again through the Holy Spirit. But this isn't a one-time event of salvation or limited to a Sunday morning experience—it's a daily, ongoing act that connects our hearts to the heart of the Father, wherever we are. Worship in spirit flows from a deep surrender, a profound understanding that we are completely dependent on God. In John 4:24 (AMP), God is described as *spirit [the Source of life, yet invisible to mankind]*. It's not just about lifting our voices—it's also offering our very lives to the Lord, our source, our well of life.

True worship in spirit doesn't come from striving; it's a natural overflow of God's presence and power within us. When we grasp the reality of who He is and what He's done, worship becomes a response from the core of our being, aligning our hearts with His in every moment.

Worship in *truth* begins with bringing our real, authentic selves before the Lord. It's not about pretending to be perfect or hiding our flaws and struggles. It's about coming to God as we are—honest, open, and vulnerable. Only then can we worship Him in truth, acknowledging who He is—holy, loving, just—and who we are in His sight—broken yet redeemed, fully dependent on His grace. God isn't after a flawless performance or worship set; He desires sincerity. When we worship in truth, we lay our hearts bare before Him, unguarded and unashamed, and in return, we receive His heart.

In this exchange, we come face-to-face with the truth of who He is and the truth of who we are in light of His grace. This doesn't mean we simply come as we are and remain unchanged; rather, we are transformed by encountering His truth. His truth begins to shower over our doubts, fears, concerns, and even our hopes and dreams. And this transformation isn't limited to a worship set or a well-played song—it's an ongoing process where our lives are continually reshaped by His truth.

Jesus says that the Father is seeking *true worshipers*. He's looking for those whose hearts are fully surrendered to Him, those who worship Him with authenticity, and in light of *His* truth. Worship is an offering of our entire lives, which means every thought, every word, every action can be worship when done in spirit and truth. It's about living in a constant posture of surrender to God, knowing He is worthy of all honor and praise, not just when the music plays but in every moment.

Worship is more than a song—it's the heart of the believer fully surrendered to God's love and purpose. Let this be the anthem of your life as you worship Him in spirit and truth.

Don't just sing a song; be the song.

Revel: Is worship something you do on Sundays, or is it a lifestyle? Do you worship in spirit, fully connected to God's presence, or are you distracted by the noise around you? Do you worship in truth, offering your real self to God, or are you hiding parts of yourself from Him?

Take a moment to worship Him, asking God to reveal areas of your life where He's calling you to worship Him more fully in spirit and in truth. Ask the Holy Spirit to ignite your heart and empower your worship beyond the confines of a song and into the fullness of your everyday life.

Day 94 Worship: More Than a Song

Align: Remember, this isn't about whether you're making progress every single day—it's about tracking your progress. That was the shift a few weeks ago. But let's be honest: if you're anything like me (or just human), you've probably missed a day or two. Maybe you forgot. Maybe you didn't check in.

That doesn't define your outcome—unless you let it. Yesterday is behind you. Still, it's worth asking: Did I move in the direction God's calling me or have I lost momentum?

If not, don't cover it up. Don't excuse it. Call it out. What tripped you up? Be real about it. Bring it into the light—and let God meet you right there. His grace doesn't just cover—it empowers. Take the time to pause. Reflect. Realign. Then rise and take the ground He's already given you. Today is a new day.

All right now—keep on keepin' on!

Dream Stack: What's one thing you can do today to move you closer to your dreams? Write it down and take that step as an act of worship—because every move you make in obedience is a way of honoring Him.

DAY 95

Breathe

God now unveils these profound realities to us by the Spirit. Yes, he has revealed to us his inmost heart and deepest mysteries through the Holy Spirit, who constantly explores all things.

—1 Corinthians 2:10 TPT

HAVE YOU EVER FOUND YOURSELF saying, "I don't know"? It's such a common response when you're faced with something you don't understand or when you're unsure of what to do next. But in our family, we've noticed that this little statement can be a hidden roadblock, especially on the journey to dreaming with God. That's why in the Gentry household, we've made it a rule that we don't say, "I don't know." It's not because we think we should always have an answer. In fact, we recognize there's so much we don't know. The problem isn't the lack of knowledge—the problem is what the sentence can do to us.

When we say, "I don't know," it's like hitting a mental roadblock that causes us to stop thinking, stop searching, and stop growing—similar to a dead-end street. It can be a cop-out, a quick and easy way to avoid the effort of digging deeper. Instead of fostering curiosity and exploration, "I don't know" can shut down the very process that leads to overcoming the impossibilities of life.

So we encourage a different response: "Hmm, fascinating! How *could* I know?" This shift in language moves us from a mindset of uncertainty and passivity to one of curiosity and active pursuit of an answer. It opens up possibilities and encourages us to think creatively, seek knowledge, and explore the unknown with hope and even joy. It makes the impossible feel more possible and the unknown not so scary.

The reality is that not knowing is part of life. We're not expected to have all the answers. But as believers, we have a unique advantage: We know the One who does have all the answers. God invites us into a relationship where we can come to Him with our questions and lean on His wisdom.

Today's verse is absolutely mind-blowing when you stop to really think about it. God, the creator of the universe, has given us direct access to His heart and the deepest truths of heaven through His Spirit. Too often we underestimate the power and significance of this. But when we truly grasp it, it changes everything.

Think about it: The Holy Spirit revealed God's *deepest mysteries* to us! This means we're not left stumbling through life trying to figure things out on our own. We have divine access to wisdom that the world doesn't even know exists. It's not just for pastors, theologians, or super-spiritual people. It's for every believer, meaning you and I have the ability to walk in the knowledge and revelation of God's ways.

If we, as Christians, fully understood the magnitude of this truth, we would be leading in every sphere of life—education, business, science, technology, or any other field. Why? Because we have access to the divine creator's insight. But here's the key: It's not about having instant answers like a magician pulling a rabbit out of a hat. It's about knowing where to turn when we need wisdom. It's about having a relationship with the Holy Spirit, who reveals things at the right time, and being led by Him.

In our walk of faith, the Holy Spirit is our greatest gift. He's not just some distant or abstract concept; He's personal, present, and powerful. The Bible describes Him as our comforter, counselor, helper, and advocate. He is with us every step of the way, guiding us into all the truth (John 16:13). The Holy Spirit reveals Himself in many ways—like a dove descending from heaven (Matthew 3:16), tongues of fire (Acts 2:3), a cloud of glory, or water that brings refreshment and life (John 7:38). But most of all, He is described as the very *breath* of God.

And this is where I want to dive deeper: *breath*.

If you've ever explored breathwork, you know it offers numerous physical benefits, including:

- Nourishing your body
- Oxygenating your cells
- Promoting healing
- Boosting your immune system
- Calming your mind
- Quieting mental chatter
- Aligning your mind, heart, and body
- Breathe in. Breathe out.

Here's the interesting part: You don't need to actively practice breathwork to experience these benefits. We naturally get them from breathing. However, when you intentionally engage in breathwork, you unlock these benefits at a deeper level. Most of us tend to breathe shallowly, almost as if we're sipping air. Take a moment now to check in with your breath—are you taking deep, full breaths, or are they short and shallow?

No matter your answer, try this: Pause and take five to seven deep breaths by inhaling deeply for seven seconds, holding for one second, and exhaling slowly for eleven seconds. Repeat this process several times. This is a simple form of breathwork. Now imagine doing that for thirty minutes. You might notice your fingers and toes tingling, your heart rate increasing slightly, or your belly feeling a fluttering sensation . That's because you're waking up your nervous system and fully engaging your body's natural power. Breathing is automatic, but with purposeful breathwork, you activate its benefits in a whole new way,

Day 95 Breathe

The same is true for the Spirit. *Breath* is translated as *spiritus* in Latin, and *spirit* is derived from the word *breath*. The Hebrew word for *spirit* is *ruach*, which also means breath or wind. The Holy Spirit is the breath of God, the life-giving force that fills and sustains us. Just as our physical breath keeps us alive, so the Holy Spirit sustains and empowers our spiritual life. We don't often think about breathing—it's automatic, happening without effort. The same is true spiritually. The Holy Spirit is always there, like breath, but when we consciously invite Him into our life—when we intentionally lean on Him for guidance, wisdom, and strength—we activate His power in a whole new way.

Breathe in. Breathe out.

What if we began to live with this kind of awareness of the Holy Spirit every day? What if we let Him breathe into our decisions, our challenges, our uncertainties, and even our dreams? Just as you practice breathwork to nourish your body, take time every day to activate the Spirit's presence in your life. Breathe Him in deeply. Invite Him into your conversations, decisions, and moments of uncertainty. Ask Him to reveal the mysteries of God's heart to you. And watch how He begins to unveil *profound realities*—truths that can guide you, transform you, and lead you to places you could never reach on your own.

So the next time you're tempted to say, "I don't know," pause for a moment. Instead of stopping there, ask yourself: How *could* I know? Invite the Holy Spirit into that very moment. Activate your breath. Activate the Spirit. Then through studying Scripture or spending time in prayer, seek Him, because He is faithful and His Word says you will find Him!

Breathe deeply today. Take time not just for breathwork but for intentionally inviting the Holy Spirit into your day and into the I don't knows you face.

Breathe in. Breathe out.

Revel: Write down any questions or uncertainties weighing on you. Then pause, breathe, and ask the Holy Spirit to bring light to the mysteries of Christ in every area of doubt. Keep seeking until His clarity and peace fill your heart.

....

....

....

....

Align: Reflect on yesterday—what's one thing you did to move toward your dream? Let the reflection cause you to pause. Regardless of your wins or setbacks, stay rooted in the power of alignment with the Lord.

Breathe in. Breathe out.

Realign and move forward in His grace.

....

....

....

....

Day 95 Breathe

Dream Stack: What's one thing you can do today to make your dreams a reality? Write it down, then go make it happen. (Oh, and don't forget to breathe!)

....

....

....

....

DAY 96

It's Not About the Boat

Shortly before dawn Jesus went out to them, walking on the lake. When the disciples saw him walking on the lake, they were terrified. 'It's a ghost,' they said, and cried out in fear. But Jesus immediately said to them: 'Take courage! It is I. Don't be afraid.' 'Lord, if it's you,' Peter replied, 'tell me to come to you on the water.' 'Come,' he said. Then Peter got down out of the boat, walked on the water and came toward Jesus.

—Matthew 14:25–29

AT THIS POINT, YOU'RE OUT OF YOUR comfort zone. Or as I often say, "You've stepped out of the boat." You're doing things you've never done, talking to people you've never talked to, trying new things, and going to places you've never gone before. With each step, you're gaining a fresh perspective on that "boat" you once found so comfortable. Perhaps you're realizing it's not as scary or difficult as you thought. And no matter how far you've come out of that boat of comfort, you should be proud of yourself.

But here's the thing—it's not about the boat!

We often spend years in the boat—our comfort zone—where we feel in control, everything makes sense, and we can measure outcomes. But then something happens. We encounter the Lord, we start dreaming again, and the Holy Spirit nudges us out of that comfort zone. Suddenly, we realize, "I've been in this boat for too long, and it's time to step out." That first step of faith can feel enormous. We overanalyze, pray hard, and break through strongholds. We seek advice, develop new habits and practices (much like you've done with this devotional), and do what we can to work up the courage to take those first couple of steps. But in the end, the only way to get out of the boat is to actually step out of it! We don't think our way out or feel our way out; we don't even pray our way out; we act our way out! We have to step out of the boat!

Today's story of Peter is the perfect example. Here we see Peter and other disciples in a boat. Up to that point, there was nothing wrong with these men being in the boat. They didn't know anything else was available to them other than sitting in a boat. Then here comes Jesus, walking on water, defying everything these men knew was possible. Yet in their humanity, they don't recognize Him; instead, they're terrified!

Why do we often respond with fear instead of awe when we encounter something unknown? These men were looking at Jesus, and yet they thought they saw a ghost. When the unknown shows up in our lives, we must learn to recognize Jesus. It's not about the unknown or for these men, the ghosts; it's about seeing Jesus in everything!

Then Jesus does what He's so faithful in doing; he calms their fear not only with His words but also with His spoken identity: *'Take courage! It is I. Don't be afraid.'* This statement is so simple and so profound from Jesus, because it causes us to remember that no matter how afraid we are, the great I AM is greater, and in that, we have no reason to be afraid.

Then Peter makes a bold statement: *'Lord, if it's you, tell me to come to you on the water.'* Peter knew that nothing was impossible as long as Jesus called him. Did you hear me?! I'll say it again—there is no miracle or dream that can't be realized if the Lord calls you to it. Peter wasn't acting out of fear but out of faith, saying, "I won't step out unless *you* call me." Here we begin to see that it's not about the boat; it's about the call. One call from Jesus gets you out of the boat, it eradicates your fear, and it allows you to walk on water!

Then with one word, *'Come,' the call*—Jesus calls Peter forth! Peter defied reason, intellect, and the laws of nature. He stepped out of the boat and walked toward Jesus on the water.

Let me tell you this, when Jesus calls, you GO! When Jesus says *come*, you better get your booty out of that boat. It's the moment you were born for, the moment you've been waiting for.

Here's the key—it's not about the boat. It's about Jesus. Stepping out of the boat is important, but the focus must remain on Christ. If we make it about the boat, the boat becomes greater than Jesus. If we make it about the waves, they become greater than Jesus. It's about keeping your eyes on Him and following His call.

Listen for His voice. Respond to His call. Keep your eyes on Jesus. And walk on water!

Revel: Where has your focus been lately—on the boat of comfort, the fear of the unknown, or the waves of resistance?

Today, shift your gaze back to Jesus. Respond to His call, repent for any misplaced focus, and realign your attention on the One who calls you out of the boat—Jesus!

Day 96 It's Not About the Boat

Align: Reflect on yesterday—where did you dare to step out of the boat and follow Jesus? Remember, boldness isn't about confidence in yourself—it's about locking eyes with Him and moving in obedience, even when it costs you.

Don't downplay those small, daily steps. They aren't just tasks to check off—they're surrendered, faith-filled acts of obedience that are building something eternal.

Today, as you fix your eyes on Jesus, align your heart with His—and trust that He'll steady you to walk on water, one bold step at a time.

....

....

....

....

Dream Stack: What's one bold thing you can do to get out of the boat and go where Jesus has called you to go? Write it down, fix your eyes on Him, then step out in faith!

....

....

....

....

DAY 97

Disqualified

The Spirit of the Sovereign Lord is on me, because the Lord has anointed me to proclaim good news to the poor. He has sent me to bind up the brokenhearted, to proclaim freedom for the captives.

—Isaiah 61:1

HOW MANY TIMES DO WE DISQUALIFY ourselves before God even has the opportunity to use us? If you've ever found yourself doing this, know you're not alone.

Throughout the Bible, God often chose individuals who, by the world's standards, seemed "disqualified"—those who appeared unfit for the tasks He had in store for them. Yet through their stories, we learn that God's purposes are often fulfilled through those the world overlooks. If you've ever felt disqualified or counted yourself out, take heart—you're in the perfect place. God has chosen you, and He will use you. But you do have to respond, even when you feel unqualified. Here are some more powerful examples:

Isaiah may not have seemed qualified by the world's standards, but he was fully called by God. When Isaiah encountered the holiness of God in Isaiah 6, his immediate reaction was to confess his unworthiness: Woe to me! I am ruined! For I am a man of unclean lips...(Isiah 6:5). He didn't try to hide his flaws—he acknowledged them. By cultural standards, he lacked the credentials: he wasn't a priest or king, and he didn't have the religious résumé that would make him a likely prophetic voice. But God wasn't looking for perfect; He was looking for available. Even though Isaiah confessed how unqualified he felt, he said yes. And though his message wouldn't be popular—he was called to speak to a rebellious group of people who often wouldn't listen—God wasn't after worldly success; He was after faithfulness.

Moses was a fugitive and a stutterer, and when God called him to lead the Israelites out of Egypt, Moses initially protested, feeling unqualified due to his speech impediment and lack of confidence. Yet God chose him to confront the pharaoh and lead an entire nation to freedom. God didn't see Moses's weaknesses as disqualifying factors; instead, He empowered him to do the impossible (Exodus 3:11–12; 4:10–13).

David was the youngest and least likely son of Jesse to be appointed as king. When Samuel came to anoint the new king of Israel, all of David's older brothers were presented to him first, but God rejected them. God saw something in David—his heart. Despite being young, inexperienced, and a shepherd, David was chosen to be Israel's king, and he eventually defeated Goliath, a giant no one else could defeat (1 Samuel 16:6–13).

Gideon, from the weakest clan in Manasseh and the least in his family, was hiding when the angel of the Lord appeared to him, calling him a mighty warrior. He doubted his ability and questioned why God would choose someone like him. Yet God used Gideon to deliver Israel from the oppression of the Midianites, showing that even the most unlikely leaders can be used for great purposes when God is with them (Judges 6:11–16).

Rahab was a prostitute in the city of Jericho, yet she was used by God to help the Israelite spies, hiding them from the authorities. Her faith in God's power and her willingness to act saved her family when Jericho was destroyed. Despite her past, Rahab is listed in the genealogy of Jesus (Matthew 1:5), showing that God can redeem anyone for His purposes (Joshua 2).

Paul, formerly Saul, was a persecutor of Christians. He was an enemy of the early church and did much harm to believers. Yet God radically transformed him on the road to Damascus, turning him from a murderer of Christians into one of the greatest apostles of the faith. His story is a powerful testimony of how God uses even the most disqualified individuals to advance His Kingdom (Acts 9:1–22).

So what's your excuse? What's holding you back from responding to the Lord? Believe me, I understand the weight that shame and feelings of disqualification can carry. But today, I want to remind you that your qualifications don't come from you—they come from the Lord. The truth is, He doesn't call the qualified; He qualifies the called. That means this has nothing to do with your own qualifications. It's all about God's mighty power and what He wants to accomplish through you.

Notice what today's verse highlights: The Lord is with you, He has anointed you, and He has sent you. This is foundational to understanding your calling.

The Lord is with you. He sees you, chooses you, and desires to work through you. It doesn't say He's chosen you because you've got it all together or because you're perfectly qualified. So take heart: This isn't about you. It's about Him and what He wants to do in and through you. He doesn't call you because you're qualified. He calls you despite your disqualifications.

The Lord has anointed you. In His grace, He qualifies you and empowers you with His Spirit. It's His anointing that will give you the strength and power to do what He's called you to do. All He needs is your yes and your active participation.

The Lord has sent you. Did you catch that? He's given you a mission! Once you say yes to Him, your new job is to declare freedom to those who need it most—and who is better to send than someone like you who gets it?! The world doesn't need another "look at me" story or influencer. The world doesn't need someone who's got it all together. The world needs Jesus, because one encounter with Him restores identity and creates a ripple effect in those around them.

That means God has called you to run toward those who mourn, who grieve, who are lost in despair. But if we're too focused on our own struggles, we'll never have the courage to step into the fire. But that's the call. And He has called you.

Day 97 Disqualified

I pray that your insecurities don't keep you from responding to the call; instead, stay humble and close to God's presence as you step out to do bold things for Him. I pray that you never think you could accomplish anything without Him, because it's His anointing that will bring about the miraculous through your yes!

May your life proclaim freedom!

■ ■ ■ ■ ■ ■

Revel: In what areas have you disqualified yourself even though God has called you? Take a moment to write those down.

Then repent and respond to His call. Ask Him to ignite a fresh fire in your heart to embrace His purpose for you and to give you divine strategies to partner with Him in proclaiming His freedom to those around you.

....

....

....

....

Align: Count 'em—what steps did you take toward your dream yesterday? How was your mind? Your heart? Your steps? Were they aligned with truth or with fear? Were you focused on where you are or where God is taking you?

As you align today, be sure to fix your eyes forward. Stay focused on where God is leading, not where you feel stuck. Keep taking bold, obedient steps of faith, trusting that He is leading you in paths of righteousness—one faithful move at a time.

Dream Stack: What's one more thing you can do to chase your bold dream today? Your steps of faith declare the goodness of God to a world that so desperately needs Him. Write it down, make it happen, and let your life be an example of God's truth.

DAY 98

What Do You Need?

Then Jesus declared, 'I am the bread of life. Whoever comes to me will never go hungry, and whoever believes in me will never be thirsty.'

—John 6:35

"I'M HEADED TO THE STORE. Do you need anything?" my husband asked.

It was a typical question—he's always been so thoughtful. And yes, I have an amazing husband, no doubt about that. But we did go through a season where we were a bit codependent, enabling each other to make choices that didn't reflect our true, God-given identities.

"Yes, please! A bottle of wine. You know the kind."

For over ten years, this was a common conversation. No one would have labeled me as having a problem with alcohol; it was just part of life. So much so that it felt *normal*—that should've been the first red flag. I didn't drink a lot, but I drank often. And because it seemed so ordinary, I brushed off the problem and ignored the deeper issues. It was Monday, or Friday, or five p.m., or I'd had a long day, or the kids were driving me nuts. Whether it was sunny or cold outside, a girls night out or Momma's night in, there was always a reason.

Addiction is complicated. It's not only a physical, chemical, and emotional problem, but it's also very spiritual. At its core, addiction is a strong physical or psychological need or urge to do something or use something, it is a dependence on a substance or activity. *Dependence* is the key word.

This pattern became so ingrained in my life that I stopped questioning it. It was just *what I did*. Over time, I felt more comfortable with a glass of wine in my hand than without. And because the world around me made it seem normal, I had no reason to stop. That is, until I had an encounter with the Lord.

At the time, we were living in Florida. I had just published my first book, we had four kids, and we were in the middle of rehabbing a five-acre farm—while living in it. Trust me, I had *plenty* of reasons to pour a glass of wine each night. I mean, who wouldn't? But here's the strange part: For the four or five months leading up to that pivotal season, something inside me started tugging at me every time I poured a glass. What once felt so normal and justified started feeling off, like it didn't sit right anymore. It was weird. I brushed it off, thinking it was just another one of those moments where I'd swing the pendulum, maybe do a short-lived cleanse, then go back to normal. "You deserve it; you've had a long day," I'd tell myself. But this time, the nagging feeling wouldn't go away.

Around that same time, my husband and I started having conversations about how much we were spending on alcohol. We were both feeling those whispers from the Lord about making some changes. We talked about the dreams we had in our hearts and how we knew we needed to shift some habits. But, as usual, *tomorrow* always became the fallback and the never-ending excuse. You know how that goes.

I still remember the day I was standing in my kitchen when I heard the audible voice of the Lord ask me, "Where do you hide?"

"Where do I hide?!" In that moment, I felt both completely exposed and deeply seen at the same time. My whole life flashed before me, and it hit me—*where don't I hide*? As a kid, I hid behind perfectionism, doing all the right things. As a late teenager, I hid behind drugs. In my twenties, I hid behind my husband. In my thirties, I hid behind success. And now, here I was, hiding behind alcohol.

It all made sense. I had been using alcohol as my hiding place. I had grown dependent on it. *Dependence*—relying on or being controlled by something else. Honestly, it allowed me to be in a room without actually being emotionally present. It let me be around people without feeling the weight of my own insecurity. It let me live in the middle of chaos without having to feel it. Up until that very moment, all the places I had found to hide made sense. All of them seemed practical. And they all worked—until they didn't.

"What if *I* could be your hiding place?" I heard the Lord ask.

My knees hit the floor. In that moment, everything changed. In one instant, I recognized the source of my addiction. I laid my heart bare before the Lord, and for the first time, my pain made sense. I felt truly seen, and my heart opened up in a way I had never allowed before. That moment marked the beginning of my life's journey toward freedom in Him.

What about you? Where do you hide? Who or what are you depending on? And what are you asking them to give you that only Jesus can truly provide?

We all have something. It may not be alcohol or drugs, but let's be honest—we all have areas where we're hiding from the Lord. When we hide, we overlook the fact that we *have* a need, and it's a misplaced need that leads to addiction. Instead of turning to *the source*, Jesus, we start looking to things of this world to fill us. We ask alcohol, success, money, or relationships to give us something they were never designed to provide. We try to satisfy our hunger and thirst with things that leave us emptier than before. I've been there. I've tried, and I'm here to tell you, nothing can fill you like Jesus can.

As today's Scripture boldly declares—Jesus is the *bread of life*, the One who truly satisfies. And as food sustains our bodies, Jesus provides the nourishment our souls desperately crave. We often try to satisfy that hunger with the things around us, but only Jesus can meet the deep needs inside us.

Every need, whether emotional, mental, or relational, is spiritual at its core. And it's not until we turn to Christ to get those unmet spiritual needs met that we will feel filled! As long as we turn to the resources around us, asking them to give us what they

Day 98 What Do You Need?

were never designed to give us, we will continue to manifest in unhealthy emotional and relational patterns. Yet Jesus promises that when we come to Him, we won't hunger or thirst again. In Him, our deepest spiritual hunger is fully satisfied. In Christ, we find not just spiritual provision but healing and wholeness in every area of life.

What does it mean to come to Jesus and be filled? It means recognizing our need for Him, feeling the feels, and choosing to turn away from temporary fixes. It means believing that only He can truly meet our deepest needs. In His presence, we find peace, joy, and contentment that go beyond our circumstances. He's with you in the process—through the pain, through the healing, and into victory.

Let's be real—my journey to sobriety didn't suddenly mean I was perfectly fulfilled and living in overwhelming joy. Actually, it got harder before it got better. Sobriety brought me face-to-face with all the things I had been avoiding. But for the first time, I had my freedom of choice back. For so long, I was bound by alcohol and felt like I had no choice. Alcohol was my choice. But with each step I took, my choice became stronger and stronger despite the pain, despite the insecurity, despite *all the feels*.

All the feels? Yes, *all the feels*. Let me tell you, feeling your emotions without numbing them with an unhealthy habit is tough. When we mask our pain with substances or distractions, we bypass the real feelings. Sure, for a moment, I could rise above my stress or insecurity with a drink, but that relief was temporary, and the pain always returned. It was a vicious cycle. When I got sober, the real work of feeling my feelings, processing my pain, and healing began. And that's no joke.

So if you've been feeling spiritually hungry or thirsty, this is your reminder to come to Jesus. If you're facing your own addiction today, and you're turning to the things of this world that you know are not designed to give you what you're asking of them, bring your needs fully to Him. You may need additional support—counseling, spiritual guidance, and a strong community. I did. Whatever it takes, don't rely on willpower alone; find the support you need and make sure that all of it points you back to Jesus as your source.

Remember, the goal isn't to feel good; it's to become whole again. Sobriety isn't just about ridding yourself of unhealthy habits; it's also about filling yourself with the Lord. It's not just something you do; it's also about healing your place of pain. Go the Lord, feed on His Word, and let Him satisfy your soul in ways nothing else can. He is the bread of life, and in Him, there is abundant, never-ending fulfillment.

Revel: Who or what have you been turning to, asking it to fill a need that only Jesus can fulfill?

Today, take a moment to acknowledge your hunger and recognize your true need. Instead of seeking satisfaction from the things around you, bring your heart to the bread of life—let Jesus fill you in ways that go beyond what you can understand. And as the emotions surface and you feel the feels, don't hesitate to ask for help. Reach out to a pastor or a Christian counselor who can walk alongside you on your journey to freedom.

....

....

....

....

Align: With just a few days left in our journey together, taking time to reflect becomes even more important—and I hope for you that it has started to feel more natural, even essential.

My prayer is that this practice has woven itself into your morning rhythm, anchoring you deeper in the Lord with your mind, heart, and steps moving fully in sync with Him.

Today, take a moment to truly relish how far you've come. Celebrate it! Go back through every page, every step, and let the realness of the journey sink in. Lift your hands in gratitude for all God has done in you and through you—and hey, don't be shy. Give yourself a real round of applause. You've come so far, and there's so much you still get to do.

....

....

....

....

Day 98 What Do You Need?

Dream Stack: What's one bold move you can make today toward your dream—fully and completely depending on the Lord to do it? Write it down. Let go. Let God. Make it happen. Then live to tell the story of His faithfulness tomorrow.

....

....

....

....

DAY 99

My Hole for His Whole

[Jesus said,] 'Come to me, all you who are weary and burdened, and I will give you rest. Take my yoke upon you and learn from me, for I am gentle and humble in heart, and you will find rest for your souls. For my yoke is easy and my burden is light.'

—Matthew 11:28–30

AS A HOMESCHOOLING MOM to five kids, I can honestly say I've learned more than I ever expected—especially about how much I don't know or, let's be real, how much I've forgotten. Did you know that when you're born, 80 percent of your body is made up of cartilage, not bone? Or that there are more stars in the sky than grains of sand on all the beaches on Earth? Or that a cat's nose is as unique as a human's fingerprint?

And that's just the beginning. Did you know that cows have best friends, bees dance to communicate, an octopus has three hearts, and a homophone is definitely not a game of phone tag? These are just a few of the mind-blowing things I've discovered. It's humbling, eye-opening, and frankly, a little mind-boggling all at once.

Back to those homophones and how they relate to your life—it might seem like a stretch, but stay with me. Homophones are words that sound the same but have different meanings or spellings—like *to*, *too*, and *two* or *there*, *their*, and *they're*. They can be super confusing, especially for a six-year-old trying to figure out which is which. Whoever designed the English language clearly didn't consider the fact that homeschool moms have to explain these rules—then also explain that sometimes we break them for no reason at all.

Here's why this matters: *Hole* and *whole* are homophones, and like the confusion between other homophones, we often confuse the hole in our hearts with things that aren't meant to fill it and make us whole. Yesterday, we dug into the reality of addiction and how we often try to fulfill needs that only God can meet. We look for satisfaction in things like alcohol, success, money, or approval from others, thinking they will make us whole. But only Jesus can fill those spaces. Today, I want to challenge you to acknowledge the hole in your heart, the unmet needs, and stop hiding, ignoring, or justifying them. Instead, I encourage you to make one of life's greatest exchanges—your hole for His whole.

Jesus came to take our sins and give us grace, to take the death that was inevitable for every single one of us and give us eternal life! And as today's verse tells us, He also came to give you *rest*, a better quality of life, on this side of eternity by exchanging our heavy burdens for His light ones. He didn't come for us to ignore our struggles or numb them with unhealthy habits. He didn't come to justify the holes we had or shame and condemn them; He came to give us so much more—wholeness in Him.

When Jesus invites us to *take my yoke* upon ourselves, He is offering us an exchange. The yoke is an image of partnership, like two oxen sharing a load. But with Jesus, the weight is lighter because He carries the heaviest part. He knows the burdens we carry—fear, anxiety, exhaustion, disappointment, the constant striving to fill the *holes* we feel inside. These holes, gone unchecked, cause us to seek fulfillment or completeness in success, relationships, or escaping through unhealthy habits.

But Jesus offers to replace those holes with something whole—Himself. When we give our fragmented burdens to Him, He gives us His wholeness in return. It's like giving up our broken pieces and receiving a masterpiece in exchange. We are no longer trying to patch together our lives with temporary fixes, but instead, we are leaning into His completeness and wholeness. He fills you in ways you can't imagine—so you can run and not grow weary, walk and not faint (Isaiah 40:31).

Think about a time when you tried to fill a gap in your life with something temporary—maybe it was a job, a relationship, or even an achievement. But after a while, that "solution" just created more emptiness. Jesus is asking you to hand over our holes to Him and receive His complete peace, His rest. This isn't a momentary fix but a long-lasting wholeness that aligns your life with His purpose and grace.

When we exchange our heavy burdens for His light yoke, we step into a life no longer driven by striving but anchored in the assurance of His love, guidance, and presence, which fills every gap we've tried to fill on our own. Let Him fill those gaps today. Instead of working harder or striving to cover the empty spaces you feel, invite Him to fill them. Don't run from or ignore the places that stir up shame, guilt, or overwhelm—bring them to Him and let His fullness bring peace.

If you want the real stuff, the key to true fulfillment on this side of eternity, give your hole for His whole. It's the best exchange you'll ever make.

Consider this your language arts lesson for today. You're welcome.

■ ■ ■ ■ ■ ■

Revel: What's your God-size hole today?

Take a moment to recognize the empty spaces within you and your life. Instead of trying to fill them with temporary fixes, pushing them aside, or powering through on your own, bring them to God. Watch as He offers you the greatest exchange you'll ever make—your holes for wholeness. Close your eyes, and let His yoke rest upon you, lightening your load as He walks with you through it all.

Day 99 My Hole for His Whole

Align: Arise and shine. Take a moment—sit back, close your eyes, and reflect on yesterday. When did your thoughts, attitude, or actions reflect His glory?

Celebrate the places where His glory showed up in your behavior. Write each moment down. Make them real. And in the areas that still need a little more of His touch, ask for grace. Let today be a day in which you let Him love you, overwhelm you with His goodness, and gently realign every part of you back into the beautiful rhythm of His grace.

Dream Stack: What's one thing you can do to chase your bold dream today? Got it? Good. Now write it down and go make it happen.

DAY 100

Miracles

You are the God who performs miracles; you display your power among the peoples.

—Psalm 77:14

WHEN WE HEAR THE WORD *miracle*, each of us reacts differently. Some struggle to believe in miracles today, as though they existed only in Biblical times. Others once believed, but after facing disappointment from seemingly unanswered prayers, they no longer do—or at least not for themselves. Then there are those who are miracle junkies, constantly chasing after signs and wonders. No matter where you stand, both doubt and fixation can lead us to miss the bigger picture, causing us to focus too much on the miracles themselves. I suggest that miracles are less about the events themselves and more about their source—God. If we're not careful, we can lose sight of the miracle worker by becoming preoccupied with the miracles.

Let me be clear: Miracles in and of themselves are, well, miraculous. They aren't events to be measured or compartmentalized. They transcend our understanding, and they happen all around us—even in ways we might overlook. Sometimes the miracle is in the process, not in the instantaneous. Sometimes, God is working not in our circumstances but within us. And yes, miracles are even in our unanswered prayers (thank you, Garth Brooks). Yet whether His miracles come suddenly or unfold over time, God is always at work. Scripture clearly states that God is the same yesterday, today, and forever (Hebrews 13:8). His power doesn't diminish, and His nature doesn't change (Malachi 3:6). Miracles are not simply for those in Biblical times. They are part of God's continuous expression of His nature and are available to us today, and they testify about who God is and the type of character He has.

Did you catch that? They are part of who He is, not just what He does. If we're disappointed by the outcome, we're too focused on what He can do or appears to not be doing instead of the nature of who He is.

The word miracle means an amazing or wonderful event. It comes from the Latin *miraculum*, meaning "object of wonder."

In Hebrew, one of the phrases associated with miracles is *oseh niflaot*, which translates to "He who makes wonders" or "miracle maker." Miracles are not just events that happen—they flow from the very identity and nature of who God is, the source of all wonders. He doesn't just perform miracles; He is the miracle worker. If we're not careful, we'll focus more on the miracle itself than on the awe and majesty of the One who performs them. He is our object of wonder!

Psalm 77 is attributed to Asaph, a Levite and one of King Davod's chief musicians and worship leaders. In this chapter we see Asaph pouring out his heart in lament. He speaks of crying out to God with no response, seeking Him but feeling abandoned. "Has God forgotten to be merciful ? Has He in anger withheld His mercy and compassion?" Maybe you can relate.

But then Asaph does something remarkable—a pattern interrupt, if you will, like a wake-up call when we forget that God is and always has been a miracle-working God. Asaph declares, *Then I thought, 'To this I will appeal'* (Psalm 77:10). An appeal, by definition, is a request to a higher authority for a decision to be reversed. What began as a sob story, the result of only focusing on what God hadn't done, shifted as Asaph made an appeal to himself. He consciously interrupted his negative thinking and chose to remember God's faithfulness and the miracles of the past.

I propose that a solid appeal would do you good too!

This appeal is a powerful reminder that God's faithfulness is not limited by our current circumstances. Just because we don't see a miracle doesn't mean God isn't moving. Just because our prayers seem unanswered doesn't mean He isn't listening or caring. This psalm teaches us to refocus on God's unchanging character, trusting that even when we can't see it, God is still at work.

Asaph continues: *'I will remember the deeds of the Lord; yes, I will remember your miracles of long ago. I will consider all your works and meditate on all your mighty deeds* (Psalm 77:11–12). In a pivotal moment, Asaph shifts his focus from the wrong source—his own limited reasoning—and from dwelling on what God hadn't done. Instead, he begins to intentionally remind himself of who God is and all that He has accomplished. By reflecting on God's past faithfulness and mighty works, Asaph realigns his perspective and finds renewed hope in God's unchanging power. Then in today's passage, he declares, *'You are the God who performs miracles; you display your power among the peoples.*

God is still the miracle worker, even when we don't understand His ways. Just because He hasn't answered in the way you expected doesn't mean He won't answer in a way that is for your good. Sometimes the miracle is in the process of learning to trust Him more deeply. Sometimes it's in the unanswered prayers that shield us from things we don't yet see. Sometimes the miracle unfolds little by little … and then all at once. Sometimes the miracle happens generations later. Sometimes the miracle happens within us. Sometimes the miracle happens instantaneously. No matter what, I am here to remind you that miracles do happen, because we have a miracle-working God.

The truth is, God is still the same miracle-working, mountain-moving God He's always been. Whether through divine intervention, gradual healing, or even unanswered prayers that turn out to be greater blessings in disguise, God is at work. He is performing miracles all around you—and within you.

Today is your pattern interrupt like the one Asaph had. Make an appeal to yourself!

Day 100 Miracles

Revel: Where in your life do you need to shift your focus from the miracle itself to the miracle worker? What prayers have gone unanswered that you need to release to God's perfect timing and His perfect ways?

Maybe today, like Asaph, you need to appeal to yourself. Instead of focusing on all that God has not done, begin to reflect upon all that He has done. Open your heart and see God's faithfulness. Trust that He is still performing miracles in ways seen and unseen. See Him as a miracle worker.

Align: You made it to 100 days! A hundred bold steps of faith. A hundred moments of revelation, surrender, and courage. You didn't just dream with God—you moved with Him.

Today, don't just glance at the finish line—own it. Look at what obedience has built. Look at the alignment He's forged in you. This is more than a milestone—it's a launching pad.

Lift your head high. Lift your hands in worship. Celebrate what God has done—and get ready, because this is just the beginning of a life lived aligned.

Dream Stack: Today, what's one thing you can do to proactively move closer to your dream? Define it, write it down, then do it!

....

....

....

....

DAY 101

Arise and Shine

Rise up in splendor and be radiant, for your light has dawned, and Yahweh's glory now streams from you! Look carefully! Darkness blankets the earth, and thick clouds cover the nations, but Yahweh arises upon you and the brightness of his glory appears over you! Nations will be attracted to your radiant light and kings to the sunrise-glory of your new day. Lift up your eyes higher! Look all around you and believe, for your sons are returning from far away and your daughters are being tenderly carried home. Watch as they all gather together, eager to come back to you! Then you will see with understanding and be radiant. Your heart will be thrilled and swell with joy. The fullness of the sea will flow to you and the wealth of the nations will be transferred to you!

—Isaiah 60:1–5 TPT

WE FIND OURSELVES AT THESE MONUMENTAL moments—much like today—where we celebrate the fact that we did it, *you did it*, and we feel a bit of sadness that it's over. It's in moments like these we realize the joy isn't just in reaching the goal, but it's also in every step of the journey that brought us here. The sweetness at the finish line comes not from just crossing it but also from looking back and cherishing each moment along the way.

Over the past 101 days, you've expanded your heart and mind to embrace more of heaven's realities, aligned your thoughts and actions with truth, and dream stacked as if your life depended on it (because you know it does). If you've been faithful in your pursuit, you've done at least 101 things to move your dream forward. Well done! Yet as we stand at the end of one finish line, may you also recognize that a new starting line is right in front of you.

This isn't the end—not even close. We're just getting started. As if you were climbing Mount Everest, you've made it to one base camp, but there are still many more heights to scale. As you continue to climb toward higher realities in the Lord, whetting your appetite for more—more of Him, more of His glory, and more of what He wants to do in and through your life—I pray you're even more convinced that yes, *"Now is the time to act!"* because God's not done making His move ... not even close!

Today's final passage is not only encouragement to you, but it's also prophetic. And I believe it is ushering us into the next era the Lord is drawing us into as His sons and daughters. It's an era in which I believe we will begin to see heaven invading earth in new, dramatic ways, both unbelievable and marvelous, and I believe the Lord is wanting to use us as His children to make His glory known. Every road, every step, every stretch of the journey has led to this moment—and I believe with everything in me: The time is now.

The beginning of today's Scripture says: *Rise up in splendor and be radiant, for your light has dawned, and Yahweh's glory now streams from you! Look carefully! Darkness blankets the earth, and thick clouds cover the nations, but Yahweh arises upon you and the brightness of his glory appears over you!.* The passage paints a vivid picture of the contrast between the darkness covering the earth and the glory of Yahweh arising over His people. This darkness refers to the original sin that entered the world when Adam and Eve chose to believe the deceiver. In that moment, humanity became disconnected from its true source—God Himself. Genesis 3:7 describes how their eyes were opened, and they saw their nakedness. This sudden awareness of their separation from God led them to hide, and ever since, mankind has been struggling with this same inclination to run from God instead of running to Him.

The fall introduced a cycle of shame, hiding, and blame. Adam and Eve, in their shame, ran from God trying to cover themselves. They didn't want to be seen in their vulnerability, just as we often run from God when we feel exposed or broken. This is the heart of humanity's struggle: We long to be fully known but fear being fully seen. The greatest lie we buy into is "If you see me, you will reject me."

Maybe you can relate.

The enemy exploits this fear in all of us by distorting our identity. He convinces us to question who we are and who God is, which leads us to search for validation and worth in places that can never fill the void. We turn to idols, whether in the form of achievements, relationships, or self-reliance, trying to cover our shame and find meaning. Truth be told, the enemy does not want the glory of God to reflect from humanity, so he relentlessly tries to keep the light out. However, we see two very powerful words in the passage that change the game.

But Yahweh ...

God's plan is always for redemption and restoration. His desire is to cover us with His glory, not for us to cover ourselves with fig leaves of shame and self-sufficiency. The thick clouds that cover the nations are not just physical darkness but spiritual blindness, confusion, and the result of humanity's disconnection from God. Yet in this passage, we see the power and brightness of God's glory appearing over each of us, transcending the darkness, the thick clouds, and the sin of humanity as His light streams through us in splendor and radiance . True freedom comes when we return to God—when we stop hiding and allow Him to fully see and fully know us. It's time to stop hiding and running and to be fully seen and fully known by God.

You were made to shine. You were created to reflect the glory of the God who made you. The darkness may be real, but it cannot overcome the light of Yahweh that *streams from you.* God's light within you isn't just for your own benefit; it's also meant to draw others to Him. Scripture goes on to say: *Nations will be attracted to your radiant light and kings to the sunrise-glory of your new day. Lift up your eyes higher! Look all around you* and believe, *for your sons are returning from far away and your daughters are being tenderly carried home. Watch as they all gather together, eager to come back to you! Then you will see with understanding and be radiant. Your heart will be thrilled and swell with joy. The fullness of the sea will flow to you and the wealth of the nations will be transferred to you!.* Did you catch that? Nations and kings will be attracted to the light of His glory radiating through you. That means you were born to shine!

It's time to rise up and let the world see who you truly are—a child of God covered

Day 101 Arise and Shine

in His glory, reflecting His light. Darkness may cover the earth, but God has chosen you to be a beacon of His light. This isn't about striving or trying to manufacture your own light. It's about stepping into the fullness of who God says you are and reflecting His brilliance. When you arise in the splendor of God's presence, it changes not only you but also the world around you.

Lift up your eyes, look around, and believe. God is moving in ways you may not yet fully see, but His promises are true. Today, embrace your calling to shine. You were made for this moment. Let God's glory arise over you and watch as His light in you draws others into His love.

We are in a new era. It is time to declare the light of God in the darkest of places and to radiate His light for all nations to see. It is time to dream boldly, create uninhibitedly, and live unapologetically for the Lord.

I encourage you to let the words of Isaiah sink into your heart and spirit. Read them once, twice, and then again and again and again. Allow them to stir something deep within you. Then share them with the whole world. The time has come.

Arise and shine!

■ ■ ■ ■ ■ ■

Revel: It's time to be fully seen and fully known by God. What would it look like for you to embrace the light of His glory and arise in splendor? How can you step into your calling to reflect His radiance in your daily life? Lift up your eyes and shine—the world is waiting for the light you carry!

Align: You made it—101 days! That means today, you're standing on the edge of your next bold, faith-filled step… step 101. That marks 101 moments of surrender. 101 days of realignment. 101 opportunities where you chose courage over comfort.

You haven't just been dreaming with God—you've been walking with Him. Day by day. Step by step. For 101 days, you've been building something sacred with Him.

Today isn't just the end of your journey—it's the beginning of a whole new way of living. Let your life declare what obedience can build. Let your alignment with Him continue to dream boldly, live big, and make an impact for God's Kingdom.

This isn't the end. This is your launch.

....

....

....

....

Dream Stack: Though today marks our final day of dreaming and stacking together, I pray it's not your last. Commit to living a lifestyle of dream stacking—beyond these 101 days.

Today, pick one thing you can do to move your dreams into reality—write it down and go make it happen. The whole world is waiting!

....

....

....

....

In Closing

WHAT AN HONOR IT HAS BEEN to spend the last 101 days with you as you've drawn close to the Lord and embraced your role as a change agent for His Kingdom. The world will be a better place because of the time you have spent with the Lord.

My hope is that you've discovered the powerful simplicity of accessing God's presence—by saying *Yes!* In that bold surrender, you encounter His heart and purpose for your life.

For 101 days, you've been conditioning your heart and mind to chase after Him while building daily practices that align your actions with His Word—mindset, heartset, and dreamset. What a beautiful accomplishment! Well done, good and faithful dreamer.

But this is not the end—it's the beginning of a lifestyle of dreaming with the Lord.

So don't quit! May dreaming with the Lord become a lifestyle as your steps are filled with purpose, conviction, and fire, and may you always know that you are not alone in this journey. I am with you, I am for you, and I am your biggest fan.

With my whole heart,
JG

Join The Community: Bold Dreamers

WE DON'T NEED ANOTHER SERVICE—we need community. We need each other.

In a world of hyper-connection, we're somehow more disconnected than ever and it's time to reclaim what it means to be intentionally together.

BOLD DREAMERS is an online community of faith-filled dreamers committed to living out their God-sized dreams and leading boldly—in faith, family, career, and community.

This is more than just access—it's **alignment** with a global movement of bold believers who are committed to dreaming with God, living on purpose, and building His Kingdom in every sphere of life. People from all walks of life and chasing all kinds of dreams, this tribe carries powerful testimonies, unshakable faith, and the kind of courage that moves mountains.

You no longer have to journey alone.

When you say YES to this journey, you don't just join a program—you join a **family**. A Spirit-led, faith-filled, action-taking community of visionaries, creatives, business leaders, moms, missionaries, and Kingdom builders who are doing the inner work AND the dream work, together.

HERE'S WHAT YOU WILL HAVE ACCESS TO:

- Lifetime access to **DREAM Curriculum** (Transformational video lessons from Julia Gentry's CORE curriculum)
- Downloadable **workbooks, devotions, and tools** to walk you through every layer of your God-sized dream
- Monthly LIVE coaching with Julia Gentry (+ surprise guest mentors throughout the month)
- Access to our **private online community of Dreamers**—a space to ask bold questions, share breakthroughs, receive prayer, and stay accountable
- Exclusive invites to Experience Nights, LIVE trainings, early access to events, and more!

Because you were never meant to do this alone.
Because your dream matters.
Because the world needs what God put inside of you.

Welcome home, Dreamer.

Let's go even bolder—together.
Join us today. You'll be so glad you did.
Come dream with us—daily.

Learn more at TheJuliaGentry.com/bolddreamers

About JG

JULIA GENTRY is the Founder of The Dream Factory & Co. and the author of the best-selling book in Christian Leadership, Dream – I Dare You.

Despite starting her professional career in real estate—and facing full-blown burnout by her early 30s—Julia experienced what she calls a "Midlife Awakening." Today, she can boldly say she's truly living the dream.

As an international speaker, author, business owner, growth coach, wife, and home-school mom to FIVE, Julia knows what it takes to bridge the gap between where you are and where God is calling you to be.

Through her signature D.R.E.A.M. Framework, she has helped thousands of dreamers around the world discover the answer to their deepest question: "Is there something more?"—and ultimately live with bold vision and Kingdom impact.

As a sought-after speaker and thought leader, Julia believes that when we change the way the Church understands dreaming with God, we become the bridge that brings heaven to earth.

If not you, who? And if not now, when?

Learn more at TheJuliaGentry.com.

www.ingramcontent.com/pod-product-compliance
Lightning Source LLC
Chambersburg PA
CBHW080832230426
43665CB00021B/2821